TO TONI HUDSON

A VOTRE SANTÉ

WWW. ALAINBRAUX. COM

WWW - HEALTHY CHEF RECIPES . COM

Healthy French Cuisine

for Less Than $10/Day

By Chef Alain Braux

C.E.P.C., C.M.B.

B.S. Holistic Nutrition

Edited by **Kathleen Thornberry**

Cover design by **Nathan Stueve**.

Back photograph by **Athena Danoy**

HEARD ON THE GRAPEVINE

"Chef Braux supplies us with a wealth of accessible dietary information that can be easily incorporated into everyday life. He gives us recipes and health tips giving the maximum nutrients for the minimum cost. Not only do the foods help you achieve an energetic lifestyle, they are inexpensive and delicious. Say goodbye to the dreary dietary statistics and hello to affordable health - not only will you spend less at the grocery store but you will most likely be spending less at the doctor's office too. Alain's book is so useful - I will encourage my patients and friends to read it."

Dr. Janet Zand - L.Ac., OMD, Dipl. Ac., CH, CAN. Author of *Smart Medicine for a Healthier Child*.

"Chef Alain Braux has inspired me yet again. As though gourmet eating on a fast food budget wasn't enough, fabulous recipes like the French Green Goddess Salad with Shrimp and Orange Grand Marnier French Crepes make this book a must have. Filled with dozens of quick tips on how to shop, food preparation, budgeting both money and time and keeping a basic pantry this book is everything you wish your mother had taught you about the kitchen. Bon Appetite!"

Dr. Amy Neuzil, ND. Author of *DIY Health: For Women*.

"No more excuses! Chef Alain Braux provides those of us concerned about eating well on a budget with everything we need to feast our bodies, minds, and spirits. Combining inspiring down-to-earth advice, expert insights, and delicious, easy-to-follow French recipes, this book is essential reading for every American household — especially those with children."

Dr. Liz Alexander - The Book Doula. Author of *Birth Your Book*.

Chef Alain Braux's approach to healthy eating is literally "down to earth" in this delightful and extremely useful guide to balanced, nutritious meals on a budget. With a passion for flavor and fresh ingredients, Braux takes us through an eye-opening grocery shopping experience (including the 12 most contaminated foods in the produce section, and what "natural" *really* means on food labels), to alternative shopping choices (farmers' markets, growing your own). Inspired by the foods he grew up with in his native France, Chef Braux's recipes will not only sate the appetite, but can feed a family of four for less than $40 per day! A truly valuable guide to nutrition, *plus* who knew French cooking could be so affordable!

Table of Contents

FOREWORD

Hello again. If you have read either of my two previous books *How to Lower Your Cholesterol with French Gourmet Food* or *Living Gluten and Dairy-Free with French Gourmet Food*, thank you for reading them. I hope they helped you become healthier through eating fresh, delicious food.

It is a fact that we live in more difficult financial times than we did only a few years ago. Our economy has still not fully recovered, no matter what "they" want us to believe, and inflation is causing prices to go up. First: gasoline. I know, we don't drink it, but we have to buy it to get to work and shop, and gasoline prices tend to restrict our food budgets. And, of course, the cost of food itself is spiraling upward.

My challenge, and my gift to you, is to prove you that a family of four can eat fresh and healthy food on a fast food budget. My goal is forty dollars a day for a family of four (two adults and two children). This will require a few lifestyle changes. You may have to go back to some old-fashioned ways of doing things, like taking a homemade lunch to work, but it is more than possible to eat well on this amount. I am writing this book, in part, to answer the complaint: "But eating healthy is so expensive!" I hope I can convince you that it is far from impossible, and can be fun too. Read my ideas carefully, implement them a little at a time, and you will be pleasantly surprised.

As I did for my last book, I would like to put my money where my mouth is and donate $2.00 per book sold to the Austin Sustainable Food Center (SFC) for the first year of publication. They are doing a wonderful job strengthening our local food system and improving access to nutritious, affordable food for all, regardless of budget. They also teach children and adults in Central Texas how to cook their own organic and locally grown food. They even have their own demo kitchen called Happy Kitchen or La Cocina Allegre™ where they teach anyone interested in basic nutrition how to prepare and cook fresh food from scratch. Additionally, they teach how to start your own garden. They encourage the community to create school and community gardens for those of us that don't have our own backyard. And finally, but not the least of their admirable efforts, they organize three weekly farmers' markets in Austin and surrounding areas which allow our local farmers to earn a decent living and connect with their customers face to face. Other programs offered by SFC are: Farm to Cafeteria, Farm to Work, and Farm to School. We are very lucky to have them in Austin. Without their hard work and dedication, we all would not have access to such wonderful food and ideas. Thank you SFC for your hard work and my sincerest thanks

for your support. For more information, please visit
http://www.sustainablefoodcenter.org.

Bon Appétit!

Chef Alain Braux

INTRODUCTION

Life on Mamie's Small Farm

As some of you already know from my previous books, much of what I know about healthful eating, I learned from grandmother, Mamie, a French small farmer. It was not that she taught me how to prepare fancy French food; that I learned later in my professional life in the food industry. What I did learn from her was that one could eat very healthy food on a tight budget.

How? My grandparents ran a small farm for the property's landlord in exchange for free lodging and whatever they could grow in their own kitchen garden and "poulailler" (chicken coop). Since my grandfather was a night guard at a local factory, Mamie ended up running the farm and feeding the family (including two of her grandchildren) by herself. Because she did not have a lot of money to feed us, her kitchen garden allowed us to survive. (You would cringe at how little we had to live on at the time. It took me a while to appreciate this part of my life!) She grew nearly everything we ate. She was very proud of her garden, and it showed on our plates. Although it was very simple peasant food, it was tasty and good for us.

Why? Because everything was always in season, freshly picked from the garden that same morning. All she had to do to create her daily menu was to walk to her garden, pick what was ripe at the time, cook, and serve it. Although I did not realize it at the time, she taught me a lot by her example, including showing me how to choose ripe tomatoes, green peas and apples. She would tell me: "Go pick six carrots out of the garden for dinner", or "go get me a salad, rinse it and dry it." I will always remember the wire basket with handles we used to shake the water off the freshly picked leaves. All she needed to add to that was radish slices and simple vinaigrette for a healthy and quick meal, loaded with true vitamins and minerals (not the kind out of a bottle). Trust me, with that kind of food we never needed to take additional supplements; it was all there in our food.

Mamie also raised a few small animals for food. Chicken for eggs and meat, and rabbits for meat (and to produce more rabbits). To this day, I can still see in my mind's eye how she tried to teach me to kill a chicken by twisting its neck, or a rabbit by holding it by the ears and giving it a sharp karate chop at the back of the neck. I just could not do it. After all, I was a little city slicker at the time, and killing a cute bunny with my own hands was beyond my abilities. If she had taught me to do the same with the school bully, maybe I would have paid attention, but not bunny "Foufou"! If she wanted more expensive meat like beef or pork, she would trade with other farmers at the market. She did the same with those huge 2-kilo loaves of "pain de champagne" (country-style bread). As kids are wont to do, when she sent me to pick up the bread at the nearest "boulangerie" (bakery), I was tempted to tear off a piece of that still warm, huge loaf of bread. But I had strict instructions not to do it or else, and trust me, I did not want to find out what "else" was. We all knew! As loving as Mamie was, she was a rough lady with very large and tough peasant hands. We did not care to feel how hard they could be on our bottoms. Her policy was to never eat fresh bread, only "pain rassis" (stale bread). That way, we would not be tempted to overstuff ourselves on bread, and waste what little money she had. Lesson learned and remembered. Although I do eat fresh bread nowadays, I tend to pay attention to how much I eat, just by remembering her big red hands.

Sorry if I rambled down memory lane a little too long there! But the point I'd like to make is that, with a little effort and ingenuity, we can still eat healthy food on a limited budget. We can't do much with no food at all, but we can sure come up with a lot of creative, inexpensive meals.

MY HEALTH BELIEFS: Ranting and Raving from a Chef/Nutrition Therapist

Portion Control: Size IS Everything

Let me address a pet peeve of mine: food portion size. Sorry everybody. I know you have been indoctrinated to believe that bigger is better, but in this case, bigger is only going to do one thing: make YOU bigger. You need to learn to not pile food high on your plate. Portion control is very important for the proper functioning of your body. When you eat too much, you tax your digestive system and make it work overtime. That's probably why you feel sleepy after lunch or dinner. Your body is taking the energy needed to digest that big plate of food away from other bodily functions. Not to mention that you may have to deal with an upset stomach and acid reflux if you keep abusing your digestive system. So please, be kind to yourself and learn to eat less food per meal. What is most important to understand is that quality *always* trumps quantity. What I would like to see you do is eat a smaller amount of better quality food, loaded with fresh vitamins, minerals and fiber, so that your body gets the proper fuel to operate at its peak. If you eat a large amount of bad quality food, not only will you strain your digestive system, you will probably feel hungry again in a couple of hours. Why? Because you fed your body with empty calories, devoid of real nutrition. Naturally your body will ask for more! You filled it, but you did not feed it. It's like trying to run your car on watered-down gasoline. Eventually your car will start to slow down, have problems and break down. Your body is like your car. If you feed it the right quality of fuel, it will function a lot more smoothly and you will stay healthy. Isn't your health worth the extra effort?

What is an Ideal Food Portion?

If you picture a medium-sized plate about eight inches in diameter, imagine you see four equal sections. You should have one section with whole grain (two ounces of brown rice or a slice of whole wheat bread for example – not two), one section with protein (four ounces maximum – about the size of a deck of cards), one section with veggies (two ounces of salad or lightly cooked vegetables) and one section with fruit (a small or medium fruit – about four ounces). It's that simple. In macrobiotic classes, we are taught we should eat no more than what our two hands forming a bowl can hold. Ideally, after eating, you should feel slightly hungry, not stuffed to the gills. You are not a fish!

If you are a visual person like I am, I'd like to offer visual cues as to what a serving should look like:

➢ A serving of protein (meat, fish or poultry) should not be more than four ounces per person, the size of a deck of cards or the palm of your hand.

➢ A vegetable or fruit serving should be four ounces, the size of a tennis ball (for example, half a large apple or half a large banana).

➢ A normal salad serving should be two ounces (it takes a lot of space on the plate), a cup or a handful.

➢ Pasta should be four ounces per person before cooking, about one-half cup (I use one-half of a Bonne Maman jar as my measuring cup), or the size of a tennis ball.

➢ A potato serving should four ounces (medium potato) or the size of a computer mouse.

➢ Small grains (rice, couscous, quinoa, millet, amaranth and so on) should be two ounces, about one-quarter cup dry per person, or one half-cup cooked; keep in mind that some pasta and grains double in size after cooking.

➢ A waffle or pancake serving should be two ounces (one waffle or two pancakes maximum) or the size of a CD or DVD.

➢ A cheese serving should be a couple of ounces or about the size of a domino.

➢ A dried fruit or nut serving should be one ounce, about the size of a golf ball or a small egg.

➢ A serving of nut butter (peanut, almond, cashew) should be one tablespoon, or the tip of your thumb.

Another playful way to picture sizes is:

➢ one cup = one baseball;
➢ three-fourths cup = one tennis ball;
➢ one-half cup = a computer mouse;
➢ one-fourth cup = one egg;
➢ three to four ounces = a deck of cards;
➢ two tablespoons = a ping-pong ball;
➢ one tablespoon = your thumb top.

Plate Size

Typically, American dinner plates are too large. Instead, find medium plates and use that size for dinner. Visually, it will look like your plate is full with less food. Since we eat with our eyes first, we are in fact telling our stomach, "That's all you're going to get." And please don't allow for seconds. Sorry! If your kids tell you they have had enough, listen to them; they know better than we do when they are full. Do not force them to eat their whole plate, like I was told when I was a kid. Which brings me to a French concept: feeling full.

I've Had Enough!

If you've ever been lucky enough to live in or be invited to a French home, you will notice that typically food portions are smaller, but a greater variety of fresh food is offered. This may be why the French tend to be healthier than Americans, even though they eat supposedly "bad" foods like butter, cream and rich dishes. Their other secret is the concept of satiety. That's when your body tells you, "I've had enough!" That does not mean you wait until you feel like a stuffed turkey, but instead that you listen for your body's signals that you've had enough food. It's hard to describe, but at a certain point while eating, you begin to feel satisfied and naturally slow down. This is the point where you should stop. If you're not used to it, start by cutting down your "normal" amount of food progressively until the amount feels just right--enough, but not too much. We need to let go of this need to stuff ourselves at all costs, or it will eventually cost us far more in doctors' bills.

Shrink Your Budget and Your Waist Size

I believe that as you start following my ideas, you will not only save money while eating exciting and nutritious food, you will most likely lose weight and your waist size will shrink as well. Although I did not write this book as a diet plan, eating smaller portions of live, vibrant, fresh food and avoiding refined sugar, processed food, trans-fats and artificial preservatives and colorings, will cause you to progressively lose weight. Do not think of it as a diet plan as much as a lifestyle change. As you start to implement some of my ideas, you will notice better quality, sustained energy as the needle on your scale goes backwards.

Shrink your Medical Budget as Well

Another hidden benefit that can add up to a lot of money is that you will not have to see your doctor as much as you used to for colds, flu and other illnesses, because your immune system will be strengthened by food loaded with fresh and powerful nutrients, vitamins, and minerals. You can even lower your cholesterol, as I explain in my previous book: "How to Lower Your Cholesterol with French Gourmet Food." As I told my son, "I would rather spend a little more money now on delicious and nutritious food, than a lot of money later on in doctor and hospital bills." Doesn't that make sense to you?

Why I Could Never Compete with your Mom's Pie

Have you ever noticed that when you are raised on home-cooked food, nothing else quite compares to it? I always tell my customers that no matter how hard I try, I could never compete with their mom's version of this cake or that pie. Why? Even if she used the wrong or worst ingredients in the world, it was fresh out of the oven, smelled great and best of all it was made with your mother's *love*. How can I compete with that? Have you ever heard of Proust's Madeleine? I have even heard some of my friends complain that they could not match their own mother's recipe results. That's because your memories add an extra glossy finish to these cherished foods. So, put on your favorite apron and add the secret ingredient, your love. Give your children great memories and create your own recipes for their delight. You will be rewarded with a never-ending supply of happy smiles and hugs.

THE COST OF NOT EATING IN SEASON

The Real Cost of Food

Being able to buy any food at any time of the year does not mean it does not cost us. For example, there is the cost of shipping that food to your grocery store. Do you really believe that all that supposedly cheap food is really cheap in the long run? Granted, labor and production costs might be lower in other countries, but what about the shipping cost and the added energy cost and the damage caused to our environment? Wouldn't you rather eat a fresh apple picked nearby than an apple picked in New Zealand weeks before it reached you?

Eat Local Food

Eating seasonally allows us to eat a wider variety of foods at their peak of freshness, flavor and goodness. Wherever we live, our bodies are adapted to the local living conditions. So is our food. Eating tropical food–created to keep you cool in hot temperatures--is not appropriate if we live in the Antarctic. On the other hand, the Inuit people, who lived mainly off local fish and seal blubber–foods considered to be fattening to us–used to lead a healthy life, well adapted to their environment, even though they do not eat vegetables or fruits. Wonderfully strange, isn't it? When the Western diet of canned and refined foods caught up with them, they started to experience the same illnesses we experience in Western societies. Dr. Weston A. Price proved that traditional local diets were perfectly adapted to their environment no matter what these different tribes or groups ate. It was only when refined food was introduced to their way of life that their overall health started to deteriorate. So, not only should your diet be adapted to the environment you live in, eating the foods that grow in your region, but you should also follow the seasons and be in harmony with your surrounding natural habitat.

Frankenfood anyone?

Another side effect of eating out of season is that the producers had to create hardy species that could withstand the abuse of early picking, packing, travelling and being dumped "pêle mêle" on that store display. What we are killing in this process is diversity and flavor. When we buy locally, we have access to heirloom fruits and vegetables specifically grown in our region and nowhere else. For example, in Texas we have a special type of strawberry grown in Poteet, and they're so happy about it that there is a Festival put

together just for these special strawberries. I agree with the folks in Poteet----
-they certainly are worth celebrating! I'm sure the same is happening in your
region. Go ahead and celebrate these traditional crops and gorge yourself on
freshly picked peaches in Georgia or Fredericksburg, TX.

Lost Nutrition

Did you know that while fancy imported organic food is travelling from
Chile, Brazil or Argentina, it looses up to eighty percent of its nutritional
value? Well duh! It's kind of like you after a long trip to Australia or
Singapore. You're not that fresh anymore, right? Why would you expect
your food to be any fresher? They have been picked green, suffered days of
travelling and arrive at our grocery store still unripe and tasteless. What's the
point of buying them?

Taste

If you buy these kinds of imported foods you are taking the risk of losing
appreciation for taste. You agree with me that produce out of season does
not taste the same as freshly picked food still warm from the sun, right? So
why agree to be disappointed? It is always best to enjoy your food in season.

Expectation

If you think about it, don't you have a certain pleasure in knowing that the
tomato or strawberry season is coming and a slight sadness by knowing we
are reaching the end of that season? But then we get excited about what the
new season will bring us, and so goes the cycle of seasonal foods. This
expectation is what makes you salivate in advance and brings back
memories of culinary pleasures. When we always get what we want when
we want it, we lose those most precious pleasures, expectation and
excitement... and we get bored with our food. Not only is the food boring,
but also your palate gets bored with so much sameness. Wake up that palate
of yours by eating freshly picked food with its taste bud-sparkling flavors.

Eating Fresh Again

This will take a little extra work but, like the commercial says, aren't you
worth it? For example, when I grate fresh carrots in my gluten-free Exotic
Carrot Cake, it means that not only is it better for you, but that it's moister
than if I used pre-grated juiceless carrots. And it makes you like my cake
even more.

Cheap IS Good

So, for your next lunch break I suggest you grate one fresh local or organic carrot at 30 cents each (I even suggest you chop up those beautiful greens and add them to your carrot salad. They're full of chlorophyll), drizzle a little olive oil and lemon juice, salt and pepper and voila! You have yourself a healthy side dish for less than fifty cents, instead of paying two dollars or more for a product that has been sitting in that showcase for God knows how long. Enjoyed with 3 ounces of ham or smoked turkey and a glass of water, you have a healthy and satisfying lunch that's better for you *and* cheaper for your wallet. What's to think about? Go fresh! It's time again to pull out those long forgotten brown bags or insulated lunch containers to bring cheap, home-prepared lunches. I don't like to use the word "cheap", because in this modern society it implies lower quality, which in my opinion is a wrong perception. We need to reverse that perception. Cheap or frugal should not be politically incorrect words. Cheap is GOOD for our budget, and we should give it more respect. If we went back to the idea of bringing lunch from home, our lunch would be only two to three dollars instead of costing us eight to ten dollars. What's not to like?

HOW TO MAKE THE TRANSITION TO COOKING FRESH FOOD

Because I have been a chef for longer than I care to admit (forty-two years), it is hard for me to even remember what it is like to be a beginner, without knowledge of the basics of cookery. But, if you are used to eating prepared and packaged foods, and eating take-out, the switch to cooking from fresh ingredients at home can be daunting. Here are some resources to get you started:

Cooking Classes

The **Sustainable Food Center** cooking program is called **The Happy Kitchen/La Cocina Alegre**.™ I have taken this class myself and they do a great job of exposing you to the basics of cooking from scratch. You will learn both cutting and cooking techniques, and they also take the time to teach you about basic nutrition. They focus on fresh produce, whole grains and low-saturated fat ingredients, and offer pointers in cost effectiveness through local and seasonal shopping and cooking. They help you understand how your dietary changes can help you reduce diet-related diseases such as diabetes, overweight, obesity, heart disease, and cancer. They also instruct you what foods are good for your children's optimal and healthy growth. And finally, if that is your interest, they will take you one step further and teach you how to grow your own food. Isn't that great! I, for one, am glad we have this wonderful organization and their volunteers (a special thanks to Joy and Anne, Sandie and Maria) to help us. All you have to do is commit to a few classes. Depending on your income level, you can take these classes for free or for a very reasonable cost. For more information on their classes, cost and schedule, please check: **http://www.sustainablefoodcenter.org/happy-kitchen**.

Culinary Schools Classes

If you are serious about learning from the professionals, there are 4 culinary schools in Austin ready to help you. You can choose from the **Auguste Escoffier School of Culinary Arts**, **Le Cordon Bleu** cooking school, the **Art Institute of Austin**, and the **Natural Epicurean School**.

My personal favorite to learn professional skills from real life-trained chefs is the Austin location of Escoffier School of Culinary Arts: **http://www.escoffier.edu/locations/austin**. Their **Classes for the Home Cook** will teach you how to gain confidence in your own kitchen. According to your level of experience, their chefs can take you on your culinary path from basic knife skills one day/night workshop to 5 days advance techniques classes. When you're ready to be more culinary adventurous, you can take their 20 weeks Culinary classes to help you gain a thorough understanding of the artistry of food, flavor components, presentation and plating, and the orchestration of entire meals. They also offer kids cooking and baking classes for those curious children helping you in your own kitchen.

How do I know so much about this particular school? I used to be a Pastry and Baking Chef-Instructor there for 2 years. I know all the chefs there personally and trust their ability to teach you in a few days what it would take years to discover on your own. It's well worth your investment in your own culinary future. It's not just for chefs in training, you can do it too.

Grocery Stores Classes

Another option would be to take basic cooking classes at your local community college, food stores or private cooking classes available in your hometown. In Austin, we are lucky to have the **Central Market Cooking School** offering many great classes at all expertise and price levels, from basic cutting techniques to ingredient knowledge, and even classes taught by food and music celebrities. See: **http://www.centralmarket.com/Cooking-School.aspx. Whole Foods Market** also offers similar classes at their Lamar Cooking Center. Please see: **http://wholefoodsmarket.com/stores/lamar-culinarycenter.**

Your Own Favorite Restaurant Classes

In Austin, even local restaurants offer cooking classes matching your culinary interests: Casa de Luz, Thai Fresh, Malaga Tapas and Bar, Lake Austin Spa Resort, A Taste of Italy, East Side Café and others. You can learn to bake at some of the above professional schools, as well as at All In One Bake Shop (their new name is Make it Sweet at a new location coming soon).

Kids Classes

Looking to expose your kids to cooking? Check out Central Market, Whole Foods Market and Young Chefs Academy. For more details, check out the Edible Austin Magazine dedicated page at: **http://www.edibleaustin.com/content/resources-resourcesmain-84/cooking-classeseducation-resourcesmain-62.**

Making a Gradual Change

Our eating habits are just as resistant to change as our other habits. Making a big change, such as changing from restaurant fare to fresh, locally grown food, might seem like an insurmountable hurdle. My clients who have experienced the most success have approached this change gradually. Be easy with yourself, and add fresh, vibrant foods to your diet a little at a time. Give yourself time to adjust.

Start with the Weekend

If you have a typical workweek schedule, I suggest that you begin by buying fresh food at the market on Saturday, and preparing a large home-cooked meal on Sunday (large enough to provide leftovers for later in the week). It will be much less stressful for you to begin cooking from scratch on a non-workday. Good items to make would be a hearty soup, a stew, or a big pot of rice and beans. Enjoyed with a side salad and fresh fruit, you will have a lovely Sunday dinner. Then, later in the week, you can use your leftovers for a quick dinner or for several lunches.

Expand to More Days

As you grow more confident in your abilities, and as you begin to savor how delicious your own efforts are, you will be eager to expand to more days. For people with very long and busy workdays, it is sometimes a good option to prepare many dishes on Sunday, to be eaten throughout the week. As your skills improve, you will find that it can take the same amount of time to make several dishes as a single one, especially if you are preparing dishes that involve long, slow cooking times, like braised meats and stews. For example, you could prepare *Provençal-Style Beef Stew*, and *Cous-Cous, Lentil, and Spring Greens Salad*, and *Cream of Carrot and Coconut Soup* on one weekend afternoon. Having these dishes already prepared in your fridge will give you lots of options to create meals throughout the week.

For those of you who have sufficient time to cook daily, simply add cooking to your schedule as it feels comfortable to you. To help you get started, I have created a week's menu for each season, located in the recipe section of this book. You will find that, the more you prepare fresh, seasonal food for yourself, the more you will prefer your own cooking. You will get addicted to the vitamins, minerals, and tasty flavors. In time, you will find restaurant fare, prepared foods, and packaged foods downright unappealing, for you will be able to taste how inferior they are.

A GRAB BAG OF ASSORTED SAVING TIPS

Shopping Tricks and Cheats

= Go to the farmer's market or grocery store with a clear and precise shopping list ("one pound of beans and one basket of strawberries") instead of trying to remember what's left in the fridge and overbuying. That's a budget buster. Also, temptation and impulse buying should be avoided. Eat something before shopping and you might be surprised at the money you can save when you're not tempted. Stay firm, with your list in hand, and your food budget will thank you.

= Avoid packaged meals. Think of them as something only for emergencies, for they will destroy your budget while not providing adequate nutrition. Stay fresh!

= Don't feel you have to eat red meat every day. Once a week is plenty. You can stay with the lower-priced cuts of meat and use them in stews and soups. You can also eat more white meat (pork, chicken, and turkey) to lower your protein costs, giving you savings that you can put toward the purchase of fresh fish.

= Don't forget good old reliable eggs. In the U.S., eggs are mostly seen as a breakfast food, but it does not have to be that way. There are plenty of egg dishes like omelets, frittatas, soufflés and quiches that can be used on a tight budget; eggs are the still cheapest and most complete protein source available. Combine them with a salad and you have a complete, cheap and very satisfying meal. I do this at least twice a week.

= If that still taxes your budget, don't forget that your cheapest source of protein, by far, is beans and pulses. Combine beans and rice and you will have a complete protein. Despite what the meat industry would like you to believe, you do not have to eat meat every day to get your protein needs met.

= Go to your local farmer's market on Saturday mornings with your shopping list in hand and find the freshest and least expensive food in season. To stay ahead of the game, ask you favorite suppliers what will be available the following week and plan your menus around these products. To help them and save money, buy only from the farmers themselves, not from wholesalers. Use my shopping tips below for more ideas.

= Buy your staples in bulk or large quantities at a wholesale store like Sam's or Costco. It's well worth the cost of the annual membership for a family of four or more.

= Bring your calculator with you and use it to find the best prices. Of course you already know about coupons, but have you noticed that coupons are rarely available for fresh food, only for processed food? Avoid them. You will end up spending more money for less nutrition.

= If you're a smart and frugal shopper, you already know that grocery stores love to play dirty and expensive tricks on you. They offer "loss leader" prices to lure you in, and overcharge you on other products. Don't fall for that. Beat them at their own game by looking for the best prices in the newspaper or online, and buy only what is advertised - nothing else. You may even look at ads from competing stores close to each other and buy only what's on sale in the first one, go to the other one and buy only what's on sale there. You may have to spend a little more time looking for these deals, but after a while you will be a shrewd shopper and will save money on your food bill.

= Keep an eye on unit price, not just package price. At my grocery store, they label each product by the package and by the unit (ounce or other unit count). Smart business people that they are, food companies know that thrifty buyers will tend to grab the larger bags or boxes, thinking it is a better deal. It's not always the case. Sometimes the medium sized product will be cheaper. Oh, and do not always trust the cost per unit on the shelf price tag. Keep your trusty calculator close by.

= Depending on the size of your grocery store and your neighborhood's ethnic diversity, you may be able to find the same product packaged differently, but at a cheaper price in the Mexican section than in the Asian section of your store. You will have to do a little detective work to find the best deals. You might also want to check out the prices at ethnic groceries in your area; many offer very low prices on superior quality meats, staples, and vegetables.

= Most of the time you will also save money by buying store brands. Consumer Reports has proven again and again that store brand products are not of lower quality. They charge less because they do not have to pay for expensive national advertising the way brand name companies do.

= Recycle your packaging. I recently found that my HEB Central Market allows me, in some cases, to reuse my own recycled containers (such as glass jars) when buying bulk food. You will have to ask an employee to pre-weigh your container, you fill it with what you need, and they will weigh and price the item in front of you. A nice lady from Albania showed me that trick last week. Another good idea to save packaging and money both for you and the store.

= My friend Aurora commented that carrying all those glass jars in her backpack made it too heavy for her to carry, so I suggested she do what the shopping ladies in France do: Buy a shopping cart on wheels and voila! If you buy products that need to stay cool (especially in Texas), another idea would be to buy one of those beer coolers on wheels (or better yet, get a free one from a beer company), stuff it with a few frozen cooling packs and drop it in the back of your car or truck.

= In the same vein, farmers love it when you bring your own recycled cloth and plastic bags to the farmers market. Since packaging is an added cost to them, they will appreciate your thriftiness and may thank you with a little extra gift here and there.

= If you're willing to take a chance, wait until the last 30 minutes before the farmer's market closes and get discounts on what's left over. Most farmers do not want to bring back home their unsold produce.

= Sometimes, if you prod him a little, your grocery store produce manager will allow you to buy overripe fruits or vegetables at a very reduced price (please note: not all of the stores will, due to possible litigation issues). From the slightly damaged produce, you could make a batch of peach sorbet or a cobbler, canned tomatoes, sauce, or pickled cucumbers. Your local farmer may also offer you a great deal on slightly overripe or damaged produce. There is no harm in asking!

= I personally love vanilla almond milk. Granted, it's a little expensive at $2.68/ half gallon or eight cups at thirty-four cents a cup. But since it's too thick for me and too sweet for my taste (fifteen grams per serving), I cut it with about one-third filtered water and voila: one cup "light" and low-sugar vanilla almond milk now costs me twenty two cents a cup and I still have the right amount of sweetness and the vanilla flavor I like. Nice! You can use the same trick to "water down" whole organic milk instead of buying low-fat or no-fat milks that taste like water anyway.

= I like to control the sweetness, flavor and cost of my yogurt so I buy a thirty two ounce plain organic yogurt (Brown Cow, for example) at $2.85 or seventy three cents per cup, add two teaspoons of all natural fruit preserves, and voila! One cup of organic fruit flavored yogurt at eighty cents and five grams of sugar per cup instead of $1.49 to $1.68 a cup and fifteen grams of sugar per cup. This way, you can control the price, quality, and sweetness of your yogurt.

= I love my cup of homemade mocha in the morning. Instead of buying "cocoa" mixes that are nothing but sugar with little actual cocoa, I buy Hershey's unsweetened cocoa powder (the same one you use to prepare your favorite chocolate cake) at $2.45 per eight ounces or ten cents per teaspoon. I put a teaspoon of that cocoa in the bottom of my cup, add an eighth of a teaspoon of Medaglio del Oro instant espresso, pour boiling milk (or alternative "milk") over it, mix it well with a plunging blender (to eliminate lumps) and "Mocha chaud maison" (home-made hot mocha) for about thirty cents a cup compared to $3.50 at Star-dollars. Keep in mind that if you don't use vanilla almond milk like I do, you may have to add a little sugar and a drop of vanilla extract to it. Please, please and pretty please, avoid all these overpriced fancy chocolate mixes (Ghirardelli Premium Hot Cocoa for example) at $3.99 for sixteen ounces or twelve servings at thirty-three cents and thirty-one grams of sugar each. You won't taste the difference and your pocketbook will be *much* happier.

What We Need to Learn or Relearn at Home

= Try to organize your time to allow for more cooking at home. By preparing two or three meals at once, portioning them and storing them properly (vacuum-sealed, refrigerated or frozen), you will be able to eat for the whole week. All you have to do is prepare a quick mixed salad and drizzle it with your homemade dressing, add some fruit and you have a quick whole meal.

= Use this book to learn simple healthy meals you can prepare in no time at all. Because I work in a kitchen all day, I do not feel like cooking long meals when I get home, either. So I use different quick cooking techniques to make easy meals that typically do not take a lot of time to prepare.

= Relearn to love your crock-pot for stews and braised meals. Planned properly, they can save you a lot of money, as well as time. Plus, you can cook a larger amount and use the leftovers for lunch the next day, or vacuum-seal and freeze them for future quick meals when you are really tired. For example, you could start your meal preparation Saturday morning and let it cook slowly while you're running errands or shopping at the farmers market, and when you come back home, finish the meal at the last minute. These slow-cooking methods never prevented our grandparents from living their lives!

= Take advantage of these slow cooking methods to buy lower-priced cuts of meat. The slow cooking method will tenderize them, and often these cuts have richer, more powerful flavor and aroma.

= Make your own salad dressing. Not only is it less expensive than store-bought, you know what's in it and can avoid added HFCS and other chemicals. I always make a one-quart batch (see my own recipe in the recipe section) and store it refrigerated in a large recycled squeeze bottle, and it provides me with salad dressing for a few weeks. All I have to do is let it come to room temperature, shake it baby, and it's ready to be drizzled on my daily salad.

= Plan for your next day's food. It does not take a lot of time to think about what you will eat the following day. Check your menu plan, pull the proper ingredients out of the freezer; soak the beans overnight; defrost a premade meal; prepare all the ingredients needed for that crock pot recipe for tomorrow's dinner. Prepare and pack leftovers for tomorrow's lunch. Planning the night before will save you from a last minute anxiety attack. There will never be a need to stop at a fast food place or to order a last minute pizza. Save yourself unnecessary hassle and save money instead.

= Another professional technique to use at home is what is called "mise en place" or advance "prep". On your shopping day, plan for a little extra time after you get home to clean and prepare ingredients so they require minimal handling when you're ready to cook dinner. Wash all your fruits and vegetables. If you bought green leafy vegetables, soak them in water, rinse and dry them and precut in quarter-inch sections. Store them in green "breathable" or paper bags so they don't spoil too fast. If you have time, precut and plastic-bag some of your veggies for snacks, soup, or stew. Precut and store your meat and fish in meal size portions in airtight containers properly labeled.

= Watch what you throw away. Your well-thought-out menu plan and shopping list should help you avoid waste, but keep a sharp eye on home waste patterns. If you live alone and buy those thirty-two ounce yogurt containers, they might go bad before you have time to finish them. If that's the case, either buy smaller containers, or start making your own yogurt from scratch. When you end up throwing food away, it is a double blow to your budget.

= Another little thing that annoys me to no end is when I see one of my young co-workers throwing away a whole tomato or cucumber, just because part of it has been damaged during transport, or there is a little brown spot on it. Most of the time, three-quarters of that slightly damaged tomato, apple, or banana is perfectly good. What a waste! Cut the bad part out and use the rest. If a bug or a bird started to eat at your fruit before you, see it as a good sign that it's ripe for eating. They know. It does not mean you have to throw away the whole thing!

= Remember the portion control section? I keep on having a vision of crowds of people (mostly men) with potbellies. I suspect it's because they eat more food (and too fast) than their stomach can handle. So to accommodate that excess food, the belly will stretch out a little at a time and 10 or 20 years later.... pot-bellied adults. The ladies can agree with me that it's not as cute as a Vietnamese pot-bellied pig. If you can manage to eat only what you need and not what you want, your waistband and belt will thank you, you will have a healthier body, and you will save a lot of money in the process. Think about how many times you've had to change your wardrobe to accommodate that expanding waistline and you'll know exactly what I'm talking about.

MY FOOD BELIEFS

What Healthy Food Means to You and Me

Over the years I have found most people, even my own clients, to be very defensive about what they eat. They'd rather tell me how much money is in their bank account than write an accurate "food diary"! So I'm not going to tell *you* what to do. Instead I will tell you what *I* do. That way I will not offend anyone. Feel free to follow my example as much or as little as you want. We are all masters of our own life and health and we should act according to our beliefs.

It's That Simple

When it comes down to it, it is very simple. Eat only fresh, living food in season. What does that mean? Eat as many fresh fruits and vegetables as possible. Eat locally raised, free-range poultry, eggs and grass-fed beef and pork. Eat wild, line caught fish. If you can, buy them fresh at your local farmers' market, or organic at your grocery store. If you can't afford to buy it that way, grow and raise it yourself. I'm not advocating we all go back to the good old days and start riding horse-drawn carriages, but in a way, when life was simpler, life was healthier as well. In a twisted way, I feel that all the forces that are making our lives more difficult–the economy, the way food corporations are serving us unhealthy food, how little protection we are offered by our own government against large scale agriculture abuses–are forcing us to reevaluate how we spend our hard-earned and shrinking food budget. Now is the time to take responsibility for our health through how we eat. We might as well stop counting on our not-so-helpful elected officials to deliver on their false promises. I also believe that as we become more aware of our society's shortcomings, we will develop friendlier, stronger, and healthier local communities. Let's regain control over our lives now by taking things into our own hands.

No Fast Food

I even hate to use the word "food" next to the word "fast". The grub that we are served in these businesses has nothing to do with real food. They may try to convince us that it's yummy food, but we know the truth--it's not. Does the word Frankenfood mean anything to you? There it is in your Styrofoam container staring back at you. (If you haven't watched the documentary "Supersize Me" by Morgan Spurlock, please watch it. It is a real eye-opener.) Making matters worse, many fast "foods" are fried in oil (most likely hydrogenated polyunsaturated oil, loaded with killer trans-fatty acids) that has been heated and reheated again to the smoke point. Two things happen here: First, the repeatedly heated oil degrades into toxic compounds. Prolonged consumption of burnt oils can lead to atherosclerosis, inflammatory joint disease, and development of birth defects. Second: even though that oil is filtered every night, microscopic burnt food particles are still present and they are carcinogenic. In other words, if you eat food fried in reheated oil, you may be exposing yourself to some ugly types of cancer. That is why I recommend you only fry with high smoke point oils such as coconut or palm oil, and that you throw the oil away after being used once. Never use olive oil to fry food; its smoke point is too low. Use olive oil on cold or lukewarm dishes only.

For Budget's Sake! Avoid Eating Out

I'm going to make some people in the restaurant business unhappy by telling you a few of their secrets. Actually, when you think about it, some of this will be obvious. A restaurant's food cost average is usually around 30% of the menu price, sometimes lower depending on the type of restaurant you go to. With the remaining 70% they have to pay their employees, buy or rent their location, pay for utilities, insurance, repair and maintenance and a slew of taxes (city, state, federal and payroll) and, if possible, make a profit so they can stay in business. So when you eat at home you save 70% off that restaurant bill, not counting the tip, for a grand rich total of 85%. Isn't this worth thinking about it when calculating your food budget?

In Europe, a typical family will go out to a restaurant very rarely and only for special occasions, such as my Maman's 80th birthday last year. If it's a small family celebration, it will be held at home, and everyone will pitch in to prepare that birthday or anniversary dinner. Plus, it's so much more intimate and relaxed when you have your celebrations at home, isn't it? You can have more fun without disturbing the table next to you, you can drink as much as you want (as long as you don't have to drive afterwards) and dance all night long as long as you invite your neighbors so they don't complain about the noise. All you have to do is order the decorated birthday cake at your neighborhood patisserie and voila! Have a great time with your family and friends and "laissez le bon temps rouler", while saving yourself a nice chunk of change.

Legal or Illegal Drugs? Pick your Poison.

Most people would recoil at the thought of taking illegal drugs or smoking pot (maybe not all people!), yet they don't have any problem poisoning themselves with a lethal cocktail of chemical preservatives, artificial coloring ,and sugar. Sugar is extremely addictive, and in my opinion should be treated like an illegal drug. After all, excess intake of refined sugar or refined carbohydrates is directly linked to thousands of deaths every year. How is one different than the other? It's all white powder. Yet I don't see the government declaring a war on sugar anytime soon. If we want to treat our body as our temple, we should give it the respect it deserves by eating only foods fit to keep it healthy and functioning optimally.

No Processed Food

Ideally, we should steer away from any form of overly processed food. The only exceptions might be home-canned and organic frozen fruits and vegetables. Why am I against processed food? Because by the time it reaches your plate it has lost much of its nutritional value. The processing has destroyed most of the life-supporting vitamins. And don't forget flavor, or should I say, the lack of it. By the time you eat it, the nutritional value of overly processed food is severely compromised. Then the manufacturer or food scientist in his lab, knowing that, will add nutrients and artificial flavorings back in to compensate for that loss. And they dare to brag about it: "Added vitamin D or C", and use that as a selling point! Aren't they ashamed of themselves? What twisted reasoning! If they did not take it out in the first place, they would not have to add it in later on. And don't get me started on the unpronounceable chemicals used to color, preserve, and add taste to that dead food. So, you may be filling your stomach, but you are not satisfying your body's need for health-supporting nutrients. And you wonder why you are hungry two hours later and fill yourself with a pick-me-up snack loaded with sugar! That's why! Nothing can replace fresh food when it comes to beauty, taste and life force.

No MSG

MSG, or monosodium glutamate, also known as sodium glutamate, is a sodium salt of glutamic acid, a naturally occurring non-essential amino acid. It is used as a food additive and is commonly marketed as a flavor enhancer. You can also find it under the trade names of *Ajinomoto*, *Accent*, "Sazón Goya" or Natural Meat Tenderizer. It was once made predominantly from seaweed, but is now made mostly by bacterial fermentation.

Why is it so attractive to our taste buds? Glutamates create a savory taste called umami (savory) usually found in fermented or aged foods such as soy sauce, miso (fermented soy bean paste), and cheese, as well as some mushrooms. It is also a component of hydrolyzed protein such as yeast extract. That's why it's used so widely in the food industry, especially in the fast food business. It has an addictive effect on our bodies and that's good for repeat business. Even the propaganda website sponsored by the food manufacturers lobby group supporting MSG explains that the reason they add it to food is to make people eat more… And we wonder why this nation is overweight!

What is so bad about MSG? In a book called "The Slow Poisoning of America", John Erb mentions numerous studies linking MSG to allergies, diabetes, migraines and headaches, autism, ADHD, and even Alzheimer's. Not only that, but MSG is believed to triple the amount of insulin created by our pancreas which could lead to insulin resistance and obesity. So far, this has not been proven in human beings, but it is a well-known effect used in labs to "grow" MSG-obese rats for research on obesity. If you don't believe me, please go to the National Library of Medicine at **http://www.pubmed.com.** Type in the words 'MSG Obese' and read a few of the 115 medical studies that appear there.

How to avoid it? The easiest way (but not so easy for most people) is to avoid all fast food and most processed food. Both are loaded with it. Unfortunately, it is well hidden under many different names such as hydrolyzed vegetable extract and hydrolyzed soy protein. For more information about this hidden threat to our health, please check **http://www.msgtruth.org** and **http://www.msgmyth.com.**

No Packaged Food

Other than staples like rice, beans, and pasta, avoid buying packaged food. Why? For the simple reason that the box, can or container costs money and the manufacturer has to make you pay for it. Usually, the actual cost of the food inside a packaged food item is only 10 to 15% of the retail price. Did you think they would give you the box for free? Of course not. All the people involved in getting that food to you have to make a profit. It starts with the grower, then the processor, the distributor and finally the store. That's a lot of people you have to pay to get that food in your shopping cart. Sadly, the grower barely earns a living when selling their goods to a wholesaler. Why not buy directly from the farmer, help him make a decent living growing fresh food for you, and get better food on your dinner table?

If you have access to bulk bins at your local store, you can even get your rice, beans, pasta, and most of your dry staples without the packaging mark-up. They will likely be fresher than the boxed food sitting on the shelves, as well. If you can, buy at a store that does a high volume of business so you know that your food has not been sitting there for a long time.

Maximum Nutrition, Not Maximum Calories

We already established that fresh food is a better choice than packaged food, but you might still ask "Why?" The answer is nutrition quality. What your body needs is as much nutrition as possible for your dollar. What it does not need is empty calories. Since packaged food is loaded with empty calories, the only thing your body will gain is extra weight. And you already know how I feel about all the additional chemicals involved in these processed foods. So, to recap: poor nutrition, the added cost of fancy packaging, poisoning chemicals... the solution: do not buy packaged processed food.

Avoid Refined Foods

By that I mean you should eat food that is as complete and natural as possible. Unbleached whole-wheat flour versus all-purpose white flour; organic or natural raw or turbinado sugar versus white sugar. Whole-wheat flour, even though processed, still contains fiber beneficial to your intestinal health and prevents a spike in your blood sugar levels. Raw sugar is also processed, but unrefined, and still contains some of the vitamins and minerals from the sugar cane or beet it came from. If you are diabetic, any excess sugar intake is bad for you; but if you're not, raw and unprocessed sugar is a better choice than white refined sugar.

How to Eat According to Me... and Many Other Nutritionists

Breakfast – You've heard it before many, many times: Breakfast is the most important meal of the day. Try to live up to this saying by going back to a solid meal in the morning. It does not have to take a lot of time. Two fried or poached eggs or an omelet, a slice of toasted whole grain bread with real butter or nut butter and no-added sugar preserves. Or, homemade oatmeal with dried fruits and nuts (see my own recipe later), a cup of coffee or a bowl of hot chocolate, and a small glass of freshly squeezed juice will provide you with plenty of long-term energy to last you well into lunch time. These days, the problem is that we have been convinced to load ourselves with an excess amount of sugar-loaded breakfast "stuff" that does us no good. White flour waffles, muffins or breakfast pastries... once a week, or as a treat on weekends, maybe. All the time, no. Overly sweetened breakfast cereals only raise your kids' blood sugar through the roof, causing them to go hyper on their teacher for a couple of hours, then crash in the middle of the morning, then "need" another sugary snack to make it to lunch. Not good at all! A lot of kids labeled ADD or ADHD by teachers are nothing more than kids high on sugar, a powerful drug. Please don't do that to them (and yourself). Eat real food. I have the same issue with sugary fruit "drinks" served at breakfast. Out with them! Real juices only, and in much smaller amounts.

Lunch - The same thinking should apply to lunch. Keep it light, get some greens, eat no more than 4 ounces of protein, avoid refined carbohydrates, and drink water. You will feel a lot lighter and will not fall into the classic after-lunch stupor. If at all possible, try to bring food from home and enjoy it knowing you are eating healthier and saving money in the process.

Dinner - Honestly, for single people like me, there is no need for complicated meals at night. In my case, I avoid eating carbohydrates at night and try to keep my meals simple. In the fall and winter, a bowl of homemade soup, a side salad and a fruit is all I need to eat. In the spring and summer (especially in Texas where summer seems to last forever), I prepare a larger mixed salad with assorted additions and dressings, top it with a quick broiled portion of fish, chicken or pork, sometimes eggs or an omelet, add a piece of fruit and there's dinner. For those of you who are cooking for a family every night, see my meal plans at the beginning of each section of seasonal recipes.

REFINED SUGAR: The Wolf in Sheep's Clothing

No Added Sugar

This is a huge subject, and thousands of books and papers have already been written about the negative effects of added sugar in our diet. In my opinion, the majority of your sugar intake should come from fruit. Fruits contain a natural fruit sugar called fructose, and unless you are diabetic you should not have any problem eating two or three servings of fruit a day. The fiber fruit contains will slow down and regulate the absorption rate of the natural sugar, preventing a spike in your blood sugar level. Our bodies and especially our brains do need glucose to function, but it should be from fresh food, not from added refined sucrose.

What is Sucrose?

Sucrose is what is commonly called sugar or table sugar - also called saccharose. It is the result of refining the natural sweetener extracted from sugar cane or beets. It usually comes to us as white or brown sugar. It is a disaccharide (two sugars) made of glucose and fructose. Sucrose in itself, coming directly from nature is not a bad thing. But the refining process makes it go straight into your blood, instead of being broken down in your body by the enzymes amylase and carbohydrase as would normally happen were you to eat sugar cane or beets.

Shockingly, it is said that the average American consumes from a low of 45.3 pounds of sugar per year (NY Times) up to 150-170 pounds of combined refined sugars (USDA). I know you probably don't think you eat that much sugar yourself, because you're thinking about that teaspoon of sugar you add to your coffee or tea, but try to imagine all the different kinds of sugar hidden in processed foods (glucose, sucrose, fructose, galactose, maltose and many more sweeteners finishing with "ose"…and let's not forget the infamous high fructose corn syrup or HFCS) and you may realize that you are ingesting far more sugar than you think. It's time for you to look at the labels a little more closely. It is also said that for one person eating only 5 pounds of sweetener per year, there is another one that ingests 295 pounds a year. Ouch!

What is Fructose?

Fructose is a monosaccharide (simple sugar) contained in fruits, vegetables, honey, maple syrup, and molasses. It is broken down by our bodies into glucose, then into glycogen. The fructose in a fresh fruit is not harmful, because of its fiber, vitamin, mineral, and flavonoid (antioxidant) content. For example, according to http://www.nutritiondata.self.com, an average eight-ounce apple contains nineteen grams of fructose, a total of twenty-five grams of carbohydrates and three grams of dietary fiber. Per ounce, you get less than two and a half grams of sugar, about 3 grams of carbohydrates and almost one-half gram of dietary fiber. Nice!

Are you Sure you want Those Innocent-Looking Cookies?

On the other hand, when you eat a couple of chocolate chip cookies or one ounce (really, who can just eat two cookies?), you ingest eight grams of sugar (glucose and fructose syrup) with a total of eighteen grams of carbohydrates (coming from the refined flour, chocolate, and other ingredients). So, to compare apples to cookies, if you were to eat eight ounces of cookies (who doesn't eat that much in a sitting while watching TV–not you of course – just saying), you would scarf down a total of sixty-four grams of sugar and one hundred grams of total carbohydrates. Per ounce, there are eight grams of sugar (almost four times as much as in the apple) and eighteen grams of total carbohydrates (almost six times as much as in the apple) and *zero* dietary fiber. Ou la, la! Not so good, eh?

Dr. Lustig's Point of view on Fructose

Dr. Lustig is a Professor of Pediatrics in the Division of Endocrinology at UCSF and specializes in children's obesity and diabetes. He is a well-known speaker regarding the negative effects of sugar on health. He postulates that the main reason why people (and especially children) are more obese and face higher rates of diabetes in recent decades is the increase of fructose in our diet. His position is that sugar is an addictive drug and, when taken over a long period of time, a "chronic toxin" dangerous to our health. I agree with him, because most people, especially in the younger population, get their fructose from an every day consumption of highly sweetened foods loaded with processed fructose, such as soft drinks, cookies, candies, and ice cream. It is an extremely valid point of view, but…

My Problem with Dr. Lustig's Point of View

Even among scientists, there is disagreement whether fructose is healthier than glucose. My problem with these arguments is that they are based on processed and refined carbohydrates only, not simple or complex carbohydrates coming from fresh food. In my humble and non-scientific point of view, that fact negates the whole argument until they start specifying "processed" fructose. As they did before with fats, they bunch together the good and the ugly in the same bag. I say it isn't so! We need to keep natural fructose coming from fresh food separate from added fructose contained in processed food. Natural fructose contained in fresh food is NOT bad for you, as long as you don't eat ten pounds of it in one sitting. Keep on eating fresh food and avoid all processed foods loaded with refined or processed sugars, wherever they come from.

What are the USDA Added Sugar Recommendations?

The USDA recommends that you ingest no more than thirty-two grams or eight teaspoons of ADDED sugar per day. Added sugar is what does not occur naturally in your food. Easy peasy! Take all the processed and packaged food OUT of your diet and you will not risk high blood sugar, insulin resistance, hypoglycemia or type II diabetes down the road. It leaves you with the sugar you add to your coffee or tea. You can even replace that with a natural plant-based sugar like stevia.

How to Recognize Added Sugar

These sneaky added sugars are trying to disguise themselves under many different names such as:

➢ Anhydrous dextrose
➢ Brown sugar
➢ Confectioner's powdered sugar
➢ Corn syrup
➢ Corn syrup solids
➢ Dextrose
➢ Fructose
➢ Fruit nectars (e.g., peach nectar, pear nectar)
➢ High-fructose corn syrup (HFCS)
➢ Honey
➢ Invert sugar
➢ Malt syrup
➢ Maltose
➢ Maple syrup
➢ Molasses
➢ Pancake syrup

➢ Raw sugar
➢ Sucrose
➢ Table sugar
➢ White granulated sugar

Caution: There are other added sugar names not recognized by the FDA as ingredient names. They are evaporated cane juice, evaporated corn sweetener, corn sugar, fruit juice concentrate, crystal dextrose, glucose, liquid fructose, sugar cane juice, and fruit nectar. Again, become a sugar hunter by reading the food labels carefully.

Killer HFCS

When it comes to plant-based sweeteners, your worst enemy is high fructose corn syrup (HFCS), commonly used in almost all processed foods, including soft drinks. It is an inexpensive sweetener refined and processed from corn. It causes huge spikes in your blood sugar. Since the introduction of HFCS to industrial food manufacturing in the 1970's, obesity and type II diabetes have increased dramatically in this country. Have you noticed that when we eat too much natural sugar our bodies, by way of the sugar-binding protein lectin, sends us a nauseating signal telling us, "Stop eating that stuff or I will throw up?" That's the body's natural defenses, telling us our organs (in this case, our pancreas) can't take any more of this sugar overload. Well, it has been found that HFCS completely bypasses this warning system and allows us to eat or drink huge amounts of HFCS-loaded food or drinks without feeling sick. Great for the food business, eh? But not so great for us. To clarify this for you, did you know that the average American consumes four gallons or thirty-two pounds of HFCS per year? Eventually we develop insulin resistance when our pancreas cannot control the dangerous blood sugar spikes we are causing ourselves. When our pancreas are completely exhausted and can no longer produce insulin, type II diabetes sets in, and a whole new, miserable phase begins. I don't want that. Do you? Of course not. So avoid HFCS like the plague.

Why does Refined Fructose Make us Fat?

Unlike sucrose, which is metabolized by all cells in our body, refined fructose is metabolized directly by our liver into fat. In the normal process, carbohydrates are broken down into glucose. When there is an excess of glucose it is transformed into glycogen and stored in our liver and muscles for emergency use. But if we overload on sugar–especially liquid sugar--our liver will turn this excess sugar into fat stored in adipose tissues around our waist or thighs.

When we ingest fructose from fruits, vegetables and complex carbohydrates, the proportion of fructose to mass is much lower, the fiber slows down the whole metabolizing process and allows our body to absorb it slowly thus giving us a steadier level of energy.

Where is Added Sugar Hiding?

They're all the processed sugars contained in that processed or packaged food I suggested you avoid above. A few examples of processed foods containing high amounts of added sugar include:

- Food
- Candies
- Cakes, pies and cobblers
- Cookies
- Desserts and pastries
- Donuts, sweet rolls and breakfast pastries
- Frozen desserts, such as ice cream, sherbet and sorbet
- Jams, jellies
- And let's not forget many, many hidden sources of sweeteners as in ketchup, sauces, salad dressings, soups, and other processed foods. Please read the labels carefully. Be your own food detective.

Drinks

ALL soft drinks, no matter what kind. Did you know they contain an average of one teaspoon of sweetener per ounce of drink? So if you drink a twenty-ounce bottle of C@&e (sounds like a drug, doesn't it?), you're drinking about twenty teaspoons or eighty grams of sweetener *per bottle*. One bottle of that liquid poison contains more than twice the USDA recommended daily amount. Drinking soft drinks can lead to the following health issues: Tooth decay, high blood sugar, type II diabetes, obesity, cancer, heart disease, and osteoporosis.

Sweet teas, energy drinks, sports or "smart" drinks, as well as the fancy drinks marketed as "healthier" than soft drinks. Bull! Some of them contain up to thirty-five grams (nine teaspoons) of sugar per serving and there are two servings in each pint. So, for example, every time you drink a bottle of sweet tea (marketed as healthier than a soft drink), you drink a total of seventy grams (eighteen teaspoons) of sweetener, double the recommended daily amount–all in one drink.

Did you know that if you drink just one twelve-ounce can of soda every day for a year, you could gain eighteen pounds? If you give up drinking that daily can, you could *lose* eighteen pounds. Something to think about!

Additionally, buying any of these drinks will add a heavy cost to your food budget. Save your money and lose weight instead.

Please know that I am not saying, "Do not have ANY sugar, ever". As in everything else in life, moderation is the key. I believe that eight teaspoons of added sugar a day is a very reasonable amount of sugar. Heck! Most days I don't even ingest half of that, and honestly, I'm not that special. I just know what to watch for, and now you do too.

What Do I Drink Then? Water… and a Little Wine

Water. Again, a simple solution. Plain ol' water. I know, I know… the commercial drink companies are trying to scare you into believing that water is loaded with pollutants and you should not drink it. This is pure BS. Certainly we should all be cautious about what is in our water, but not to the point of being paranoid. For everyday use, I have installed a good quality water filter on my kitchen faucet and use that for drinking and cooking water. I have a pitcher of cool water always waiting for me in my fridge and to make it less boring, I add ¼ of a squeezed lemon or lime per cup of water. Try it. It's very refreshing. Once in a while, I will add natural sparkling water to it for a little fizz.

If you are addicted to sweetened drinks I suggest you try this healthier drink: Mix equal amount of one hundred percent fruit juice with sparkling water and you have a sparkling fruit drink at less than half the sugar content. Reduce the amount of fruit juice progressively and one day you will be free of sweetened drinks forever.

On a slight side note and for adults only, I drink a glass of red wine once in a while to get my quota of antioxidants from grapes. It's good for you and helps you relax too. Just don't overdo it.

THE FAT CONFUSION: Good fats, Bad Fats and Ugly Fats

Unfortunately, due to an intense marketing effort by the margarine industry, fat in general has gotten a bad rap for the past forty years or so. Wanting to sell their supposedly healthier product, they went after saturated fats with a vengeance. Little did we know at the time that their form of fat–hydrogenated fat–was much worse for our health than saturated fat. It was practical for the food industry to adopt this new fat because of two major advantages for them:

➤ It was a lot cheaper to produce than animal-based fat and…
➤ It never turned bad or rancid.

Meanwhile, the processed food manufacturers jumped at the opportunity to:

➤ Replace animal fat with artificial fat because of its benefits to their bottom line and…
➤ To start a whole new trend of low fat, healthier-for-you food products with higher profit margins.

Remember, we are still talking about processed food here. This whole fight should have stayed within the confines of that industry, but it spilled over to perfectly good-for-you foods like whole milk and yogurt, pork fat, and even coconut oil and butter, all of them perfectly wholesome foods appreciated for centuries for their health-giving properties.

Why did this margarine fiasco become a health problem? Because it was created in a lab by food scientists, not by nature. During the manufacturing of margarine, parts of the unsaturated oils are converted into hydrogenated fats or trans-fats in order to give them a higher melting point, so they stay solid at room temperature like saturated fats. The problem is that trans-fatty acids had not been studied long enough to discover their negative health effects. It took a couple of generations to discover that this artificial fat was not accepted normally by our bodies, and helped create all sorts of health problems like coronary heart diseases by raising levels of LDL (bad cholesterol) and lowering levels of HDL (good cholesterol). So, avoid hydrogenated and trans-fats as much as possible.

Is Cholesterol Bad For Us?

What people were not told is that, in reasonable amounts, cholesterol is essential for the creation of several important hormones produced in the adrenal glands, ovaries, and testes. Every cell in our body uses cholesterol to help build its protective cell membrane. Cholesterol also helps to produce the very important vitamin D when we expose ourselves to the sun every day. If we did not ingest some natural cholesterol in our diet, our bodies would produce its own cholesterol in order to survive. How can it be bad for you if our own body has to produce in order to function properly?

So we come back to saturated fats. Unlike margarine, which is an artificial trans-fat, good saturated fat (in moderation) contains essential fatty acids. It means that they are essential for the proper functioning of our body. There are many good books written about fats if you would like to learn more. I will try to cover the basics below.

Essential fatty acids are separated into to major groups: saturated and unsaturated.

Saturated Fats

These can be animal-based fats (suet, tallow, butter, or pork lard) or plant-based fats (coconut oil, palm oil, and palm kernel oil) as well as fats from pastured-raised eggs and grass-fed meats. As long as they are naturally produced, a reasonable amount of saturated fats are not only recommended, but also necessary to our health.

Saturated fats provide the building blocks for cell membranes and a variety of hormones. In addition, they act as carriers for important fat-soluble vitamins A, D, E, and K. Dietary fats are also needed for the conversion of carotene to vitamin A, for mineral absorption, and for a host of other biological processes. They contain the antiviral agent, caprylic acid. They also contain an effective anti-cavity, anti-plaque, and anti-fungal agent called lauric acid. The palmitic and stearic acids in saturated fats have been shown to actually *lower* blood cholesterol. Another one, butyric acid, is a modulator of genetic regulation and a possible cancer prevention agent. Better yet, when you eat fats as part of your meal, they slow down food absorption so that you can go longer without feeling hungry.

Unsaturated Fats

These usually come from fruits (olive and avocado), nuts (almond, macadamia, pecan, walnut, peanut, etc.), seeds (sunflower, sesame, safflower, etc.), and plants (soy, corn). They are further broken down into monounsaturated oils (i.e., olive) and polyunsaturated oils (i.e., corn, sunflower, safflower, and canola).

They all contain different ratios of polyunsaturated fats called omega-6 and omega-3 fatty acids. They are both beneficial, but our modern diet tends to privilege omega-6 fatty acid oils over omega-3 because they are easier and cheaper to produce. The ideal ratio of omega-6 to omega-3 should be 3-1 (some say 1-1). Unfortunately, our modern diet is extremely unbalanced towards omega-6 fatty acids, and the current ratio is more like 20-1 to 30-1. Omega-6 fatty acids are known to promote inflammation and inflammation is the cause of many health problems.

What so terrible about a skewed ratio, you might ask? Well, it is said that our brain is made of about 60% of fat, most of it being omega-3. Omega-3 fatty acids are known to keep our brain cells membranes flexible which allow good nutrients to come in and toxins to exit. Omega-6 acids, on the other hand, tend to make our brain cell membranes less flexible and prevent good nutrition from feeding our cells. Some researchers claim that our imbalance of omega-6 over omega-3 may be the reason for a host of brain-related diseases such as depression, bipolar disorder, schizophrenia, ADD/ADHD, autism, Alzheimer's, and even strokes.

The best food sources of omega-3 fatty acids are fish oil, cod liver oil, and some plant-based oils such as flax seed oil.

My Favorite Fats for Eating and Cooking

For eating: Extra virgin olive oil for salad dressings or as a light drizzle on top of steamed vegetables. If you cannot afford or do not care for the strong flavor of extra-virgin olive oil, light olive oil will be fine. Be aware that the lighter the oil is, the more processed it is.

My own take on canola oil: I know a lot of people swear by it, but I am cautious about using it. There is no such thing as a "canola" plant. The oil is extracted from a plant called rapeseed (not a very marketable name, wouldn't you agree?), which in its natural form is poisonous for human consumption. So it had to be crossbred or genetically engineered to make it "safe". A smart marketer came up with the idea of combining Canada (the major source of "canola") with oil (ola) and voila! Canola oil was born. As I personally refuse to eat any genetically engineered food, I cannot recommend it.

<u>For cooking</u>: For pan-frying, coconut oil or a blend of half coconut oil and half butter. Please note that although I sauté, I do not deep-fry my food. I like a pat of butter on my steamed corn and in my mashed potatoes, but if you are concerned with saturated fat, feel free to substitute olive oil.

OUR GOVERNMENT'S INVOLVEMENT WITH OUR FOOD

No Chemicals Should Be Allowed On or In our Food

Avoid pesticide-sprayed produce. Do not eat meat that has been raised in crowded and filthy feedlots. These poor animals are pumped with bovine growth hormones and fed antibiotics constantly to prevent the sickness and failure to thrive that would naturally occur under these wretched conditions. It is the same with pork and chicken. Do not eat farm-raised fish unless they are certified organic (which is still very rare). Farmed-raised fish suffer the same unhealthy living conditions as their hoofed friends. Where do you think all of these unnatural hormones and antibiotics end up when you eat them? In your own body and that of your children. Why do you think doctors are seeing kids growing into puberty younger and younger? Those marvelous (not!) growth hormones used to pump up those poor animals. Our commercial food is killing us, and the vast majority of people are not even aware of it. It is sad to see kids afflicted with diseases we used to see only in adults, like type II diabetes, obesity, heart problems, osteoporosis, and so on. Enough already! This country and other developed nations are digging their own graves with their mouths. But the powers that be are not helping, because it would be against the corporate bottom line. The less we know about it, the more money they make.

What is our Government Doing About It?

I feel that the American government is failing its people when it comes to our national food safety. Other than small efforts at the local level, the major agencies in charge of protecting and educating us–the USDA and FDA--are asleep at the wheel, if not downright blind to the nasty effects of our food policies in this country. Commercial food producers have powerful lobbies in place in Washington whose job is to protest loudly against any challenge and water down any law trying to make our food cleaner and healthier to eat. Enough! This is a fight we need to fight ourselves. Obviously our government is not doing its part. Folks like you and me are becoming more aware of the negative health effects this commercial food is having on us. We end up paying in unnecessary pain and increasingly large medical bills. We need to regain control and fight the good fight to stay alive and healthy in this beautiful country. Let's not allow corporate greed to overwhelm our healthy lives.

No GMOs in Our Food! Update Our Food Labels!

It is getting becoming clear that GMOs (Genetically Modified Organisms) have a negative effect on human health. GMOs, or genetically engineered organisms (GEOs) are organisms whose genetic material has been altered using genetic engineering techniques. These techniques use DNA molecules from different sources, which are combined to create a new set of genes. This DNA is then transferred back into the original organism, giving it the newly modified genes. Some of these transplanted genes can also come from completely different species, like using animal genes in vegetables like the "fish tomato" proposed in 1991. Germany, France, and most European countries ban GMO crops, but they are allowed in the U.S and much of the globe.

I am doing my best to avoid GMOs, but I'm not getting any help from my food labels. For one thing, most of the processed foods available in grocery stores already have GMOs in them. It's a big hush-hush headache for the food companies and our government. They know from prior experience in Europe (where GMOs are clearly labeled, after a long and hard fight) that the vast majority of educated customers will never want their children to eat these Frankenfoods. If consumers are able to avoid GMOs, it would be very bad for both the chemical labs that create these mutant foods, the food conglomerates' stock market quotations, and the government would have a harder time protecting its processed food friends with the deep pockets. They all claim that they created these food-like mutants to increase food production so that all human beings in the world have something to eat. That is a bold-faced lie. It has been proven again and again that if we follow proven organic ways of growing our food, there will be plenty for all to eat. The beneficial side effect is that organic production methods will not destroy our environment in the process. We have the right to know what's in our food, and manufacturers should be forced by the government to clearly label such content. Meanwhile, avoid processed food unless it is certified organic or you personally know the farmer that grows your food. To help with this issue, check the Organic Consumer Association at http://www.organicconsumers.org/ and get more information on this subject.

Fresh News: The National Leafy Green Marketing Agreement

What's that? In my opinion it's another attempt from large agricultural conglomerates to eliminate the growing competition from small local farmers. Growing awareness of the major problems in our industrial food system has led us to buy more local food from growers we trust. In the past ten years, farmers' markets have more than doubled all over this country. It's starting to show on the Big Ag radar and they want to squash to competition the only way they know--brute force with the help of the USDA. They convinced the USDA to create a set of new rules favoring their industry at the detriment of small local and organic farmers. It is called the National Leafy Green Marketing Agreement. It's a new set of rules drafted by large vegetable growers' lobby that would drive small farmers out of business with expensive regulations. It feels to me that the USDA, while paying lip service to improving our food safety, is being strongly influenced by their old friends in giant agribusiness. Existing organic standards (that we the people had to fight for to protect from the same people's undue influence) contain adequate rules that help prevent food-borne illnesses. The recent rashes of food-borne illnesses were all connected to large agribusinesses, never to small farmers. So why try to make their lives more difficult? Because we, not trusting the "normal" food growers, have helped our local fresh food suppliers to grow to the point of being seen as competition by Big Ag. Isn't it what capitalism is all about? Let the people choose their favorite source of food and may the best win–fairly–at least that's what the naive amongst us believe. If Big Ag has his way–and it has deep pockets to push their nefarious agenda – they will try to eliminate what they see as completion, our cherished local farmers. Don't let them! For more information, see **http://www.FoodDemocracynow.org**.

Is Prohibition Back?

Are we living in an Ubu Roi (a famous French play about the deleterious effects of French bureaucracy on its citizens) where everything is upside down? I have to ask because it's becoming more evident that the same people that are supposed to protect us from the abuses of giant food, agricultural and pharmaceutical companies are, in fact, acting like they are trying to protect these same entities from regular folks like you and me. Why am I telling you these troublesome stories? Because, according to Mike Adams at NaturalNews.com, on August 4th, 2011, in a magnificent show of power, a multi-agency SWAT-style armed raid was conducted by helmet-wearing, gun-carrying enforcement agents from the LA County Sheriff's Office, the FDA, the Department of Agriculture and the CDC (Centers for Disease Control) against a private buying club offering raw milk and raw milk products. What did they do that was so wrong and against the law? They were charged with 'conspiracy' related to the sale of unpasteurized raw milk products and of mislabeling cheese? On top of that, they "seized" all the cash on hand and forced the people present to dump all the milk and cheese right on the spot. Thousands of dollars down the drain. See: **http://www.naturalnews.com/033220_Rawesome_Foods_armed_raids.html**.

This private club (not open to the general public) called Rawsome Food offers customers interested in such products the opportunity to buy shares of the production from cows and goats raised at Healthy Family Farms in Santa Paula, California–the victim of a similar raid on the same day. Apparently it's now illegal to sell raw milk and cheese. I have also read that the FDA did the same to an Amish farmer in Pennsylvania. The same abuse happens all over this beautiful country of ours. They go after all sorts of fresh foods sold at farmers' markets or private farms. When will they stop? If this abuse of power from our government agencies (paid by our own taxes, I might remind you) continues, they will force us to eat that industrial crap that passes for food in this country against our will. We know better. We don't want to feed our children that stuff. That's why farmers' markets and smaller famers are so successful. We know about these big guys' twisted games. If we don't stand up for our rights now, soon everyone that grows food in their own backyard could be arrested. You think that can't happen. You wait!

Why is the government doing these things? After all, they're supposed to work for us. The way I see it, all these huge businesses–processed food, milk, meat, poultry, and agriculture–see the writing on the wall. Our "grass-roots" movement of not buying their poisoned food makes them shake in their boots and they use their good friends in high places to clamp down on the competition. I thought we lived in a free country where any legal business was allowed to compete with others based on the quality of their product. Apparently not! Explain to me why the FDA and USDA would go after small potatoes like family farmers and yet allow these large conglomerates to poison our food?

A few examples and believe me, I can't tell them all. It would make this book far too long!

= Consumer Reports says that two-thirds of all fresh chicken meat sold in grocery stores today is contaminated with salmonella. Good thing I eat only farm-fresh chicken. Oh wait! Maybe the FDA will claim this chicken and their eggs to be a danger to society. Watch out!

= Diet soda is sweetened with aspartame, a chemical sweetener made from the feces of genetically engineered bacteria. Nice!

= "Natural" corn chips are made from genetically modified corn plants linked to widespread infertility when consumed by tested mammals. Another proof that "natural" does not mean anything.

= Most of your deli's processed meats are laced with cancer-causing sodium nitrite.

= Everything from soups to salad dressings is "enhanced" with the chemical excitotoxin known as MSG, which not only can cause severe allergic reactions, but also promotes obesity.

= Most dried "blueberries" in your breakfast cereal are fake, containing artificial colors, corn syrup and antifreeze liquids. Wow! That's a new one for me.

= The homogenization process artificially modifies fats found in milk, which makes them dangerous for human health.

= The high fructose corn syrup used to sweeten soda causes diabetes. Nothing new there.

= Chicken "My Noggings" (not its real name; its name was changed to protect its producer) are made with a chemical used in silly putty.

= The soy protein used in most protein bars is extracted from a toxic chemical called hexane.

= Did you hear that thirty six million pounds of ground turkey meat was recalled recently by Cargill–a huge food conglomerate–for causing a nationwide outbreak of salmonella? One person in California has died in the outbreak and at least seventy-six people have fallen ill, including at least nine in Texas. See: **http://www.statesman.com/news/nation/36-million-pounds-of-ground-turkey-recalled-in-1691995.html**. Now, did you see the USDA raid the factory and arrest everyone in sight? Why not? There was a death, after all. Isn't that supposed to be an actual crime?

= You also know that all the food recalls–spinach being the most recent–and many others come from huge industrial farms using sludge to "feed" the growth of their plants. You never see a small farm involved in these kinds of outbreaks, do you? Did anyone involved go to jail? I don't think so. A slap on the wrist and back to business as usual.

= All the toxic chemicals and highly processed ingredients that cause cancer, diabetes, heart disease, and nutritional deficiencies are all perfectly good for your health, the FDA says... because *they're dead!* According to an FDA spokesman, only living foods pose a health risk to us poor defenseless folks. We could never survive these nasty live foods unless the FDA and the USDA approve them to protect us. Is that why they arrested the owner of Rawsome

Foods? As far as I know, no raw veggie food has ever been proven to kill anyone. Never! So, what the deal? We need to ask them why and make them justify their actions. Only public outcry will show them we do not believe their lies and will not allow these abuses of power to go on.

Food as Fuel? What the Heck?

Here's another example of Big Ag influencing the cost of our food: by using their powerful connections, they managed to convince our government to back the policy of using corn ethanol as car fuel. How did they do that? Most of the gasoline at the pump now contains about ten percent ethanol. Ethanol or ethyl ethanol is an alcohol similar to the type of alcohol found in your favorite hard liquor. It can be refined from common crops like sugar cane, potato, manioc, and corn. But it is highly debatable that using food as fuel is an efficient way to power our vehicles. It's not enough that agribusiness is getting subsidies from the government (in reality shifting the tax money we pay to them) to "help" them grow corn, now they are fattening their pocketbooks at our expense by growing food as fuel. Besides, growing corn is much more energy intensive, as well as using more land and water and pesticides than diversified small farms. How is that fair? It's not. It costs all of us in added taxes and added food costs because of the large amount of corn used for fuel instead of food.

Some people may say, "But biofuel allows us to reduce pollution, makes gasoline less expensive to buy and reduces our dependence on foreign oil." True to a certain extent, but have you really noticed a lower cost of gasoline at the pump since ethanol has been introduced? It is possible that pollution is minimally reduced at the individual car level, but have we really calculated the environmental cost of growing and processing ethanol? In my modest opinion, we would better off not driving gas guzzling four-wheel drive monsters and just drive smaller cars like they already do in Europe. That would make a much bigger difference.

Vote with your Pocketbook

All of us food-eating and tax-paying citizens should complain to the USDA about unjust subsidies to the large agricultural companies. Instead of subsidizing industrialized corn, wheat, and soy--most of them GMO--which helped destroy small farmers in this country, demand that these subsidies go to support organic or local farms offering us fresh, healthy, and unpolluted food. Of course, I do realize that our politicians are influenced (bought?) by these huge lobbies with the deep pockets. We might have to do like the

French did, revolt and cut a few heads off for the sake of our food safety! But seriously, if more people like us refuse to eat this subsidized crap (oops!) that makes us sick and instead, buy fresh food from the markets, less of their "stuff" will sell and the price of real food will go down. It will increase demand for wholesome foods and reduce prices. Am I naïve in believing we can pull this off? You tell me. Meanwhile, you have the power of the pocketbook. It's your money! You work hard for it. Use it to influence the future of our food. Stop buying GMOs and subsidized foods and buy more fresh food. The market will adapt to your demands... eventually. It always does. They are wrong when they think they are in control--we are. We need to use our shopping money to create pressure. Look how the organic market has expanded over the last two decades! We can do the same for locally grown food. We have the power.

THE NEWEST USDA FOOD PYRAMID

Are You Ready for the New USDA Round Food Pyramid?

Did you know that the newest USDA food pyramid is now round? Wow! A big change, and a good one in my opinion. It now looks like a regular plate of food divided into four sections. On the left half of the plate (fruits and vegetables), the vegetable section (about 30%) is slightly larger than the fruit section (about 20%). On the right half of the plate (grains and proteins), the grains section (about 30%) is slightly larger than the protein section (about 20%). On the top right side is a glass of milk (can't forget that milk, can we? I'd rather it be water). It is visually much easier to understand because you can relate it to that plate in front of you during dinner. The great part is that they reduced the amount of grain (especially refined grains) and increased the amount of fruits and vegetables. Nice! Now that's what I call an improvement. See more at **http://www.choosemyplate.gov/**

What to drink? Water and (Ideally) Only Water

I'm also very glad they replaced sweetened drinks with water. For proper hydration, nothing beats water. Really! In my opinion, you should forget about any other drink. Not even those fancy waters loaded with "vitamins" at a premium price. No soft drinks. Sugar-loaded drinks may damage your health in the long run by contributing to insulin resistance, diabetes, osteoporosis, and many other health problems. To stay healthy, your body needs only one form of liquid…water.

A Few Additions from my French Plate Point of View

As a chef and nutrition therapist, I deplore the USDA's position about fats. Although they explain the difference between oils and what they call solid (saturated) fats, they do not differentiate between good and bad oils. There are important differences between them (see above), which should be pointed out very clearly. They also do not explain the differences between good and bad solid or saturated fats. They throw all solid fats into the same bag as artificial fats and transfats. It is inexcusable for the USDA to not warn the public about the potentially negative results of eating transfat-loaded shortening, partially hydrogenated fats and margarine.

Dairy

When you look at the dairy serving next to the plate, you will see a glass of milk. The USDA recommends you drink low-fat milk. Again, I (Frenchly) disagree for two main reasons.

1. We need full fat in our diet as explained above.

2. The processed milk we are told to drink is nowhere near as health giving as the good old fashioned fresh milk from a cow--as long as it is grass-fed and raised in a humane environment.

Although the pasteurization process was created to destroy harmful bacteria, I believe that the overheating inherent to the pasteurization process causes the destruction of vital vitamins and enzymes. Also, it has been proven that bacterial infections due to raw milk are extremely rare. Some scientists also claim that homogenization (the process used to suspend the cream throughout whole milk) could be the cause of increased hormone-based cancers as well as atherosclerotic plaque. Is animal-based milk fit for consumption by humans? I'll let you ponder that question for yourself. But, if you're going to drink milk, I suggest you drink whole raw milk if you can find it. Did you know that in some states, a farmer caught selling raw milk to the public could go to jail? There is a groundswell demand for the states to allow raw milk to be sold to the public, but the dairy industry has powerful lobbyists on their payroll. It is another fight we need to fight for our own health. For more information please see **http://www.westonaprice.org.**

Another factor to consider in consuming dairy products is their source. Is the milk you're drinking coming from poor scared animals raised in horrid conditions on commercial feedlots? Has the cow been pumped with bovine growth hormones? Has it been injected multiple times with antibiotics? Do you really believe that all of these chemicals do not eventually end up in the milk? Why are we seeing an increase of hormone-dependent cancers in children? Growth hormones! Why are we seen children growing faster and taller and little girls reaching puberty a lot sooner that nature intended it? Growth hormones! Why are we finding more and more super bacteria resistant to normal antibiotic treatments? Antibiotics! Because these bacteria evolved to resist antibiotics over generations of cows transmitting them through their milk. Another factor: These cows are mainly fed corn, which is a known source of omega-6 fatty acids. If you are drinking commercial milk, you are getting this added omega-6 with your daily breakfast, and we know omega-6 fatty acids are known to cause inflammation in our bodies. Do you really want your children to "get milk?" Again, if you drink milk, please drink milk from happy cows raised humanely and fed on grass loaded with omega-3 fatty acids.

So when you look at the new USDA food plate, keep in mind that eating your dairy products full fat and from healthy cows is actually a good thing, as long as you don't overdo it. Even when something is good for you, eat it in moderation.

Food Labeling

We have the right to know what is in our food. Yes, we already have nutrition labels on our processed food. It is a step in the right direction, but what worries me is, what KIND of food is in our food? By that I mean that more and more genetically modified organisms (GMOs) and engineered foods are invading our food supply. If we have to pay for our food, shouldn't we at least know what's in it? We should DEMAND that our food be labeled properly regarding genetic manipulation. In other words, food containing genetically modified organisms (GMOs) should be clearly labeled. Food corporations will fight us tooth and nail on this because they already know (from Europe's example) that people will not eat genetically modified food.

Mrs. Obama Efforts

Little ol' insignificant me commends Mrs. Obama for her efforts in trying to reduce childhood obesity through her program "Let's Move." She is supporting organic food certification efforts and being a good example by planting an organic garden and placing beehives at the White House. It is a great start and as parents, we must encourage the spread of this program locally. See if there is anything you can do at the local level. Be aware, it won't be easy, but I believe this is a grass root effort indispensable for our nation's health.

It's the Food Stupid!

Do you remember Bill Clinton's campaign motto in 1992? "It's the Economy, Stupid!" (He said it, not me!) Well, I feel the same way about food. I should make it my slogan: "It's the Food, Stupid!" I firmly believe that the vast majority of modern diseases afflicting us in the West are caused by the very bad SAD (Standard American Diet). I won't go into details here, because many more qualified people have already written and spoken on this subject, but it saddens me that so few are paying attention. It's really simple: Eat healthy food and you will be healthier.

Of course, I am not referring to genetic diseases, but I suspect that a switch to a healthy diet would impact even these. It makes perfect sense to me that children raised in a family eating an unhealthy diet will grow up to experience the same diseases as their parents. Type II diabetic parents will tend to raise Type II diabetic children, and obese parents will tend to raise obese children. It's the type of food they eat! The sad part is that most of these families are on a very limited budget and for them, a "Dollar Meal" seems like a good deal. True, on the face of it, but they don't realize that in the long run, the poor quality food will affect their health and force them to spend a lot more money on drugs and hospital bills, not to mention feeling bad and constantly drained of energy. Is that the life we want to live? Poor nutrition also adds enormous additional health care costs to our economy. But only the private healthcare system is getting rich here, not you and I. We should try not to support its never-ending expansion.

Lack of Proper Food Education

It is simply a shame that our educational system does not teach children how to prepare fresh and healthy food. Whatever happened to home economics? Even though some schools are making an effort to provide healthier food in their cafeterias, it's not enough. Children should be educated about healthy food choices. Of course, we also have to do our part at home. Education and prevention are extremely important, and all parents should insist that these basic skills be taught in our public schools. We are spending increasing amounts of money for education in this country, and yet our kids lack basic life skills such as cooking fresh food and budgeting money. It's a shame. An enormous effort is needed to change that. But let's not forget our own responsibility as well. As parents, we are responsible for the health of our children. We can begin by educating ourselves. In Austin, some pioneer schools and the SFC are doing their part to educate people on how to shop, cook, and grow their own food. We are lucky to have them in our midst and should support them the best we can.

A Little Dirt Never Really Hurts. My Two Centimes

One thing that keeps on amazing me in this country (remember, I'm from France) is the near-panic attitude most people have towards bacteria and germs. You are being brainwashed. Many big businesses want to keep you scared, to keep you buying their anti-bacterial soaps, hand washes, and antibiotics. What you really need is a strong immune system, and the best way to develop one is to be exposed to germs a little at a time, so that your body can learn from minute exposure. The best time to learn, as usual, is when you're young, but it's not too late to teach your body to learn to defend itself. I remember playing in the dirt with my buddies, and even though our mothers always asked us, "Did you wash your hands?" we did not *sterilize* them. We were exposed to a cocktail mix of bacteria and germs parents would probably run scared of these days. Did it make us sick? Not really. I would rarely get colds (and I still don't), and I may have caught the flu a time or two, but I had built a strong immune system by then and recovered quickly. I have been suspicious of pharmaceutical drugs ever since, and I still am. It would take something major for me to take a chemical drug and I would still argue with my doctor about it. I see him once a year for my routine physical–that's it.

You may be wondering… what is this French guy's point with his rambling comments? What I'm getting at is that eating fresh food pulled from the ground will expose you to a host of tiny, tiny bugs your body will get to know, get used to, strengthening your immune system in the process. I know I'm pushing the envelope here, but have you noticed that older folks that were raised on farms (like me) or grew their own food tend to have what was called, not too long ago, a "strong constitution?" I believe that this obsession over assorted invisible bugs and the need to eradicate them by all means is actually weakening our own natural defenses and opening us to all sorts of infections. We should cultivate and grow our friendly bacteria and not eradicate them with the overuse of antibiotics. Good health starts with a healthy gut. Friendly bacteria are our first line of defense and will attack foreign invaders. If these bad guys still manage to get through, our strong immune systems should take over and get rid of these nasty invaders. You can smile at my description. It may not sound scientific, but my reasoning is backed by plenty of studies telling us a healthy gut is our best defense against sickness. There! I said my piece. You think about this, do your own research, and come to your own conclusions. Bonne chance!

EATING DINNER TOGETHER

Having dinner together as a family sounds like a quaint idea from the olden days, doesn't it? Well, maybe June Cleaver had the right idea. Of course, life wasn't so hectic then. Most likely there were not two wage earners trying to keep their financial heads above water. Back then, dad went to work and mom stayed home to be a homemaker, take care of the children, and cook homemade meals. Life is more complicated and stressful nowadays; dad goes to the health club after work; mom has her yoga class; the kids have after school activities, and the whole family rarely ends up eating together. But everyone is a little worse off because of it, including the food budget.

How? Think about it. Most likely, everyone ends up either buying fast food, grabbing something out the fridge, or reheating a prepackaged meal. All of these habits are hurting their health *and* your food budget. Aren't those good enough reasons for the whole family to slow down for an hour, and gather around a good meal at the family dinner table? A home-cooked meal is always cheaper to prepare than anything you buy from the take-out showcase or the drive-through window. It will be a lot healthier, too. Best of all, it can be done for a reasonable cost. Another benefit is that you can model good eating habits and portion sizes for your kids. This will help your kids learn good eating habits and keep them strong and healthy. I personally believe that reorganizing or limiting our extracurricular activities is worth the additional time spent around the dinner table as a family.

Many studies have proven that when families eat dinner together, they consume more vegetables, fruit, and juice, and fewer soft drinks. Children who eat dinner with their family eat less fatty foods and receive higher amounts of essential vitamins, minerals, and fiber. One study noted that children who ate family dinners more frequently had healthier eating habits overall, even when eating away from home. A couple of cautionary notes: Be careful not to use food as a reward, or a punishment. Don't force your kids to "clean their plates." Children are well attuned to their bodies and know when they have had enough to eat. Try not to use food as a way to calm or make your children feel better when they are upset or hurt. It could lead them to an eating disorder later on.

Working Parent or Homemaker?

When my sister calculated the amount of money she would earn versus the cost of an additional car to go to work, child care costs, and additional stress, and compared it with the savings she would make while shopping carefully and staying home to care for her family, she told me the best choice for her and her family was for her to stay home. Maybe it's the best choice for you too.

There is no shame in you taking care of your family and raising well-balanced and healthy children. There seems to be a subtle stigma put upon stay-at-home caregivers, but not everyone is meant to be a careerist. If it makes sense for you economically, make it your career and be the best at it.

On a personal note, I had to cook dinner for my younger brother and sister because my Mom had to work to support us. I knew why she had to work, but I missed the days when she was taking care of us. Is that why I am a chef now? I am sure it had something to do with it! That's probably why my sister and her husband decided the whole family would be better off if she stayed at home to take care of the family. She still goes to her exercise class twice a week and volunteers at an animal shelter, in addition to taking care of her home and feeding her family. They chose to live a more balanced life. My brother- and sister-in-law also made that decision, and both moms did a great job raising two healthy and smart girls each. It's all about balance. Is that why French people have "la joie de vivre'?" I'm not sure, but I envy them once in a while when I observe their lives, compared to my crazy life in the U. S.

Other Good Reasons to Eat Dinner Together

Families who eat dinner together benefit in many ways. Eating together helps families achieve better communication and build stronger relationships. Children do better in school, are better adjusted as teens and adults, and the entire family enjoys better nutrition. Family meals also help improve school performance. In a recent survey, researchers found that seniors in high school who regularly ate dinner with their family four or more times a week scored higher than students who ate family dinners three or fewer times a week. The same result showed up with elementary students. Preschoolers whose families ate together had better language skills because mealtime was an opportunity for them to hear more spoken language, giving them a chance to learn from adult conversations.

Family meals are also a good time to teach kids good manners and social interaction skills, and for the adults to model proper table etiquette. Old fashioned concepts? It may seem like it, but good manners should never go out of fashion. Sharing a pleasant conversation around the dinner table helps improve children's social skills.

Chew Your Food

Old-fashioned wisdom had it right. Take your time when eating. There are many reasons for this. First, our food should be chewed properly, so that we puree our food in very small pieces. Remember, your stomach does not have teeth; it cannot do this for you. Another reason for thorough chewing is that it allows our salivary enzymes, salivary amylase, and ptyalin, to start the digestive process, especially of carbohydrates. The macrobiotic philosophy suggests that we chew each bite of food at least 50 times before we swallow it. I know, who has the time? But we should still make an effort.

No Distractions

When you are eating, there should be no distraction from the enjoyment of the food except the company of your family. No TV, no telephone or texting, no computer, no reading of books or magazines. We should focus on our food and our dinner companions. It is the perfect time to talk about what happened to everyone in the family during the day, current affairs, and even silly stuff so everyone can have a good laugh and snort milk through their noses, the way family dining is meant to be.

HOW TO KEEP YOUR FOOD COSTS DOWN: Growing, Shopping and Cooking

GROWING YOUR OWN FOOD

<u>Disclaimer</u>: I need to preface this chapter by coming clean, so to speak, on this subject. Although I was partially raised on my grandmother's farm, I am the worst gardener in the world. Some people have a green thumb; mine is black and a killer thumb at that. Every living plant I come in contact with dies within days. But of course, that won't stop me from putting forth a few ideas. Just don't expect gardening tips from me! I may be a food geek, but my work is done in the kitchen. Like I always tell my friends: If you grow it, I'll cook it!

Can We Still Trust our Food Supply?

As you probably know already, the food grown in this country is increasingly grown with chemical fertilizers like nitrogen and phosphorus designed to make plants grow faster, but to the detriment of their nutritional value. And what about pesticides? Peaches, at the very top of the "Dirty Dozen" high pesticide residue list, are sprayed with a cocktail of 50 pesticides you would not drink by choice. If you really want to be scared, go to this site and see a list of the chemicals used on peaches in California: **http://pesticideinfo.org/DS.jsp?sk=5004#TopChems**. Similar amounts are sprayed on the rest of the Dirty Dozen list (**http://www.ewg.org/foodnews/**).

It's also common knowledge that some of the government agencies in charge of protecting our food quality are doing a poor job, and are often headed by past executives from large food chemical conglomerates. How can we possibly trust them? We can't, and people all over this country are finally taking charge of their personal food supply--where they buy it, how they grow it and how they cook it. It is a vast grass-root movement. Food conglomerates are fighting this trend and trying to introduce more genetically modified organisms in our food supply, but we are aware of their tricks now, thanks to courageous and outraged citizens. Let's not allow them to poison us. One way to fight back is by growing some of your own food.

Why Growing Our Own Food Also Makes Economical Sense

Our economy is not getting any better, no matter what the government wants us to believe. If you do your own shopping (who does not, except the super rich?), you know that grocery shopping is more expensive by the month. Inflation is here, and here to stay for a while. Food and the cost of shipping it are becoming increasingly expensive. Therefore, next to buying your food locally, growing your own food can be the most economical source of cheap, wholesome, and fresh food for your family. You can even make it a family project and teach your children important lessons about nature and self-reliance. Have fun with it. Who knows, this tough economy might turn out to be a good thing for our communities, our local economies and us. We may rediscover the beauty of human connections.

When I was growing up on Mamie's farm, there was no way we could have survived financially if she did not have her own kitchen garden, chicken coops, and rabbit hutches. She traded for the other staples she could not make herself such as butter, bread, and other meats. If the dollar goes to hell in a hand basket, we could always go back to the old days and trade again. Who knows? I sure don't, and our government does not seem to know either, the way they are spending dollars they don't have. If we all spent our money the way the government does, we would have been out on the streets a long time ago. Watch out for dollar devaluation and inflation, both bad events for our food budget.

A few years ago when I had the opportunity to live in the Ukraine, helping out small businesses, I learned another good lesson. The average worker there lives on about fifty dollars a month. Yes, per month, not per day. The only way they could live and eat fresh food was to grow their own at the small country "dacha" passed on in each family for generations. They would work for one week full-time, and take the following week off to go tend their garden in the countryside. It was an accepted way of doing things in that region. They hired two crews which alternated working shifts, a very interesting concept!

Herbs in Pots on Windowsills

Even if you live in an apartment, you can grow fresh herbs on your balcony or on a sunny windowsill. Most herbs are pretty hardy and will happily help you flavor your food at very little cost. Ask your local garden center for help. Be sure to plant the right herbs for each season, as every herb has preferred temperatures. That's the way my "working" mom did it, and even when we did not have a lot to eat, it was always tasty, thanks to our potted herbs.

Backyard (or even Front Yard) Food Garden or Kitchen Garden

Why not make part or whole of your grass patch an edible kitchen garden? You might as well. Lawns are a notorious waste of water and soon enough, water will be our most precious element. Make every drop count and grow food with it.

I know it costs money to start, but there is plenty of help available. If you don't know how to get started, there are plenty of books on the subject. Better yet, go to the local garden center and strike up a conversation about how to get started. They will know best what to grow in your region. They will be glad to share that information (and sell you supplies). We're lucky and thankful in Austin to have quite a few excellent gardening stores.

Have a Garden Built for You

If you really don't have the time to do the hard work yourself, there are a few small and qualified businesses willing to create anything from a square yard garden to a gorgeous kitchen and flower garden combination. Garden organically and do not spray your food with all sorts of nasty chemicals. Remember, you and your family will be eating that food! You will save a lot of money in the long run. On the other hand, you should be aware that the animals living in your neighborhood will want their share of your garden. Call that the angels' share. After all, some of those birds are your cheapest helpers, eating many of the bugs feeding on your garden. Don't they deserve to be paid with food too? That's the natural way. If you live in Texas, you may also want to invest in sturdy fencing, as our local deer, not to mention other wild critters, love everything that comes out of your garden.

Composting: Another Way to Save Money

Instead of using chemical fertilizers, recycle your food scraps and make natural compost out of them. That's another way to save money. Compost is the best fertilizer you can possibly use, providing plants with not only major nutrients, but also important micronutrients and trace minerals. Just throw all your food leftovers, fruit and vegetable peels, unusable food scraps, egg shells, coffee grounds and tea bags, dead leaves and yard trimmings, even clean cardboard and paper, into the compost bin There are many books and websites devoted to helping you start composting, or just chat with any experienced gardener. They're out there and will be glad to help you. Even if you don't have a garden, you may want to offer your compost material to a neighbor and get a little of the crop in return!

In Austin look at **City of Austin- Solid Waste Services**:
http://www.ci.austin.tx.us/sws/zerowaste_composting.htm; Natural
Gardener our local radio and garden hero can be found at:
http://www.naturalgarderneraustin.com.

Outside of Austin, check out Vermi Composting at:
http://www.wormmainea.com/Worm_Bin_Instructions.pdf; and
HowToCompost.org at: **http://howtocompost.org/default.asp**.

Need More Help Getting Started?

You can take food gardening classes locally. Sometimes, your own city will
offer these at a reasonable cost. In Austin, the Parks and Recreation
Department of the City of Austin offers such courses. See:
http://www.ci.austin.tx.us/greengarden/. The Lady Bird Johnson Wildflower
Center also offers free classes at: http://www.wildflower.org/. If money is
tight and you qualify for it, the Sustainable Food Center offers free gardening
classes. See: http://www.sustainablefoodcenter.org/grow-local.

Shared Garden Anyone?

If you do not care to work your garden for any reason (health or time
constraints, for example), but still would like to have access to cheap and
fresh food, there are programs that match people with unused plots of land
to gardeners that live in apartments who would love a chance to work your
plot in exchange for half the crop.

Sharing Food with a Neighbor

You may even strike a deal with one of your neighbors to share crops. If they
love to grow vegetables that take up a lot of ground space that you don't
have room for, and you love to grow tomatoes, why not cross share? You get
to grow what you like to grow and eat other veggies your may not care to
grow yourself. A great deal for all concerned. A nice side effect: It builds a
better neighborhood where people care about each other.

Community Gardens

If you live in an apartment or condo and do not have access to a plot of land
or you simply like to hang out with like-minded food growers, you may
want to consider community gardens. In Austin only there are about 30
community gardens available for your growing fancy and more and more

are being started everyday. The trend is growing as people become more concerned about the cost of food. Most of the time you have to pay a rental fee to offset expenses such as water but in some cases, if you qualify economically, you may be able to get a plot for free. Check around for more information. In Austin, see: **http://communitygardensaustin.org/**.

Pick your Own Food

Another way to reduce your food cost is to pick it yourself, and it's fun! Picking ripe peaches and eating them while they're still warm is an unknown pleasure to city folks. Look around, read your paper, or check your local Edible magazine for farms that will allow you to pick your own fruits and veggies. Eat all you can while its still fresh, and can or freeze the rest. With our slower economy, home canning is coming back in fashion. Look up canning books; there are plenty of new ones being written every day. I even saw a whole section at my local Central Market about canning with a display of books, mason jars, canning jars, and all that jazz. If you can, talk to your grandma. She may still have secret family canning recipes. Home canning is not that difficult; some might even call it fun and it can save you a lot of money. And don't forget your well-deserved pride when you offer your neighbors a jar of that wonderful preserved food as a gift.

FRESH FOOD SHOPPING

Farmers' Market Shopping: As much as possible, shop for your fresh produce, meat, and artisan products at your local farmer's market. Get to know your providers. Go visit their farm–it's a fun trip for your kids, too. The more you know about the food you eat, the more confident you will feel in the quality of your food.

Grocery Store Shopping: I created this list while walking through all the aisles, from produce to check out, at my favorite grocery store, Central Market. It should be of some use to you no matter where you shop, whether it is at a grocery store, a health food store, or on the Internet. I do understand that not all people are trained chefs as I am, so I created this list to help you learn how to shop for fresh food. I hope this list and my suggestions will help simplify your life. Do as I do: keep a sharp eye on all product labels. You are your own best health detective. Bonne chance and Bon Appétit!

Chef Alain Braux

AT YOUR LOCAL FARMERS' MARKET

Not all farmers can afford the cost to get certified as organic, even though they do not use pesticides or harsh fertilizers. So my best advice is to get to know your local farmers in person, and visit their farm if you can. If they conduct a clean operation, they will be proud of it and have no problem allowing you and your family to visit their farm. You may have to respect their visiting hours, but that is the same situation as with any good friend. Enjoy visiting with them, their family, and their animals. In season, they will have the freshest products and possibly the best prices, though you may have to haggle a little. Once you get to know each other, they may even give you a freebie once in a while as a nice gesture.

Another shopping trick to save money on your groceries: If you're willing to take a chance, wait until the last thirty minutes before the farmer's market closes and get discounts on what's left over. Most farmers do not want to bring back home their unsold produce. It probably will go on their compost pile. You might as well take advantage of this, but do not expect the best of the crop or the best choices. Those will have been picked over by the full-price paying crowd. Sometimes the farmers will holler it to the wind for anyone to hear, "Half price on everything left." Sometimes they keep it a secret for the precious few. So, it pays to be on friendly terms with your favorite farmers to get the special deals when they are available. They're more likely to give you the discount than a complete stranger. Offer them a decent price to take a big amount off their hands and see what happens. That's when your best negotiating skills will come handy. Have fun with it.

It also pays to take a first tour of the market and note the prices before you actually start shopping. You may be able to save a little money that way.

Special Federal and State Food Programs

Do you remember food stamps? Well, nowadays they have a fancier name. The USDA calls them SNAP for Supplemental Nutrition Assistance Program. In Texas, the SNAP card is called the Lone Star card. Did you know that most of Texas farmers' markets accept Lone Star cards? Not all of them will, but if you check online, you'll be able to find which ones do. Why not take advantage of them? For example, in Austin, all SFC farmers' markets accept the Lone Star card. All you have to do is go to the information tent, exchange your stamps for wooden coins, and go shop with them. For more information, please go to **http://www.benefitscheckup.org**.

If you are a mom with little children, you can enroll in the Women, Infant and Children (WIC) Farmers Market Nutrition Program (FMNP), and you can have access to additional discounts.

The GoLocal card is available in Austin but also in many other cities in the U. S. See: **http://www.thegolocalcard.com** for more information. For a very reasonable ten dollars a year, you can receive discounts from ten percent and up on your food (and many other businesses) for a whole year. It makes your food bill even less expensive.

More Resources for Local Farms and Farmer's Markets in your State

Additional information about local farms and farmers' markets in your area can be found at: **http://www.localharvest.org/**.

Other Food Shopping Choices

My second choice recommendation would be to buy organic produce at your local grocery store, but coming from farms located in your state. Most likely they will be advertised as much. Your local grocer is very much aware of the trend for buying local and fresh. I have seen helpful signs at both Central Market and Whole Foods Market, advertising in-state farmers' products.

As much as your budget permits, buy organic, but from the United States. As a last resort, buy from Latin America and Canada. Sorry, but I'm a little suspicious of organic produce coming all the way from China or the Far East. The distance is way too long for organic produce to be shipped fresh without suffering nutrient loss. Besides, think about the amount of energy spent in shipping these products to you! Local and fresh is always better.

AT YOUR GROCERY STORE

No Buying in the Middle Aisles

This principle has been known and espoused by many nutritionists over the years. Do not shop in the center aisles except for the bulk section. That's where all the processed food sits, waiting to damage your health. Shop on the outside aisles only (produce, fish, meat, and dairy, with some reservations of course. See my shopping suggestions below. Why the outside aisles? Because that's where fresh food is sold in your typical grocery store. Grocery stores are laid out in this manner to place the refrigerated food storage as close as possible to the receiving docks. The less distance that food has to travel from the refrigerated trucks to the refrigerated storage, the better. The same goes for the distance between the refrigerated storage to the showcases. In some cases, – for example, the dairy cases, – the showcases are the visible part of the refrigerated storage and are fed from the back to the front to make sure that the freshest food is always in the back.

Chef's Shopping Tip: Always pick your refrigerated food from the back of the showcase; you will extend the freshness date by a few days and avoid early spoilage.

PRODUCE DEPARTMENT

My General Produce Shopping Advice

When buying produce, try to buy the freshest picked, with the least impact on the environment. If you can, shop locally and in season. If you have access to it, buy from your local farmer's market, farmer's co-op, or directly from the farm. Many farmers offer weekly or monthly baskets where you receive an assortment of vegetables and fruits in season for a certain price. Eating food harvested in season from the area in which you live is the best way to ensure that your food is at the peak of its freshness. It also supports your local economy and avoids damaging the environment with long-range shipping. Typically, local farmers are too small to be able to afford to go through the "Certified Organic" certification process. To make sure they're not unloading produce from somewhere else in their own crates, talk to them at the market. Ask to visit their farm, take a tour, and ask a lot of questions. Local farmers are proud of the products they sell, and will be happy to show you around their farm. In Austin, our best-known local farms are Boggy Creek Farm, Springdale Farm, Green Gate Farms, Rain Lily Farm, HausBar Farm, or one of the many other high-quality farms nearby. Use the Internet to find local farmers markets or farmers advertising their fresh wares.

Another good solution is to buy flash-frozen organic vegetables. They are frozen as soon as they are picked and keep most of their nutrients in the process. Only defrost what you will use. To prevent freezer burn, use containers with tight-fitting lids to store the unused portion. Do not refreeze defrosted vegetables.

If none of the above suggestions are possible for you, buy conventionally grown produce, but only in season. Wash it carefully in cold water with a few drops of organic soap or a special produce-washing solution like grape seed extract.

If possible, avoid buying from countries that may not have the same health and environmental laws we have in the United States. Their laws may be more relaxed than ours and your produce may be covered with pesticides that are banned here.

The Dirty Dozen and Cleaner 15

It could be a movie title about our food quality, but it's not. It's the name given by the *Environmental Working Group* (http://www.ewg.org/foodnews/) to a list of the fresh produce items that contain the highest pesticide residues. Try to at least buy these foods organic only so that you do not accumulate these poisons in your body.

If you cannot afford to buy organic food or they are not available at your local grocery store, I have heard of a few ways to clean the outside of the contaminated foods properly. Some people use a few drops of bleach when they fill their sink to wash their food (I don't recommend that); some use distilled vinegar and some use food grade (three percent USP) hydrogen peroxide. Please rinse well before eating. I personally use a few drops of an organic and biodegradable all-purpose cleaner called Orange TKO (**http://www.tkoorange.com/**) made in Canada. It's a wonderful product and is part of my personal goal of getting rid of all chemical cleaning products in my house. Please keep in mind that washing your produce still won't take care of some of these chemicals absorbed by the roots of the plant.

Chef's Shopping Tip: It's a good idea to write the following lists on a piece of paper, fold it, and carry it in your wallet or purse to be referred to when you get to the market.

12 Most Contaminated

- Apples
- Blueberries – domestic
- Celery
- Grapes – imported
- Kale, collard greens
- Lettuce
- Nectarines – imported
- Peaches
- Potatoes
- Spinach
- Strawberries
- Sweet Bell Peppers: Red, Green, Yellow

If you can possibly afford it, try to buy the above items organically grown. If you can't, wash them as well as you can.

15 Least Contaminated

- Asparagus
- Avocado
- Cabbage
- Cantaloupe – domestic
- Eggplant
- Grapefruit
- Onions
- Kiwi Fruit
- Mango
- Mushrooms
- Pineapple
- Sweet Corn
- Sweet Peas
- Sweet potatoes

> ➢ Watermelon

If you must, you can buy these items in the non-organic section (many of them aren't even generally available organic). Make sure to clean them properly. Another way to save money is to buy non-organic fruits or vegetables where an inedible peel takes the brunt of the pesticides. When you peel them, you peel away most of the pesticides. For example, apples, bananas, onions, pineapple, avocado, all sorts of melons, kiwi fruits, oranges, and citrus in general. I still would like to remind you that if the peel is edible and you can afford it, eating the peel is important for its high fiber content and antioxidants. Also keep in mind that by peeling them you are not *entirely* eliminating the pesticides.

Garlic – Here is another case where you could skip going organic if you're on a tight budget. On the other hand, the price difference is so minimal; it might not be worth it. The same goes for fresh ginger. But please, please, please, do not buy peeled garlic coming from God knows where. It is way too expensive and does not save that much time. Nothing beats freshly crushed garlic in a soup or stew.

BULK FOOD SECTION

Nuts

I recommend raw, unroasted nuts, as the roasting process damages the healthy oils contained in them. Buy them in the bulk section; they will be cheaper and fresher. Buy only what you need, as they will oxidize and turn rancid unless you store them in your freezer. If you want roasted nuts, roast your own. Do not buy sugar or honey-coated nuts; they are oil-roasted and coated with added sugar.

Raw Nuts: Almonds , walnuts, pecans , pistachios (not colored), pine nuts, peanuts , macadamia nuts, cashews, hazelnuts (filberts), Brazil nuts.

Chef's Cooking Tip: If you want to prepare your own roasted, salted nuts, toss them with coarse sea salt and eggs whites that have been lightly beaten with a fork. Place them in a single layer on a baking sheet and toast them lightly at 160-170º F, so you do not damage their delicate polyunsaturated oils. Another way I like my roasted nuts is tossed with gluten free tamari sauce and dried as above.

Nut Butters

A good source of protein to spread on a cracker, a vegetable chip, or a corn chip as a healthy snack. Some stores will even provide you with a grinder to make your own freshly made nut butter. Avoid "regular" peanut butter loaded with hydrogenated fats and, in some cases, sugar. If you can find them, get raw nut butters and keep them refrigerated, as they will go rancid at room temperature within a couple of weeks.

Nut butters: Almond, cashew, coconut, peanut, pecan, pistachio, pumpkin seed, macadamia, and tahini (sesame seed butter). My favorites are almond and hazelnut.

Chef's Cooking Tip: To create your own homemade chocolate nut spread, warm one part nut butter in a bain-marie until it reaches body temperature. Separately, melt an equal amount of seventy percent dark chocolate, mix well together, and Voila! Homemade Nutella.

Seeds

Seeds: Sesame seeds, pumpkin seeds, sunflower seeds, chia seeds, flaxseeds. Only buy what you need, as they turn rancid if kept too long. Coconut flakes and shredded coconut are also a good addition to your pantry, just watch for added sugar.

Dried Fruits

Dried Fruits: Avoid if you have any kind of high blood sugar issues. Otherwise, and if possible, buy unsulphured and without added sugar. Also, be aware that some dried fruits are coated with an additional layer of fruit juice to make them sweeter. If you are trying to control your sugar intake, read the labels in order to avoid these.

Zante currants, pitted prunes, Medjool Dates, Monukka raisins, Chilean flame raisins, organic seedless raisins, goji berries, diced pineapple, organic unsulphured apricots, dried blueberries, tropical papaya spears, dried cranberries, tart cherries, Cali Myrna dried figs, and organic dried mission figs.

Chef's Eating Tip: For a healthy and yummy snack, eat a dried fruit and nut combination. You will get some of the sweetness you crave, but in a natural form, and with the fiber and healthy-oil goodness of nuts. My favorite combinations include apricot and almond; date and almond; apricot and dark chocolate (oops! I let that one slip in); cranberries and pine nuts; raisins and pumpkin seeds, and any combination from your imagination.

Grains

If you are not allergic to gluten, any of the following grains are great sources of fiber and complex carbohydrates for you. Please use whole grains as much as possible, and avoid refined grains like white flour and white rice. Instead, eat breads and products made with whole wheat and brown rice.

Grains that contain gluten: Barley, kamut, oats if not certified gluten free, rye, spelt, and whole wheat. Also, all products made from wheat, like pasta, couscous, semolina, and tabouleh.

Grains without gluten: Amaranth, buckwheat, brown rice, brown basmati rice, quinoa, millet, teff, and wild rice. For more information, check my previous book, "Living Gluten and Dairy-Free with French Gourmet Food."

Rice

In this category, buying bulk keeps you from paying for expensive packaging. You only buy what you need and you get a fresher product. Who knows how long that Uncle Bob's rice has been sitting on the shelf?

I recommend brown rice over white rice. Its bran content will make you feel full and slows down the breakdown of carbohydrates, avoiding blood sugar spikes. It is said that eating brown rice twice a week will reduce your chances of type II diabetes while eating white rice will increase your chances by ten percent.

Beans

Adzuki, fava, mung, garbanzo, kidney, black, red, white, navy, and many more. Dried beans are the least expensive option, but if you do not have the time to cook them from scratch, feel free to buy them canned. Just make sure to rinse and drain them properly to avoid the added sodium most of them contain.

Legumes or Pulses

Lentils: Green French lentils, brown lentils, red lentils. Since lentils require no soaking time and take so little time to cook, it's not worth paying extra for a canned or packaged version.

Dried Pasta

Nowadays, you can find good quality whole-wheat pasta in the bulk department. If it is available, buy organic. Either way, whole wheat is always better than white pasta because of its bran content. If you are allergic to wheat, buy rice, buckwheat, or quinoa pasta.

Herbs and Spices

I try to buy all my dried herbs and spices in bulk and in small quantities. It's so much cheaper that way. I reuse the same glass containers I bought before and refill them. For a few cents, you will have a supply that will last for weeks. It's hard to find organic herbs and spices, but it's possible. Avoid irradiated spices if you can get information about this issue from your bulk person. Food irradiation is the process of exposing food to ionizing radiation to destroy microorganisms, bacteria, viruses, or insects that might be present in the food. Irradiated food does not become radioactive, but in some cases there may be subtle chemical changes. On the other hand, Dr. Weil's position is that "irradiation is the safest and most effective way to preserve and sterilize herbs and spices". The implication is that since we use herbs and spices in such small quantities, it should not affect us. I see his point, but if you have any kind of food sensitivity, I would be cautious. If you are lucky and grow your own herbs, you can hang them to dry during the good season, and use them the rest of the year. This option is ridiculously cheap, and the herbs will taste fresh and potent. Once you try it, it is hard to go back!

Basic Dried Herbs and Spices: Basil, cinnamon, cumin, dill weed, oregano, paprika mix, curry mix, Herbes de Provence mix, Italian seasoning mix, cardamom, ginger, mint, allspice, rosemary, thyme.

Chef's Eating Tip: When I don't have access to fresh herbs, I either use the frozen herbs trick I describe in the freezer section below, or use an assortment of organic dried herbs. My personal favorite is the Herbes de Provence blend with lavender from Central Market.

Salt

As with sugar, salt is available in a coarser, more natural form (sea salt), and a more processed, refined form ("table salt"). Choose sea salt. I use only coarse sea salt for cooking my pasta and for my oven-roasted rosemary potatoes, and home-ground fine sea salt for all other uses. Any good quality sea salt will do. Remember, you will get more salty flavor out of sea salt, so you can use less of it.

The best unrefined natural salts, such as Himalayan salt, contains eighty four percent sodium chloride and sixteen percent other naturally occurring trace minerals, like magnesium, silicon, calcium, potassium, bromide, phosphorous, and vanadium, all essential ingredients for proper biological function.

Salt is Necessary for Health

= It is a major component of our blood plasma, lymphatic fluid, extracellular fluid, and even amniotic fluid.

= It helps carry nutrients into and out of your cells.

= It helps the lining of our blood vessels to regulate blood pressure.

= It promotes and regulates the propagation of nerve impulses.

= Through the sodium-potassium exchange, it helps our brain to send communication signals to our muscles, so that we can move on demand.

If you are concerned about iodine content, iodine is actually found in small trace amounts naturally in sea salt, as it is in most seafood, so you are still getting iodine in its natural, untouched form. It is typically enough for most healthy people.

The processed "table" salt on your grocery shelves has gone through a great deal of processing before it gets to your table. It contains approximately ninety seven and a half percent sodium chloride and two and a half percent chemicals (iodine and drying agents). It is heated to over twelve hundred degrees Fahrenheit. This high heat alters the natural chemical structure of perfectly good salt. It was found in the early twentieth century that people eating refined salt that lacked iodine developed conditions like goiter and mental retardation. So they added back iodine and made a big deal about it, but oops! They forgot to add back the other eighty-three missing minerals beneficial to our health. Because of this refining process, every gram of excess sodium chloride that our body has to neutralize uses up twenty-three grams of cellular water. The result of the consumption of table salt will cause fluid to accumulate in your tissues, as well as other potential health problems such as:

➢ Cellulite
➢ Rheumatism, arthritis, and gout
➢ Kidney and gall bladder stones

➤ Hypertension (high blood pressure)
➤ Cognitive problems

Chef's Tip: My favorites are, in descending order: Himalayan pink mineral salt, Fleur de Sel from Brittany, France, or Mediterranean sea salt from the Camargue region of France, then Celtic sea salts from the Atlantic northwest region of France. I suggest you buy the coarse sea salt and grind it finer in small amounts in a coffee grinder. This will avoid the use of binders/fillers. Avoid flavored sea salt; it is a waste of money. It's very easy to create your own flavored sea salts by simply adding your favorite herbs and spices. Play with it! I like to mix mine with chili powder and sprinkle it over everything I eat. Another favorite is to combine coarse sea salt and Herbes de Provence (or Italian herbs) in a salt grinder and grind away. Beware of pure white sea salt: it is refined. Less so than table salt, but is still overly processed. Sea salt should have a grayish cast.

Pepper

I prefer that you use freshly ground pepper, as it has a stronger, fresher flavor. As an added side benefit, you will use less of it.

Peppers: Black peppercorn (to be used in a pepper mill), cayenne pepper, white, pink or a blend of different color peppercorns. Assortments of dried chili pepper mixes (there are a lot of varieties from mild to hot to spicy hot) are a good way to spice up your food.

Chef's Eating Tip: I prefer to use cayenne pepper. It is known to increase your basic metabolism and has the reputation of being healing to the stomach.

Tea and Coffee

Teas: Bulk "whole-leaf" tea is out of reach for most reasonable budgets. Try to brew "family size" tea bags, make a big batch and reheat carefully to stretch your dollar. If you drink iced tea, please brew your own at home, and flavor it yourself with natural lemon, orange, or mint extract; or, crush fresh mint in it, and allow it to steep. You will save money on packaging, not to mention avoiding all that added sugar.

Coffees: Unfortunately, most bulk coffee is out of reach for folks on a tight budget. Try to find a decent quality store brand and brew it thin. Even instant coffee can be fairly expensive. I use Medaglio del Oro Instant

Espresso, which costs around three dollars for thirty cups, or ten cents a cup. If having a cup of excellent coffee or tea is very important to you, you may be able to scrimp in another area in order to savor that one very special cup in the morning.

Maple Syrup and Honey

If you're lucky, as we are in Austin, you will be able to find local, unfiltered honey in bulk. It's a little more expensive, but well worth the few extra cents per serving. Bring your own jar. If you buy filtered honey, whether in a cute bear dispenser or a regular jar, be careful to buy from a reputable producer. Imported honey is overheated, filtered, and often stretched with high fructose corn syrup (HFCS), and is known to contain pesticides. If you cannot find a good local honey, try to find honey from Florida. Florida honey has had purity standards since 2009.

The same is applicable for maple syrup--bulk is best. Try the Grade B maple syrup; it is thicker, darker, and has a stronger flavor, but contains more vitamins and minerals per serving, as it is less refined. Avoid commercial pancake syrups loaded with HFCS and colored with caramel.

Chef's Cooking Tip: If money is really tight, make your own pancake syrup: Mix one part water (one cup) with one part brown sugar (one cup) and bring to a boil. Cool down with two parts (two cups) grade B maple syrup to take advantage of its flavor and health goodies. Use it sparingly, however; is still liquid sugar!

FRESH FISH AND SHELLFISH COUNTER

Fresh fish is a very good source of protein and biologically necessary omega-3 fatty acids. Avoid large fish on the top of the food chain, since they most likely contain an unhealthy amount of mercury. If you can afford it, go for line-caught wild fish and shellfish. Ideally, I suggest you eat at least one four-ounce serving of fresh fish or shellfish per week, and an additional serving of flash frozen or canned fish. Just make sure to stay with my recommended four-ounce serving size per person. When averaged over a period of one week, this should allow you to serve fresh fish while balancing the cost with inexpensive dishes like rice, beans, pasta, and potatoes. Check out the lists below to see which fish are safe (and not safe) to eat.

Wild Fish and Shellfish Safe to Eat

King salmon; sockeye salmon; Coho salmon; canned wild pink salmon; canned sardines; anchovies; canned mackerel (except king mackerel); squid or calamari; domestic shrimp; scallops (except from U.S. mid-Atlantic) and oysters.

Farm-Raised Fish and Shellfish Safe to Eat

Striped bass; rainbow trout; char (small salmon); shrimp (domestic); catfish (domestic); crayfish (domestic); tilapia; scallops; oysters; clams, and mussels.

Fish and Shellfish Safe to Eat Once a Week

Canned white tuna; whitefish; Atlantic cod; Pacific cod; haddock; herring; Dungeness crab; spiny and rock lobsters.

Fish and Shellfish Safe to Eat Once a Month

Line-caught albacore/yellow fin tuna; bluefish; Pacific halibut; Pollack, and Maine lobster.

Avoid the Following Fish – They Are Not Safe to Eat

Domestic swordfish; tilefish; marlin; shark; blue fin tuna; king, ono (Wahoo) fish.

Farm Raised Fish or Shellfish NOT recommended

Salmon have been found to contain PCBs and artificial coloring; farmed salmon are sold under the name Atlantic and Norwegian salmon.

Imported shrimp are usually loaded with antibiotics and artificial preservatives. Imported scallops contain artificial preservatives.

Wild Fish and Shellfish to Avoid Because They Are Either Overfished or Not Sustainable

Sea bass, flounder, Atlantic halibut, sole, grouper, mahi-mahi (unless pole-caught), marlin, orange roughy, Atlantic-farmed salmon, shark, Swordfish, Asia-farmed tilapia, tuna (unless pole-caught), Chilean sea bass and orange roughy, Pacific snapper, Pacific rock cod, rock fish, red snapper; wild monkfish; wild catfish; wild king crab; wild Atlantic flounder; wild sturgeon; and imported crawfish and shrimp.

For more information, please see:
http://www.montereybayaquarium.org/cr/seafoodwatch.aspx.

FRESH MEAT COUNTER

These are my recommendations regarding the meats at your local grocery store, meat market or farmers market. I recommend small portions of quality meats, as they are a great source of beneficial proteins, vitamins, minerals, and omega-3 fatty acids–all nutrients necessary for your good health. The important word here is "moderation." I suggest one to two meat servings a week at four ounces per person. The rest of the meals should be fish/shellfish and bean and vegetable sources of protein.

Beef

Buy grass-fed, locally raised, or organic beef. Grass-fed beef contains a respectable amount of healthy essential fatty acids, such as omega-3 fatty acids. Feedlot steers, in contrast, are fed corn and grains, which give their meat an excess of unhealthy omega-6 fatty acids. Additionally, feedlot animals are fed bovine growth hormones, antibiotics, and genetically engineered grains that have been doused with pesticides, all of which will disrupt your digestion and immune system.

Bison

Bison is grown in a grass-fed environment and allowed to roam freely and without stress until they are mature enough to be butchered humanely. There are more and more local sources of this healthy meat available. Check your local farmer's market, ask around, or check on the Internet. You may even have it shipped to you.

Venison

In Texas and many other states, you can go hunting and obtain your own wild game. Since deer feed only on what nature is offering, venison is healthier than any farm-raised meat. If you are not a hunter, it is still possible to obtain venison from Broken Arrow Ranch (**http://www.brokenarrowranch.com**), Hudson's Market (1800 South Congress, 445-6611) and at Central Market.

Poultry

Buy free range, locally raised chicken and turkey. You will get more usable meat per pound, and it is much tastier. You can also buy organic or "natural"; but be aware, the "natural" label is not particularly meaningful. Check your local ordinances for more details.

Eggs

I much prefer fresh eggs from local farms. They taste so much better and make wonderfully yellow omelets; cakes made with them rise higher, and they are better for you. If they are pasture-raised, they will also contain that good fat I already talked about–omega-3 fatty acids. Besides, eggs are still the cheapest source of complete proteins around. I eat them at least twice a week, sometimes more. If you live too far from a farm or farmers' market, choose organic eggs. The information about feedlots in the meat section, sadly, is equally true for industrial chicken and egg farms.

Dairy

This is the place where you may want to take a stand with your pocketbook. Buy organic dairy products instead of their "regular" cousins. Unfortunately, it is a well-known fact that "normal" cows are mistreated animals fed corn (more inflammatory omega-6 fatty acids in your food) and even ground up dead animal carcasses. Yuck! Let's not forget that to force them to grow faster and produce more milk, they are pumped with rBGH (Recombinant Bovine Growth Hormones or BST (Bovine Somatotropin). Because these drugs are known to cause hormone-based cancers, they have been banned in Europe. The European Common Market refuses to buy American beef and dairy products unless certified organic. Lastly, to keep these poor animals living under such horrid conditions from being sick, they are injected with regular doses of antibiotics. All of these chemicals are absorbed in our bodies as we eat them, and I certainly cannot recommend that you buy them. Organic dairy products are becoming increasingly available and cheaper by the day. With that organic milk, you can even make your own cheap homemade yogurt, buttermilk (just add lemon juice and let sit for a while), sour cream, and soft cheese.

Deli

Eat only certified natural cold cuts. Ask your friendly deli person about the ingredients of any sandwich meat, and avoid anything containing nitrates and nitrites. Central Market brand oven baked ham, turkey breast, roast beef, and bison cost about ten dollars a pound. They contain no additives, no preservatives, and the few slices you need for a sandwich will set you back less than two dollars.

YOUR HEALTHY PANTRY

Healthy Pantry Staples

Breakfast Cereals: Unsweetened muesli mix, steel-cut oatmeal, whole bran cereals, and organic corn cereals. For more GF choices, see my previous book, "Living Gluten and Dairy-Free with French Gourmet Food."

Bread: These days, I eat only gluten-free bread and very little of it. So it won't go bad or dry out before I can eat the whole loaf, I buy it frozen and sliced, store it in my freezer, take one or two slices at a time, and toast them back to life in my toaster oven. You can do the same thing with your regular bread to keep it fresher longer. Try to eat only whole grain breads, and eat as little bread as possible.

Whole Grain Crackers: Some of these contain dried fruits and seeds. I love them as a quick snack with nut butter, fruit preserves, or cheese. For my gluten free friends, there are plenty of gluten free crackers available.

Canned products: Sardines and tuna in olive oil are a good source of omega-3 fatty acids. Organic beans: Black, fava, garbanzo, and others.

Tomato sauce: Organic crushed tomatoes with basil. I use this to make my own easy tomato sauce with no added sweeteners.

Oils: For cooking, virgin coconut oil. For salads, cold and warm dishes, extra virgin olive oil. Other good choices for cooking are sesame oil and macadamia oil.

Vinegars: I try to keep two or three flavors on hand for variety. My favorites are apple cider vinegar, red wine vinegar and herbal vinegars. You can also create your own flavored vinegar by soaking fresh herbs in them. For more information, see: **http://www.fcs.uga.edu/pubs/current/FDNS-E-1.html**.

Mustard: I only use Dijon mustard. There are a few very good brands in most grocery stores. Grey Poupon makes an acceptable substitute.

Natural sweeteners: I rarely use added sweeteners in my food. The only exception would be to sweeten my tea, coffee, or hot chocolate. On my kitchen counter, you will find:

Raw or organic turbinado sugar: It is not refined and still contains all the vitamins and minerals contained in the sugar cane.

Organic light or dark agave nectar: It's a liquid sweetener extracted from agave plants. It is about one and a half times sweeter than table sugar and has a lower glycemic index, thus recommended if you have blood sugar problems. The better quality is raw and unheated as well as unfiltered. It's a good source of sweetness for vegans as well as raw food followers.

Local, unheated, unfiltered honey: I recommend local honey for hay fever sufferers, as the bees feeding on local plants and flowers provide you with a natural homeopathic dose of pollen, which can lessen your allergy symptoms.

If you are diabetic or want to reduce your sugar intake, use stevia leaves, powder or liquid. Do not bother with flavored stevia; it's not worth the extra money.

Yacon syrup, which is made from a tuber containing a sweet soluble fiber substance called inulin, an indigestible sugar. It is recommended for people with blood sugar issues and diabetics.

Cocoa Powder: I use Nestle or Hershey's unsweetened cocoa powder only. I personally don't care for the Dutch-processed version. It's true its makes a darker chocolate cake, but the slightly bitter cocoa flavor is gone and you have a dull and bland result. Never buy sweetened cocoa mixes; they contain way too much added sugar. Raw cocoa powder and cacao nibs are loaded with antioxidants, but they are expensive; they can be bought as a luxury item when you save money elsewhere in the budget. I love raw cocoa powder in my chocolate smoothie. Yum!

Chef's Eating Tip: My favorite chocolate protein smoothie: Ten ounces of unsweetened chocolate almond milk, four ounces of frozen bananas (one whole), one scoop raw cocoa powder, one-half scoop protein powder (soy, whey or rice), one teaspoon of lecithin powder, and one teaspoon of vitamin C. You can make it more exotic and add even more antioxidants by adding one-eighth teaspoon of cinnamon powder.

Chocolate bars: I only eat dark chocolate with at least seventy percent cocoa content and no hydrogenated fats. If you can stand the bitterness, you can go up to eighty five percent. Any of the good quality European or boutique American chocolate makers will do. As an alternative to chocolate, you can use carob powder or chips.

Chef's Eating Tip: One of my favorite snacks is one square of dark chocolate and one raw almond. You satisfy your craving for chocolate yet have the antioxidant goodness of cocoa, and the healthy cocoa butter and almond oil. Add to that the almond fiber and it's all good. Just don't eat a pound of it. Promise?

Healthy Refrigerator Staples

Dairy

Milk: If possible buy fresh, non-homogenized, raw or lightly pasteurized whole milk. If not, buy organic whole milk. For people with lactose intolerance, use organic almond, soy, hazelnut, rice, or hemp milk. My personal favorite is vanilla almond milk.

Butter: Of course, being French, my fat of choice is butter. I buy French butter for sentimental reasons, but also because it tastes better. Otherwise, if you can afford it, buy organic cultured butter. Culturing the cream helps develop a better flavor. I have found that in my professional kitchen, unsalted Land O' Lakes butter does a great job. Because pesticides accumulate in the milk of domestic animals, and particularly in milk fat, butter is one item you really should try to buy organic.

Chef's Cooking Tip: When I sauté or pan fry, I use half coconut oil and half butter.

Cheese: I prefer my cheese local and unpasteurized. But I will not deny that buying a good quality French cheese, even when it is pasteurized (that's the only way the U.S. government will allow any cheese to enter this country) is still a "péché mignon" of mine. I also have a weakness for goat cheese. For most people, even if you are lactose intolerant, you should be able to digest cheese, as the fermentation and enzymatic process created during aging eliminates the lactose. Please do not ever buy the make-believe cheese they call "American" cheese, or the similar pale yellow stuff some people melt over their sandwich. There should be a law against calling them cheese!

Omega-3 Supplements: Because overfishing has depleted the oceans while industrial farming practices have decreased the amount of this essential nutrient in its non-seafood sources, it is wise to add an omerga-3 fatty acid supplement to your diet. A teaspoon a day per person will do the trick. Please keep these supplements refrigerated.

Healthy source of omega-3 fatty acids: Organic fish oil, organic cod liver oil, and organic flax seed oil.

Fruits and Vegetables

Fruits: I always keep an assortment of seasonal fruit on hand. That is when they taste best, are cheapest and are at their peak of nutrition.

Vegetables: I always have a bag of fresh organic mixed field greens in my refrigerator. I also have cherry tomatoes and avocados. Keep a variety of vegetables on hand according to what's available in season for a quick stir-fry. See shopping tips for more information.

Seasonings: It is good to keep fresh ginger and a head of garlic on hand. I like to keep my fresh sliced ginger in an equal blend of apple cider vinegar and gluten free tamari sauce and use it as a pickle, or in my vegetable stir-fry to add extra flavor. My good friend Marie does the same, only she stores the peeled and sliced ginger in a jar of sherry, as her Chinese cooking teacher taught her years ago. Marie also recommends keeping a knob of ginger in the freezer; frozen ginger is easily grated for use in recipes.

Fruit juices: Honestly, I do not drink any bottled or boxed fruit "juices", as most of them are over-sweetened with high fructose corn syrup and contain only ten to fifteen percent of juice. Plus, they are pasteurized, a process that destroys much of the vitamin and enzyme content. I prefer to drink filtered water with a squeeze of limejuice in it. If you have the time, squeeze your own juice, or buy freshly squeezed juice at your local quality grocery store. Just make sure you see them squeeze their own juices. Even in that case, I would suggest you cut that juice with equal amount of filtered or sparkling water to reduce the sugar load.

Water: For me, the simplest and most economical solution is to buy a good quality countertop or under counter water filter and use that for drinking and cooking. Fill up your stainless steel water bottle before you go to work and you're all set. No need to buy expensive bottled water unless it's a special treat.

Freezer Staples

Herbs: Here is a trick I learned during my last trip to France. To keep some fresh herbs "fresh" longer, pick or buy them fresh, separate the leaves from the stems and store them in the freezer in small freezer containers with tight lids, lined with a paper towel. They will keep fresh for a long time. Rosemary and thyme are perfect examples. Chop for use as needed, as with fresh herbs.

Chef's Caution: Some herbs with fragile leaves like basil or mint will not survive the freezing process. A way to "save" them will be to make your own pesto sauce without the cheese in it and freeze it. Scoop it out as needed and its flavor will come alive in your dish.

Frozen Fruits: Fresh fruit is always best, but frozen fruits can be useful for making smoothies and sorbets. Buy organic and unsweetened. Blackberries, blueberries, black cherries, peaches, raspberries, strawberries, and tropical mix.

Frozen Vegetables: Same as above--fresh is always best. Organic flash frozen vegetables, however, are preferable to pesticide-laden fresh ones.

Frozen Desserts: I would prefer you eat fruit sorbets or frozen desserts made with coconut milk. Better yet, if you have the inclination, make your own frozen desserts at home.

Chef's Tip: You can create an antioxidant smoothie with unsweetened cranberry juice, frozen acai berry, frozen strawberries (or raspberries or blueberries), and vitamin C. Or, a low-sugar protein smoothie with unsweetened almond milk, frozen bananas, almond or cashew butter, protein powder (soy, whey or rice), lecithin powder, vitamin C, and a sprinkle of cinnamon. Pour the smoothie into frozen bar or "stick" molds and freeze. This is a perfect frozen dessert for your kids, and you can sneak in all sorts of healthy goodies.

More Freezer Ideas to Keep Your Budget in Line

If you can afford to buy a chest freezer (or find a cheap one online), it will pay you back many times over in savings. A few ideas:

Soup or Stew - When you cook a pot of soup, chili beans, or beef stew, make extra, portion size it in tight-fitting containers, label and date them, and store in your freezer for future use when you are in a hurry or tired.

Chef's Organization Tip: For a stand up freezer, keep the labels in the front of the container so they will be visible without having to disturb the well-planned stack of goodies. Always rotate to the back: Oldest in front and freshest in the back. Use a large, plainly visible black marker. For chest freezers it's a little trickier: Label the tops of your containers, and rotate bottom to top.

Fruits - Take advantage of lower seasonal prices and buy more fruit than you can eat. Clean them, lay them on paper towel-lined sheet pans one layer deep and freeze them. Put them in vacuum-sealed, or use freezer-safe plastic bags and freeze until needed. You can use them for smoothies, fruit purees, toppings, or desserts.

Chef's Tip: Some fruits like strawberries do not freeze well in a home-style freezer (the best way is flash frozen in a cryogenic chamber or tunnel, but I can safely assume you don't have one of those stashed in a corner of your garage). The best way is to puree part of the cleaned strawberries with one-third of their weight in sugar, and a squeeze of lemon (to keep the berries color bright and enhance its flavor) in a food blender. Place in a large bowl; add an equal amount of freshly sliced strawberries. Mix them well and store them in your favorite way in the freezer until needed. Defrost overnight in your fridge and you can use it as a fruit sauce or puree to make your own fruit sorbet or fruit bars in the winter. The same technique applies to all berries.

Bread - it freezes well too. Bake two loaves at a time; cool, slice and freeze them. When needed, take one slice at a time and toast it to revive it. Yum! Freshly toasted, home baked bread in the morning.

Bread crumbs – Speaking of bread, do not throw away the end of your bread loves. Freeze them. When you need them, toast them dry and grind with your food processor. They can be used in *Provençal Crab Cakes, Provençal Meatloaf,* or to bread chicken medallions in recipes like *Chicken with Sugar Snap Peas and Herbs.*

Pizza crust – If you make your own pizza dough, why not roll out a few more and freeze them between wax paper sheets? Another idea is to buy frozen pizza crusts without the toppings, save them for pizza night and make a game out of it. Prepare a few pizza toppings: Sliced organic tomatoes, peppers, meat, cheese, and other goodies and allow everyone to create their own personal pizza. Sound like fun? Give it a try and you'll see.

Pesto - It can be quite expensive at the store. When basil is abundant, process big batches of homemade pesto sauce (see recipe) and freeze it in ice cube trays, then store in freezer-safe plastic bags. Use as needed. If space is tight, process basil and olive oil together and freeze. When needed, defrost gently in your refrigerator, add pine nuts or almonds, grated cheese, salt and pepper, and presto! You have fresh pesto sauce.

Beans and rice - Either bake a large pot of my beans and rice recipe (see recipe section) or cook a large pot of bean stew with vegetables. Portion and freeze. Serve on top of cooked rice, with a side salad and a piece of fruit, and you have a healthy dinner.

Frozen cookies - You'll have a hard time with this one, but we'll try anyway. Bake an extra large batch of cookies, fill your cookie jar, and freeze the rest. Take out and toast as needed. Are you sure you can resist from eating all of them before they make it to the freezer?

Lemon juice cubes - Sometimes when a recipe calls for one-half of a lemon and you don't know what to do with the other half, you can either do like me and squeeze the other half in a glass of fresh filtered water as a refreshing drink or zest the lemon, place the zest in the bottom of an ice cube tray, and squeeze the rest of the lemon over the zest. Freeze and bag. Use as needed.

Stoup – What's that you might ask? A Southern friend of mine recently told me about it. I first thought he had a speech impediment and mispronounced soup! But no, he really meant stoup, a contraction for stew and soup. This is what is seen in the South as the king of leftovers. You throw all kinds of leftovers, cooked meat, bones (for flavor) and about-to-be-too-old veggies into a pot and make a stoup out of it. Portion, freeze and use as work lunch. You can't beat that for a cheap meal and it tastes great. Just go wild with your own combinations. If someone asks you for the recipe, take on your most mysterious face and say: "Sorry, it's a family secret."

Chef's Caution: Never refreeze defrosted food. It's too dangerous and not worth the risk. That's why you want to pre-portion everything and take out only what you need.

Use loss leader buys and store them. Keep a close eye on special grocery store sales and buy as much as you can afford and freeze them. For example, did you know that butter stores very well frozen? You can even freeze grains and flours.

A Few Additional Freezing Tricks

This is something we are taught by our local health inspectors to be very careful about in the restaurant business. You want to cool down your food as soon as possible before you refrigerate or freeze it.

Do not place your large pots of soup, stew or stoup to cool directly in your refrigerator. You will heat up the whole fridge and make other foods spoil or dangerous to eat. Instead:

Make a cold iced water bath in one of your sinks. Place your pot carefully in it and cool down as fast as possible while stirring once in a while. If it's cold outside, you can cool the food on a screened porch or patio. Watch out for hungry critters or folks, though! When cold or cool, portion in freezer containers or bags, label, and freeze.

If it's a thicker stew or rice and beans meal, you can spread it in a baking pan with sides. Cool down to room temperature, then refrigerate. When cold, portion and freeze.

If you freeze in a vacuum bag or freezer-safe bag, freeze flat on a sheet pan so the cold will get to the core faster. You can stack the bags later.

Use the right containers. For space's sake, I prefer square or rectangular containers. Round ones waste too much space. My friend, Patricia, recently showed me a neat freezer container with an air vent on top. It allows steam or condensation to evacuate while you freeze. When the food is frozen, close the vent and you will not have a layer of frost sitting on your food.

How to Organize Your Freezer

I personally prefer stand-up freezers, as I know from experience frozen food gets lost in the deep Siberia of chest freezers. Typically, professional restaurants use the upright kind. A few ideas:

First, clean up time. Time to explore that nether land you call your freezer. I'm sure there are quite a few unlabelled or strange-looking foods in there. If it's covered with frost, don't even bother--trash bin. If you're not sure what it is, but does not seem old, defrost and see if it's edible. If it is freezer burned, throw it away. Keep only food you can recognize, or that is clearly labeled.

Try to organize your freezer in separate sections and allocate a certain amount of space for each one. You can even draw a layout and tape it to the front or top of your freezer, so everyone knows where everything is. That way, they don't have to stand there with the door wide open. One space for homemade food, one for meat, one for ice cream, one for frozen fruits and vegetables. Try to keep some flat space for freezing food on baking sheets.

Label each container or bag clearly with the content's description and the date made. I would have one for the top and one for the side so it's easy to read.

Make sure to constantly rotate your containers. Fresh ones in the back and oldest ones in the front. First in, first out.

If at all possible, plan for potential emergencies, good or bad. If you fall sick and no one else knows how to cook at home, make sure you have some emergency frozen food that can be easily heated, even by the most incompetent cook in your household. Also make sure to let them know about these emergency meals and how to handle them. You may go as far as print and stick cooking instructions on the container.

If you are very, very organized like my aunt Maud was (she was the mighty organizer, and all the other wives in the family hated her for being so organized and "perfect"), you could make a list of the frozen foods and stick it to the freezer door. Not that organized? Not to worry. That makes the two of us.

MY HEALTHY KITCHEN

A lot of people might assume that, because I am a chef, my kitchen is overflowing with all sorts of electric gadgets and cooking finery. Not so! I will admit that I find my blender very useful, but I use my food processor only rarely. It turns out that most of the time, a good knife will do as good a job almost as fast... and you don't have to clean the darned machine. As I mentioned before, I love my toaster oven and I do the vast majority of my toasting, reheating, baking, and cooking in it. I could not live without it. So, in case you need a little help to set up your kitchen, here is a list of equipment and tools I use regularly in my own kitchen:

= My small Black and Decker toaster oven - Even if you have a large family, you'll be surprised how many times you will use this amazing tool. It can be useful in many ways: Toasting, reheating, baking, cooking, and broiling. Some of them even have a "rotisserie" setting that allows you to roast a whole chicken at once.

= Hamilton Beach blender - If you buy one, make sure to get one that has two sets of blades, one looking up and one looking down, to make sure it blends perfectly from top to bottom. It does what the most expensive fancy blenders do, and works perfectly. I could buy twenty-four of these cheaper ones for the price of one fancy one.

= Kitchen Aid stand mixer - I use the cheaper one, the four-quart Artisan with the tilt head feature. You can find it online or a local store for a very reasonable price. I use it for all my baking and pastry recipes. It's very similar to the larger professional stand mixers I have used all my professional life. As a matter of fact, this is the exact same model I use at work to produce the gluten-free cakes for all four Peoples Pharmacy stores. So far, I have used for almost five years of daily professional use and it has never failed me.

= Electronic scale - Being a pastry chef by trade, I have always weighed the ingredients in every single recipe I have made during my entire professional life. See detailed instructions later just before the Recipes section.

= A good set of knives - You may have noticed that I did not say the most upscale set of knives. Over the years, I have learned that super expensive knives do not do a better job than a cheaper set of good quality. I do have a couple of really expensive knives in my kitchen (a gift from my son), but it turns out that I much prefer using my nine- inch Victorinox Fibrox. Its blade is thinner which makes slicing easier, but wider so I can use it to pick up food from the cutting board.

= Robot Coupe food processor – This one is leftover from when I owned my own French bakery and café. It is very useful in a professional kitchen when you have large volumes of food to handle, but less so when you cook for a family. Nevertheless, I love mine, but you do not have to have professional model. A regular Cuisinart will do a great job.

= My olive wood cutting board - I am very attached to my cutting board because it's made from an olive tree from my part of France, Cote d'Azur. I bought it years ago on one of my trips back home and splurged a little. All I need to do is wipe it and oil it once in a while to keep it like new. Some people will comment that a plastic cutting board is better, but I would argue with that. Hardwood cutting boards have been found to be more sanitary than plastic cutting boards, because the knife does not cut through and something in the wood kills bacteria. At work, I use a plastic board and at home I use my olive wood board. At work, I have one side marked "pastry" and one side labeled "food" to avoid cross contamination. If you can afford it, you can now buy different smaller color-coded cutting boards for each type of food you cut: Red for meat, green for vegetables, and white for fruits or baking. They're easy to maintain. Just wash them in your dishwasher and you're done.

= Le Creuset pots and pans – They were one of the few cooking utensils I saved from my divorce. We bought them more than thirty years ago at Macy's in New York City and I still use them to this day. They are made of glazed cast iron and are world famous for their cooking qualities and durability. They are not cheap, but well worth the money. You can pass them on to your children when it's time for you to rejoin the great Chef in the sky. You can find them on sale once in a rare while. Build up your set a little at a time. They will never let you down. On the other hand, do not let them down on your foot or you will break a toe or two! They are on the heavy side.

= Electric instant-read thermometer – It helps me check the core temperature of my meats and baked goods. Very cheap and very useful.

= Wooden rolling pin – Another vestige of my professional career. I only use straight French style rolling pins. Always did, always will. I honestly don't understand how anyone can roll a flat piece of dough with these curved rolling pins I see once in a while. I have used the "heavy duty" pins with handles and a metal rod, but I cannot "feel" the dough with them, so I prefer not to use them. When you buy one, make sure to roll it on a flat counter to make sure it's not bent or damaged. Rolling pins are not that expensive and last for a long time as long as you take good care of it. To keep it alive and well, scrub it gently and wipe it clean with a wet towel. Dry it right away. Never wash it in water or in a dishwasher. The wood will absorb water and warp it.

= Donvier cylinder ice cream freezer – I have found it to be the easiest and best working ice cream, yogurt, or sorbet freezer. It's very simple to use and gives you amazing results in about fifteen minutes. Its only drawback is that it is hand-cranked. It's a good excuse to get help from your kids. After all, they have to work for their ice cream, right? If hard work is not your thing, Hamilton Beach makes and old fashioned electric-cranked version with ice and salt.

= A vacuum machine – Like the FoodSaver V2440 we use at work. It's solid and does a great job. It's not cheap but well worth the initial investment.

= Assorted utensils – A can opener that I use very rarely; a wine steward (a French-style bottle opener) I use once in a while; a set of stainless steel measuring scoops I use mostly to scoop out ingredients, not to measure; a set of measuring stainless steel spoons; a very useful food strainer (I also use it as a flour sifter); a solid and a slotted stainless steel spoon; a silicone rubber spatula; a medium size hand whisk; a funnel; a large metal container with lid to hold my oatmeal breakfast mix; a couple of wooden spoons; a four-ounce and eight-ounce ladle, and a metal spatula for hamburgers.

Chef's Shopping Tip: I never buy my machines, tools, or utensils at fancy cooking stores. They're way too expensive and prey on your inexperience. I know exactly what I want and how much I'm willing to spend. I first shop online to find out a price range for any equipment, find the cheapest, print the page with the price, go to a local brick and mortar store, and ask them if they are willing to match that price. Most of the time they will. I also buy some of my tools at a restaurant supply store. Most of them are open to the public and offer professional quality tools at reasonable prices. If you are not in a hurry, check out craigslist or put in an ad looking for what you want. You may be lucky and find your "bonheur" (find) there. Bonne chance!

OTHER MONEY SAVING IDEAS

Canning and Preserving

This is the subject of whole books and, unfortunately, not one of my specialties. My grandma used this preserving technique a lot, as I'm sure your grandparents did during tough times or the Depression. Lately, there has been a renewed interest in canning and preserving. If you have the time or a bumper crop from your garden, it's something you should look into.

Avoiding Unnecessary Waste

Have you looked into your refrigerator's bowels recently? Let's be honest, most of us could make progress on this front. Did you know that an average American household wastes up to forty percent of the food they buy? Surprised? How long ago has it been since you really looked at what was lurking in the back of your fridge (a moldy jar of pasta sauce) or at the bottom of that veggie crisper (a wilted rotting salad)? You may find some ugly surprises in there. I know I still do once in a while, and I'm a pro. I should know better! Here are a few ideas that may help you save food and money. For starters, think twice about filling your fridge or freezer to the gills. See if you can live with a half or three-quarter filled cooler with clear lines of sight so you can see at a glance what's in there. Also, do like we do in the professional world and take a complete inventory of your food before you write your shopping list. And don't forget to use those leftovers.

Use Your Toaster Oven

Why heat up a whole oven and waste energy when your counter-top toaster oven will do the trick? I have used my toaster oven for so long I don't even remember how to use my regular oven. I kid you not! Even if you are a family of four, there is an amazing amount of things you can cook or reheat in that small oven.

Shaving a Few Extra Cents Here and There

Most of the time, peeling that fresh carrot, beet, root, or new potato is really not necessary. Use a small scrubbing brush to clean it.

If your carrots come with their own beautiful greens still on, wash them well, chop them, and add them to your soup or stew. They are loaded with vitamins and chlorophyll.

Same thing for the long broccoli stem. Don't throw it away. Peel it and slice it thinly and add it to the rest of your broccoli. All the health benefits of broccoli florets are in the stem as well. The same goes for artichoke stems.

The green part of leeks, outer leaves of cabbage, and stems of cauliflower and broccoli can be added to vegetable soups or used to make stock. Just put them in a freezer bag and use when needed.

You can even save the water used to cook your vegetables or potatoes as a vegetable soup base by adding a bouillon cube or two.

A little trick to save energy: When you cook food in boiling water, once it has reached the boiling point, reduce the gas or heat element to sustain that boiling temperature, but no more.

To save money on oil or fat expenses, use a few drops of oil and spread them with a pastry or silicone brush. Or use an oil spray. My grandmother used a dried "quignon" (the end part of a baguette), kept it in a lard pot and used it to spread a thin layer of fat at the bottom of the pot or pan before cooking.

Menu Planning

If you want to save money while grocery shopping, you need to get used to planning your menus before you go shopping. I know... who's got the time? As it is in most cases, it only takes a *little* extra time to save a significant amount of money. After a while, you'll be a pro at it and it will only take you a few minutes. For example, go through this book and pick and choose the recipes you like. Make the list of ingredients, taking into account waste factors like peeling and coring.

FIFO: First In, First Out

In the restaurant business, one of the basic rules for a chef to keep his food cost in line is to do what is called FIFO or First In, First Out. It's simple, really. Move everything older in the front of your storage space (fridge, freezer, and cupboard) and place the items you just bought in the back, and no cheating please. You have to use that older bag of chips before the new one, even if you want to try that new flavor first.

Shopping List

A good shopping list is worth its weight in gold. Here's my trick: On my smart phone or PDA, I created a shopping list that matches the layout of my favorite grocery store from the produce to fish and meat department, the bulk section, drinks, etc. On it, I indicate what is called my "par stock" which is the minimum amount of that food I need to eat for the week and right next to it I enter the actual amount I need to buy. For example, let say that I need three bottles of sparkling water per week but I have one left, it looks like this:

= Sparkling water, one liter each: 3 − 1 = 2 or for short 3 − 2 or

= Salmon filet, one pound: 1 − 0 = 1 or 1 − 1

The number three is my par stock, the number one indicates what I have on hand, and the number two is what I need to buy. So, I go to my kitchen with my PDA/smart phone in hand, open my fridge, freezer and cupboard, go down my list, and add or change what I need to buy this week. Don't forget to plug in the special ingredients you need to buy according to your menu plan.

The advantage I see by doing it this way is I do not have to rewrite that darned list every week (admit it, it's annoying to have to do that every week) and I'm not wasting paper (another saving). Plus, if you don't have the time to do the shopping that day, you can copy and paste that list into a message and email it to your partner's smart phone. Just remind them not to waste paper by printing it! Just to read it and shop step-by-step as they go through the store.

If you do not have one of those fancy gadgets, create your own shopping list according to the suggestions above and make copies of them. Make sure to leave some empty spaces at the end of each section for out of the ordinary items.

Shopping by Weight

When you shop by weight (meat, fish, or bulk) make sure to check that the person that helps you does not "add" extra weight by accident. You are the customer and have the right to buy as little as possible. When I started to cut down my meat and fish portions, my fishmonger and butcher used to tease me and asked me if it was for my cat. Without going into details, I told them I was on a strict diet and that's all they needed to know. Again, you are the customer and you pay the bills. Stick to your guns.

Tip Your Friendly Counter People to Save Money Later

Once you know your butcher or fishmonger well, ask them once in a while to give you extra free bones for your dog(s) or beef stock. Ask your fish man to give you fish bones for added flavor in your fish broth or soup. Don't forget to slip them a nice card with a tip or a little gift during the holidays to grease the wheel! It will save you money in the long run. Just be discreet about it.

Expiration Dates

Without making yourself sick, use common sense when using food just after its "official" expiration date. Food companies always give themselves a few extra grace days before your food really goes bad, so they will not get sued if the food does go bad. Smell that food, taste a little bit of it and if it looks good and tastes good, it probably still good. Be cautious with seafood, though. Don't tell anyone, but I have been known to eat fresh salmon a few days after its official expiration date and I'm still alive to confess it.

Leftovers

Leftovers do not have a good reputation but really, these poor leftovers could save you money. If you have to eat at work and lunch costs are becoming prohibitive, what's wrong with bringing some good food from home? If possible, avoid using the microwave at work. I hate the thing (see more below on why I feel that way). See if you can get your company to pay for a small toaster oven to warm up your food. To bring it alive, bring a small fresh salad and a piece of fruit and voila! A whole new meal, and its practically free.

Portion Size

I know, I already mentioned that earlier but it's worth repeating. To help you further, there is a web site called LoveFoodHateWaste that can help you size up your meals portion, and it's free!

Say No to Seconds

Say NO to seconds. Calculate your portions properly and stand your ground. I know how it feels--when your family asks you for seconds it makes you feel good all over because you they're basically telling you, "I love your food. Can I have some more?" We all need that extra serving of love, but if you do what they ask, all they will end up with are extra large love handles. Stand firm.

Plate Size

Another trick I use is to reduce the size of my dinner plates. When we use large plates we tend to fill them up. It's a normal reaction. Who wants to eat from a half-empty plate? So find nice smaller plates and use them instead of the large ones and they will pay for themselves in no time at all. We tend to eat too much anyway. For small kids, use dessert plates for their meal. This way, they will not waste food.

Learn to Compost

If you grow your own garden, what better way to recycle your food and help grow another season of beautiful fresh food than composting? Save all your food leftovers, fruit and vegetable peels, unusable food scraps, egg shells, coffee grounds, tea bags, dead leaves and yard trimmings, even clean cardboard and paper. Not being an expert gardener, I will not pretend to tell you how to do it, but there is plenty of free help available in your community or on the Internet. Even if you don't have a garden, you may want to offer your compost material to a neighbor who does, and get a little of the crop in return.

Bulk Food versus Packaged Food

We are getting better at recycling food packaging. But what about avoiding as much wasted packaging as possible in the first place? Buy as much bulk food as possible, keeping in mind its expiration date. When we buy bulk, because we are used to buying prepackaged food, we tend to overbuy. To get some help, look at one of those prepackaged products you were about to buy, find the net weight, and that's exactly what you need to buy, no more. Eventually you will know exactly what amounts to buy to use in your kitchen for a week.

Use glass jars with a tight-fitting lid such as Mason jars to store dry staples. It will keep the bugs out. If you're not sure whether the grains you just bought have their own live inhabitants, place that bag in the freezer until it is frozen solid, and that will do the trick.

Buy and Use a Bread Machine

It may sound counterintuitive, but sometimes pending a little extra money upfront will save you a lot of money in the long run. If you scour local ads or craigslist, you may even find a good used machine for a very reasonable price. Once you get the hang of it, you can make your own fresh bread from scratch for great savings. It takes a little planning, but most of these machines have timers that allow you to start the baking process the night before. Pre-weigh all the ingredients in the mixing bowl. Cover, set the timer, and voila! A warm loaf of bread in the morning.

Chef's Buying Tip: If you choose to go that route, I suggest you buy the highest bulk bread or high-protein flour with at least four grams of protein per serving and buy dry yeast. It makes a world of difference in the final result and flavor. My friend Thierry–one of my "pétanque" buddies–always brings one of his freshly baked loaves scented with fresh herbs from his garden. It's full of flavor and crusty, just the way I like it. It's so good that it feels like a treat for me. All I have to do is add a nice piece of (French) cheese to it and I am in heaven.

Leftover Bread? Make French Toast

Did you know that what is now considered a fancy French brunch dish was a way for French peasants to use their dried-up leftover bread? I learned that from my grandmother Mamie. She would always make a point of not allowing us kids to eat fresh bread, because you tend to eat too much of it out of "gourmandise" and make your tummy hurt. Instead, we were only allowed to eat stale bread and she saved money. Now, we only had these large one-kilo "pain de campagne" (whole wheat bread) and those did not go stale as easily as the white bread city folks used to eat. All we had to do was to wrap it with a humid towel and keep it in the breadbox. Nevertheless, some of it would still get to the point of being too hard to eat. So, she prepared what is called in France "pain perdu," literally, "lost bread," which is now called French toast in this country.

Buy and Use a Yogurt Machine

The same advice offered for the bread machine applies here. In Europe, many people use a cheap yogurt machine to make their own fresh yogurt. You can find such a machine able to make six yogurts at the same time for very little cost (milk, a yogurt starter, and a little flavor). I suggest you buy the machine with individual pots so you have portion control already built in. As with the bread machine, all you have to do is mix the ingredients, set the timer and before you know it, healthy homemade yogurt! Besides the cost advantage, the flavor is wonderful (slightly acidic and very refreshing), you receive all the health advantages of the natural probiotics, and you get to control the quality of the ingredients (fruits, sugar, vanilla…). Just Google "yogurt machine" and you'll find quite a few good choices, and you'll save a lot of money.

<u>Chef's Cooking Tip</u>: If you feel a little more adventurous, you can also make your own yogurt without the hassle of having another machine in your kitchen, but it takes a little more work. See my recipe in the recipe section below.

COOKING TECHNIQUES

UNHEALTHY FOOD PREPARATIONS

Techniques you will never see in this book are: Deep fat frying, grilling, barbecuing (sorry, Texas!), high temperature cooking, and worst of all, microwaving.

Deep Fat Frying

Even though French fries are cooked by this method (and I do admit that, a couple of times a year, I will indulge my love of French fries. Hey, I never claimed I was perfect!), in the long term, it is a very unhealthy way of cooking your food. First of all, vegetable shortening (also called hydrogenated vegetable oils, a trans-fatty acid known to clog your arteries far worse than saturated fats) will most likely be used. Your average serving of French fries can contain up to seven grams of transfats. These artificial fats are now known to create more health problems than saturated fats.

There is a new, "healthier" replacement to hydrogenated fat now used by some of the fast food chains. It is called interesterified fat, – a type of fat where the fatty acids are moved in a food lab from one triglyceride molecule to another in order to make it hard at room temperature and avoid spoilage. A study published in the January 2007 issue of *Nutrition Metabolism* found that interesterified fats and transfats had similar, negative effects. There you have it. Since it's another artificial fat and we haven't had enough time to judge whether it is actually better for us, I will not touch the stuff, nor should you.

Even if they use high-oleic sunflower or safflower oil, when this oil is repeatedly heated it breaks down, turning a friendly cis-fatty acid to a nasty trans-fatty acid.

To make things worse, even when it's filtered every night, small food particles and flour coatings have been cooked all day in that cauldron of hell. This creates carcinogens that may bring you an assorted menu of cancers. Even if oil with a high smoking point is used, the repeated heating process will oxidize these oils and damage your health. Never, never, NEVER eat at fast food establishments (notice, I did not use the term restaurant), as their food is always fried and very unhealthy. If you're curious to know more about fast food effects on your health, please watch the documentary

"Supersize Me" by Morgan Spurlock. This movie will open your eyes to the dangers of fried food. If you must deep fry your food, do it at home and be very careful to not overheat your oil, and never reuse that oil again. Sorry guys, but I cannot possibly recommend fried "fast food", no matter the kind of fat they use.

Grilling

Although grilling is touted as a healthier way of cooking than frying, it is not. Unfortunately, grilling creates a toxin called heterocyclic amines (HAs), which are well-researched carcinogens. Another compound created by direct flame grilling is called polycyclic aromatic hydrocarbons (PAHs), which may be as equally harmful. That charred flavor you love in your grilled food is not that friendly to you. Beware!

Barbecuing

I know I'm going to make enemies here in Texas, but I must be honest with you: Barbecuing is as bad as grilling when it comes to the creation of unhealthy compounds. When the free amino acids from protein, creatine (or creatinine), and the sugar in the barbeque sauce used to baste and flavor the meat combine, they create our old friends the heterocyclic amines (HAs), compounds known to be carcinogenic.

High Temperature Cooking

Research conducted by the Mount Sinai Medical Hospital found that foods cooked at high temperatures contain a greater amount of compounds called advanced glycation end products (AGEs) that cause more tissue damage and inflammation than foods cooked at lower temperatures. That is why I recommend the lower cooking temperature techniques above.

Microwaving

In my opinion, this is the worst of all cooking methods and the most dangerous to our health. Did you know that the Soviet Union banned the use of microwave ovens in 1976? And, here we go, eating food cooked in a way that destroys all the healthy attributes of our food and even of *water*. Maybe the Russians had good reason for not telling us!

Microwaves are a form of electromagnetic energy, like light waves or radio waves. Every microwave oven contains a magnetron, which creates microwaves of energy. When you push that button on your microwave oven, the microwaves generated from the magnetron agitate your food's molecules--especially water--a million times per second, creating friction which heats that food. So far, so good. Unfortunately, it has been found that this same friction deforms the food molecules and makes them dangerous.

In 1992, Dr. Hertel, a Swiss scientist, was the first scientist to conceive of and carry out a quality clinical study of the effects microwaved nutrients have on the blood and physiology of the human body. His small but well controlled study showed the degenerative force produced in microwave ovens and the food processed in them. His scientific conclusion showed that microwave cooking changed the nutrients in the food. Changes also took place in the participants' blood that could cause deterioration in the human system. Hemoglobin levels decreased and overall white cell levels and cholesterol levels increased. Lymphocytes, the foot soldiers of the immune system, decreased, opening the way for disease.

My mother never trusted her food to this newfangled electronic gizmo. I never cook with it and neither should you. Throw the darned thing away. You will be better off in the long run. You don't have to take my word for it, but for your own sake, please do your own research if you need further convincing.

HEALTHY FOOD PREPARATION

In order to keep the good qualities of the food you buy at the market, it is important not to damage it with the cooking techniques you use. Although I am not a raw foodist, I believe many foods should be eaten either raw or lightly cooked to preserve their nutritional qualities. Raw food contains a lot of vitamins and minerals that are important to our health. It does not make sense to destroy these qualities by over-processing or over-cooking.

Raw Food

Preparing raw food preserves all the vital nutrients of the quality food you have taken pains to obtain. It retains all the vitamins, minerals, antioxidants, phytonutrients, and enzymes necessary to keep your body healthy. I am not purely a raw food advocate, but I do believe that we should eat at least half of our food raw, usually in the form of salad and fresh fruit.

Light Steaming

I prefer to use steaming instead of boiling to cook my vegetables. It is the best cooking method for vegetables and fish. This form of light gentle cooking can tenderize asparagus or artichokes and make them easier to digest, and bring out the carotenoids locked in raw carrots and tomatoes.

You should not steam for more than 5 to 7 minutes to keep your vegetables al dente (crunchy) and full of nutrients. To steam, I use a stainless steel insert expandable basket. Pour one inch of salted hot water in a large pot with a lid, add your basket, bring the water to a rolling boil and only at that time should you add your precut vegetables. Cover and cook. I suggest you use a kitchen timer to avoid overcooking. If you cook more than one vegetable at a time, layer them, placing the denser ones at the bottom and the most tender at the top. For an easy and quick meal, you can steam fish and vegetables at the same time. To bring additional goodness to your food, drizzle them with a light pour of extra virgin olive oil complemented by a squeeze of fresh lemon, fresh herbs, a pinch of sea salt, and freshly ground pepper.

Vegetables best suited for steaming: Artichokes, asparagus, broccoli, carrots, cauliflower, green beans, haricots verts, and zucchini are all great choices because they're sturdier and won't turn to mush too easily. Leafy greens — baby bok choy, Chinese broccoli, collard greens, kale, mustard greens, beet greens, spinach, Swiss chard, and turnip greens — also steam up nicely, but take less time. If you want to try something new, steam some radishes or quartered new potatoes.

Fish best suited for steaming: Oily fish like salmon, tuna, trout, and mackerel.

Blanching

To blanch vegetables, bring a pot of water to a rolling boil, drop them in the water, bring the water back to a boil, and cook for *no longer* than one minute or until they turn bright green. Take your vegetables out the boiling water with a slotted spoon and drop in iced water to stop the cooking process and keep your vegetables crunchy. Take them out of the iced water and drain. There will be a little more loss of nutrients by this method, but it still is a very healthy way to cook.

Simmering

This technique relates mostly to soups and stews, where the food is cooked for a longer time at a lower temperature. This method allows the food to tenderize while blending all the wonderful flavors together. Many of the nutrients are preserved in the broth or the sauce.

Quick Sautéing or Stir Fry

It's no secret that I do not recommend deep frying (see below), but quick sautéing is an acceptable method of cooking if you follow my directions. Do not overheat your oil; if it smokes, it means it is oxidized and potentially dangerous to your health. Throw it away and start over. An easy way to find out when your oil is hot enough to cook is to sprinkle your oil pan with a little water. When it "sings" (that's the way I like to call it; some people prefer to say "sizzles"), I know the oil is hot enough to cook. Quick sautéing is a good cooking method for a yummy omelet or sautéed vegetables. The oil will bring out the carotenoids in many vegetables. Make sure to *never* reuse the oil you cook with.

Quick Broiling

I learned this method in the restaurant business. I also discovered by accident that it is a very healthy way to cook some foods, especially fatty fish like salmon. It also works well on chicken breast and pork tenderloin. To quick broil, preheat your oven to Broil; place a glazed cast iron or stainless steel skillet in the oven. Allow the pan to heat for at least ten minutes; take it out with oven mittens and place your fish or meat in it; put it quickly back in the oven and cook for a few minutes. As a matter of fact, this is the only way I cook my fish and meat nowadays. It is quick (2 to 3 minutes depending how thick your piece of salmon is); it preserves the healthy qualities of your food (in salmon's case, its omega-3 fatty acids) while offering a pleasant mouth feel. Your food is crunchy on the outside while moist on the inside.

"En Papillote"

This is a method rarely used outside of the restaurant business, as it can be a little involved, but it is fun to eat and will impress your family or guests. You create a parchment paper pocket wherein you place all the ingredients you want to cook, fold the paper over on itself tightly so it forms a sort of envelope, and you bake it in the oven. The advantage of this method is that all the ingredients simmer in their own juices and flavor one another. It is a wonderful method; you might want to try this on a weekend when you have more time and feel more adventurous.

Broth Poaching

This is one of my favorite ways to cook asparagus and other vegetables. Pour a small amount of a good quality broth (vegetable, fish, beef, or chicken, according to the dish) in the bottom of a stainless steel pan or skillet; bring to a simmer. Place your vegetables in the broth and cook for 3-4 minutes on one side; turn your vegetables over and finish cooking for another 3-4 minutes. Drizzle with a freshly made vinaigrette or olive oil and lemon juice, sea salt, and ground pepper and voila! A quick, simple, and healthy dish.

Best meats for poaching: Besides eggs, poaching works great for chicken, especially chicken breast. It will keep it moist and flavorful by absorbing the poaching broth flavor. I don't mean to sound English (no dirty looks from the other side of the Channel please), but poaching beef is popular in Europe and can be a welcome change on your menu, similar to a stew or soup. For poaching, use the same cuts of beef you would use for roasting, such as sirloin strips or rump roast.

Best fish for poaching: White fish (such as sole and cod) are usually thought of as the best choice for poaching, but salmon and tuna are good choices too.

Best vegetables for poaching: Carrots, celery, asparagus, and root veggies are good poaching choices. Sometimes when I feel fancy, I will poach baby veggies such as carrots, zucchini, and mini squash, and serve with an aioli (garlic mayonnaise).

Fruit poaching or compotes: Don't forget that fruits can be poached. In most French hotels, they will pass along a cart loaded with an assortment of poached fruit according to season. I use to poach strawberries, peaches, prunes (a classic), pears (in red wine), and even apples. And no, they are not just for old folks with bad teeth and sluggish digestive systems! Of course, the poaching method will soften the fruits' fiber, but it will also bring out some of the vitamins locked in raw fruit. For eight ounces of berries: Rinse your berries and place them in a bowl; bring one pint of water with four ounces of sugar, the juice of half a lemon and one-half teaspoon of vanilla extract to boil; pour the hot syrup gently over the berries, cover, and allow to cool. This compote can be used as a topping for vanilla ice cream or is wonderful by itself. See more compote recipes below.

How to Poach Fish or Meat

= Use a pot large enough to contain the fish or meat and tall enough to allow one inch of liquid above the fish or meat. Use a fish, chicken, vegetable, or beef broth of your choice. Or, if on a tight budget, use water with two bouillon cubes of your choice per quart of liquid.

= Add a form of acid, vinegar, or lemon juice. You will need one-quarter cup of acid for each quart of broth. Now, add herbs (fresh or dried), spices, and vegetables to add flavor to the broth. These will add flavor to your meat. Feel free to be creative. No need to use your finest cutting skills to cut your veggies. Rough cuts will do just fine.

= Bring your poaching liquid to a boil; add your fish or meat. Make sure the liquid is one inch above the fish or meat to make sure it cooks evenly. Make sure the poaching does not boil but stays at a gentle simmer, no bubbles showing. If you have an instant read thermometer, fish poaching should be at 175-185ºF; chicken or beef poaching temperature should be 160-175ºF. Cooking time will vary according to your product's size: An eight ounce portion of fish should take about ten minutes; an eight ounce serving of chicken should take fifteen to twenty minutes; beef will take a little longer, about thirty minutes.

Whether you're on a diet or not, poached food is usually served with steamed vegetables (see above) or rice or pasta. Couscous has a wonderful way of absorbing the cooking juices and is traditional in Northern Africa. If you feel like having a sauce, steam your favorite vegetable and puree it with some of the poaching liquid until you have a healthy sauce. Salt and pepper to taste.

A Note about Nutritional Values

I suppose some of you may expect to see a nutritional analysis with every recipe. I decided not to include them, as it would go against the spirit of this book. I want this to be all about eating healthy food for the pleasure of it. What I do not want is for you to obsess about counting calories, fats, and beans. The recipes are designed to be both flavorful and healthy. Trust them to provide that and enjoy the journey into better health.

RECIPES NOTES

Chef's Notes about the Recipes

Welcome to my favorite healthy recipes. This is where the fun begins, the hands get dirty, and the rolling pin hits the dough.

Although this book wasn't originally designed for me and my gluten and dairy-allergic friends, I made every effort to offer alternative substitutions to regular recipes. So, I am proud to say that 100% of the recipes I offer here are either GFCF or can be made GFCF with a few simple substitutions.

Even though my French cuisine is essentially Mediterranean, I will also include healthy foods from other countries to offer you some diversity and additional fun, so you can play with your food even though your mother told you not to do that.

Although I personally try to avoid products made with processed flours, I will still offer you healthier versions of your favorite breakfast goodies like muffins, pancakes, and cookies. I will also give you a few good cake recipes, but I will try to focus on easy and less expensive desserts based on fruit. After all, these are supposed to be healthy recipes, even if we are on a budget!

French Food is Not Only for the Rich

A lot of people are under the assumption that all French food is expensive, but the best known French dishes are peasant meals beautified for restaurants: "Soupe a l'oignon" (onion soup); "cassoulet"--a bean dish cooked with sausages, duck or left over meat; "pain perdu" (French toasts); ratatouille (a vegetable stew); "pot au feu" (meat stew); "poule au pot" (chicken soup); "gratin Dauphinois" (scalloped potatoes with cream, eggs and cheese); "soupe de poisson" (fish soup made from all sorts of small fish too small to eat whole); "clafoutis aux cerises" (cherries cooked in a milk and egg custard); "quiche Lorraine" (ham hocks, bacon, and cheese baked in an egg custard); "lapin a la moutarde" (rabbit cooked with a mustard sauce); "omelette du pauvre homme" (poor man's omelet); "pomme de terre farcie" (baked potato), and so on.

Weighing Instead of Measuring Baking Ingredients

Being a pastry chef by trade, I have always weighed the ingredients in every single recipe I have made during my professional life. I eventually translated all my professional cooking recipes into weight, as well, for consistency's sake. As a pastry and baking teacher, I have always insisted that my students do the same. Why? Because, while pastry making is an art, it's also a science. Since a lot of pastry science has to do with chemical reactions, everything needs to be weighed precisely. I know some of you will groan at the idea of weighing everything but, once you get used to it, you will thank me. Cup measuring is just too inconsistent. By weighing, you will get consistent results every time you bake. Therefore, in the baking and pastry sections, all the recipes will be labeled in weight unless the measurements are too small, in which case I will use tablespoons and teaspoons. You'll see, it's really not that difficult, and once you get used to it, you will never want to go back. Don't worry, I did not write the food recipes in weight.

Find a cheap electronic scale at your closest kitchen equipment or discount store. There is no need to spend a lot of money. A couple of suggestions: Make sure they can weigh up to six or seven pounds; check that they have a "tare" (zero out) button; and make sure they offer pounds and ounces as well as metric measurements (kilograms and grams). I will not torture you with metric recipes, but it could be useful if you find French or foreign recipes online that you wish to try. I wonder why the U. S. hasn't shifted their measuring system to metric yet? I thought that was supposed to happen in the 1970s. Oh well. I'm used to it by now.

You will also find that using a scale will cut down on your dishwashing, as well as saving you time. To use, place your mixing bowl or container directly on the scale and push the start button; that will zero it out automatically; add your first dry ingredient; push the "tare" button again, add the next ingredient, and so on until you're done with the dry ingredients; switch containers for your wet or liquid ingredients, press the tare button and finish weighing all your wet ingredients. I always use the mixing bowl as my measuring bowl so I don't have to wash an additional container.

Measuring Conventions

To save space, I used the contractions commonly used in the baking business. Please remember that 1 lb = 1 pound; 1 oz = 1 ounce; 1 qt = 1 quart; 1 pt = 1 pint; 1 cp = 1 cup; 1 Tbsp = 1 tablespoon; 1 tsp = 1 teaspoon.

Mixer

All my baking and pastry recipes are written with a Kitchen Aid stand mixer in mind. These are very similar to the larger professional Hobart 20-qt stand mixers I have used all my professional life.

Oven Temperatures

As many of you already know, the oven temperatures I give you are only an indication. Every oven is different, from gas to electric to convection. For these recipes, I have used a standard gas oven as a basis for the temperatures. At work, I use a convection oven. If you do too, I suggest you lower the suggested temperature by 25ºF from the standard temperature given in the recipes. Another suggestion: Turn your product halfway through the baking time so that your product bakes evenly. Most ovens do have hot spots, and this can cause uneven baking.

Special Nutrition Considerations

This book was written with an average healthy family in mind. If any member of your family is overweight, this book should help them attain a healthier weight, but it is not designed to be a diet plan. I did hear some of my clients on a custom-designed diet I created for them marvel, "Wow! Not only does your food plan taste great, but I'm losing weight on it." Although I am glad to see my client happy with this side effect, it was not designed with that particular goal in mind. If there is a diabetic person in your family, although I suggest ways to reduce your sugar intake, this book was not written for that particular condition, either. For my gluten and dairy-free friends, I will do my best to give GFCF indications or substitutions for each recipe wherever possible. For any other food allergy or health condition, please consult a dietician or nutrition therapist. I do firmly believe that, given a little basic education, everyone can eat and stay healthy on a budget. I hope I have accomplished that goal with this book.

Notes on Pricing

According to my son, an expert in the matter (I know, I should not brag about it), eating at fast food establishments will easily cost you fifteen dollars a day per person. Originally, I thought I would go for that figure, but my good friend, Chef Keem, challenged me to do it for ten dollars a day per person, or forty dollars a day for a family of four. I will try my best to beat his challenge and offer you healthy meals on a fast food budget. Keep in mind that you may spend a little more one day on a fancier dish, but save money the next day by taking leftovers to work or cooking a less expensive meal. If you keep track of your weekly budget, you should be able to keep to that average daily amount.

Even though I recorded retail prices as close to my publication date as possible, I am aware that inflation will play its tricks on us and very possibly change the final cost of each recipe. In pricing my recipes, I tried to be as accurate as possible according to current prices in Austin, Texas. For produce, eggs, and some of my meat, I first checked what was available at my favorite farmers' market, then went to my grocery store and plugged the holes with the organic versions of the Dirty Dozen. Otherwise, I would buy produce found on the least contaminated list. For dairy and bulk, I went for organic. For the rest of my shopping list, I bought regular products. I also realize that prices may be different in different regions of this vast country of ours. I hope you will be understanding of this if you find some inconsistencies. Thank you, and happy shopping!

MENUS PLANS and COSTING

How I Calculated the Food Costs for my Menus

As mentioned on the cover, I offer you a range of menu options that, over a week's time, will cost you less than $10.00 a day per person. But first I need to make some assumptions; assumptions that you are welcome to break at any time! Like most people I have a pretty set routine: a workday routine and a weekend routine.

Breakfast Cost

During the workweek, I eat the same breakfast every single day: oat cereal, enjoyed hot or cold. My variety is in my choice of dried fruits and nuts, and in my seasonal fresh fruit. To that, I add a cup of hot homemade mocha almond milk (at $0.38 per serving). So my weekday morning breakfast costs me $1.06. ($0.68 oatmeal and $0.38 mocha). My glass of water does not cost me anything.

As for my weekend routine, I eat the same weekday breakfast on Saturday, and treat myself on Sunday with a 12 oz bowl of mocha ($1.02), a potato or mushroom omelet with 2 eggs ($1.20), 2 slices of toast ($0.30), butter ($0.25), all natural fruit preserves ($0.10) and a fruit ($0.75) or sometimes a small mixed green salad ($1.00 with homemade dressing) for about $3.65 to $3.75, and I skip lunch.

Since we are all different and I don't know what your favorite breakfast is, for the purposes of this book I will use a somewhat typical American breakfast the way most people might like it: 1 cup of home-brewed coffee at about $0.15 a cup, 2 eggs cooked any style at $0.67 (organic) or $0.33 (regular), 1 cup of cereal with milk at about $0.45 and an 8 oz glass of orange juice from carton or concentrate at $0.25, for a total of approximately $1.18 to $1.52 per person. It turns out my oatmeal breakfast is a little cheaper, but it's not a typical American breakfast. If I add 1 egg ($0.34 organic or $0.17 regular) for additional protein, mine comes up to about $1.40 per person. For this pricing exercise, let's round up our breakfast cost ~**$1.50 a day per person**.

Lunch Cost

For lunch, I typically eat ½ sandwich with one slice of whole wheat bread ($0.15 ea), 2 oz sliced turkey breast, roasted ham or chicken ($1.12 to $1.25), a slice of cheddar, Swiss or Jack cheese ($0.37 to $0.43), tomato and lettuce

($0.30) for a total sandwich cost of about $2.00; add to that a side salad at with dressing ($1.00) and a fruit ($0.75) and water for a grand total of ~$3.69 to $3.88 on the high side (I used the best quality for the higher price). Sometimes I bring leftovers or a soup from home (no additional cost) plus salad ($1.00) and fruit ($0.75). So 3 days of a sandwich lunch at $3.75 (average) plus 2 leftovers lunches at $1.75 each = $14.75 per 5 days working week per adult or about $2.95 per day.

The kids may have the same ½ sandwich, without salad (typically kids don't care for salad for lunch, so I've been told), a fruit (ideally) or a protein bar (watch out for added sugar) for a total of about $2.75 per kid. Each "leftovers" lunch will run about $1.75. If we assume that there will be leftovers two days of the week and 3 days with sandwiches we'll have a weekly cost of about $11.75 per week or $2.35 per day per kid. So, if we average 2 parents at $2.95/day and 2 kids at $2.35/day, we end up with an average cost per lunch at **~$2.65 per person**.

Dinner Cost

So far during the working week, we have an average breakfast cost of $1.50 per person and average lunch cost of $2.65 per person. If all goes well we still have $4.15 left for dinner. I hope I can feed you for that amount! Please keep in mind that some dinners may be a little higher, but others will be lower so that the average will still work out.

I am realistic enough to realize that, unless you are an at-home mom, you will not be able to cook dinner fresh every night. But for the purposes of this exercise, whether you use my suggestions or not, I want to demonstrate that, yes, it is possible to eat fresh food for an average of $10.00 per day per person over a week's time.

Side Dishes Cost

As far as the side dishes are concerned, they can range from a side salad (organic mixed greens, 2 broccoli florets and 2 cherry tomatoes plus dressing per person at $1.00/person), to steamed greens ($0.85 with dressing), mashed potatoes ($0.78/serv), as well as others suggested with the main dish recipes.

Dessert Cost

For dessert, I typically eat a fruit ($0.75) and a square of dark Swiss chocolate ($0.15) as my special treat. I usually do not eat desserts, pastries or cakes unless it's for a special occasion (birthday, holiday, or anniversary). But I will give you a few dessert ideas to play with during the weekend when you have more time to cook. Have fun with them!

This plan is for one week only. I have written it as a guide to help you get started. If any of the entrée recipes do not appeal to you, feel free to substitute a different recipe; there are plenty. Eat well and stay healthy!

SPRING SEASON

SPRING FOOD CALENDAR

- Apriums **
- Arugula *
- Asparagus *
- Bamboo shoots **
- Basil **
- Beets *
- Blackberries *
- Blueberries *
- Braising greens **
- Broccoli *
- Brussels Sprouts *
- Cabbage *
- Cabbage greens **
- Carrots *
- Cauliflower *
- Celery *
- Chard *
- Cherries **
- Chives **
- Cilantro *
- Collards *
- Coriander **
- Cucumbers *
- Currants **
- Cut flowers **
- Dewberries *
- Dill *
- Fava beans **
- Fiddlehead ferns **
- Fresh herbs **
- Grapefruit *

- Lemon balm **
- Lettuce–Head and leaf *
- Mint *
- Mushrooms *
- Mustard Greens *
- Oranges (March) *
- Oregano **
- Parsley *
- Pea vines **
- Peaches *
- Peanuts **
- Potatoes *
- Radicchio **
- Radishes *
- Raspberries **
- Rhubarb **
- Sage **
- Scallions **
- Shelling peas **
- Squash *
- Squash blossoms **
- Spinach *
- Spring Onions *
- Spring greens **
- Strawberries *
- Sugar snap peas **
- Sunchokes **
- Sweet salad onions **
- Tarragon **
- Thyme **
- Tomatoes (greenhouse) *

- Green Garlic *
- Hazelnuts **
- Kale *
- Leeks *

Please note:

* = TX and other southern states.

** = All other states.

- Tomatoes, cherry (greenhouse) **
- Turnips *
- Wild mushrooms **
- Wild foraged greens **
- Wild sea beans **

And many more...

Also available: Artisan breads and baked goods, confections, pasture-raised meats (pork, beef, lamb, goat, poultry, sausages, jerky), coffees and teas, eggs, dairy products, gourmet cheeses, fresh seafood from the Gulf, salmon, shellfish, honey, ciders, hard ciders, dried fruits, dried herbs, dried wild mushrooms, pickles and preserves, seasonal cut flowers and tacos.

SPRING MENUS and COSTING

<u>Monday</u>: Breakfast $1.50; Lunch $2.65; dinner: **Alain's Quick Way to Prepare Salmon Filet** $3.33; **Side Spring mixed salad** $1.00; **Fruit and chocolate** $0.90. Total day: **~$9.38** per person.

<u>Tuesday</u>: Breakfast $1.50; Lunch $2.65; Dinner: **Potato and Chicken Salad** with **Mixed Field Greens and Honey-Tahini Dressing** $3.03; **Fruit and chocolate** $0.90. Total day: **~$8.08** per person.

<u>Wednesday</u>: Breakfast $1.50; Lunch $2.65; Dinner: **Broiled Pork Tenderloin and Watercress Apricot Salad** $3.50; **Fruit and chocolate** $0.90. Total day: **~$8.55** per person.

<u>Thursday</u>: Breakfast $1.50; Lunch $2.65; Dinner: **Spring Vegetable Quiche** $1.08; **Side salad** $1.00; **Fruit and chocolate** $0.90. Total day: **~$7.13** per person.

<u>Friday</u>: Breakfast $1.50; Lunch $2.65; Dinner: **Chicken with Lime and Spices** $2.48, Brown rice $0.26, **Side salad** $1.00; **Fruit and chocolate** ~$0.90. Total day: **~$8.79** per person.

<u>Saturday</u>: Breakfast: $1.50; Lunch: **Spring Asparagus Frittata** $1.02. **Side salad with dressing** $1.00, Fruit $0.75; Dinner: **Quick Broiled Turkey Burgers with Warm Potato Salad** $2.75; **2 scoops vanilla ice cream with 4 oz strawberries** $1.43. Total day: **~$8.45** per person.

<u>Sunday</u>: Brunch: $3.75; Dinner: Soup: **Colorful Spinach Salad with Creamy Blue Cheese Dressing** $1.58; Dinner: **Elbow Pasta with Italian Sausage and Arugula** $2.00; Dessert: **Flourless Chocolate Cake with whipped cream and strawberries** $1.12. Total day: **~$8.45** per person.

<u>Total for the week</u>: **~$58.83** or **~$8.40** average per day per person.

SPRING RECIPES

PETIT DEJEUNER et BRUNCH - BREAKFAST and BRUNCH

Petit Déjeuner A Votre Santé. *A Votre Santé Healthy Home-made Breakfast Cereal*

This recipe is one I created for myself based on the work of Dr. Budwig of Germany. It is low in sugar, full of soluble fiber, fruit and beneficial omega-3 fatty acids. The soy or coconut yogurt will provide live probiotics as well.

Servings: 56

Prep Time: 10 min

Finishing Time: 10 min

Cost per person:

- Mix: $0.56 at 1 oz ea
- All done: $0.68/serv

INGREDIENTS

To Start:

- 1 box of Quaker Oats rolled oats, or 2 lbs rolled oats, or 1 bag of GF Rolled Oats (Bob's Red Mill for example)

Add:

- 4 oz sliced raw Almonds
- 4 oz raw Walnut or Pecan pieces
- 4 oz raw Sunflower seeds

PROCEDURE

Premix:

1. In a large mixing bowl, mix the cereal with the dried fruits and nuts.

2. Place in a glass or metal storage container with a tight lid.

When ready to eat:

3. Measure 1/3 cup (1 oz) into a bowl.

4. Top with the ground flax seeds or whole chia seeds (good for omega-3 fatty acids and good fiber for digestion).

5. Pour in 2 ounces of milk or alternative milk of your choice.

6. Add 1 heaping Tbsp of yogurt, soy or coconut.

7. Top it off with 1 Tbsp of fruit-flavored Fish or Cod Liver oil, or Flaxseed oil.

8. Add any fruit of choice: banana, berries or other.

9. Mix well. Let it sit for 10 minutes to let the oats absorb the liquid.

- 4 oz raw Pumpkin seeds
- 4 oz Raisins or Dates, Currants or dried Cranberries
- 4 oz candied Ginger

Just before eating, mix together:

- 1/3 cup or 1 oz of the oatmeal, fruit and nut mix ($0.18/serv)
- 1 tsp Flax seeds (ground) or Chia seeds (whole)
- 2 oz Milk, Soy, Almond, Coconut, Hazelnut, or Rice milk (your choice)
- 2 oz unsweetened yogurt, Soy or Coconut Yogurt
- 1 Tbsp Fish or Cod Liver oil (preferably fruit flavored) or Flaxseed oil (optional)
- ½ banana or any berries of your choice

✓ <u>Chef's Tip 1</u>: In Winter, I let my breakfast warm up at 200F in my toaster oven for another 10 minutes while I get ready for work. Then I add the fruit.

✓ Another way to do it hot is to boil your milk and add to your cereal mix, stir, and then add the additional ingredients.

✓ <u>Chef's Tip2</u>: This recipe is GFCF if you use certified GF oats.

Pain Perdu de ma Grand-Mère. *My "Mamie's" French Toast*

The way my grandmother taught me, French toast is not a fancy dish the way it is perceived in America. It's only a poor folks' way to use up stale bread that's too hard to eat. In French, "pain perdu" means lost bread. So, in order not to waste precious bread, someone came up with this tasty way to rescue the lost bread. It is best done with stale "pain de campagne" or country style whole wheat bread, but you can try other breads. I hear making it with stale Challah bread gives great results.

Servings: 6

Yield: 12 slices

Prep Time: 10 min

Cooking Time: 15 min

Cost per Person: $0.52

INGREDIENTS

- 1 cup whole milk (or soy, almond or hemp milk)
- 4 Tbsp raw sugar
- ½ tsp vanilla extract
- 5 eggs
- 1 pinch sea salt
- 4 Tbsp butter
- 12 slices of stale country style whole wheat bread or GF Bread

PROCEDURE

1. In a saucepan, mix the milk with the sugar and vanilla extract, and warm to body temperature.
2. When the sugar has dissolved, pour into a shallow dish.
3. In another shallow dish, beat the eggs and salt as you would for an omelet.
4. Add a pat of butter (or ghee, clarified butter) to your frying pan until hot.
5. Dip each bread slice into the milk, back and forth. Do not allow to soak.
6. Then do the same in the egg mix.
7. Place in your frying pan. Add as many bread slices as your pan will accept comfortably.
8. Cook on the first side for 1 or 2 minutes, until golden.
9. Flip carefully. Cook the other side.
10. When done, reserve on a plate covered with a clean "torchon" (kitchen towel) folded over the toast to keep it warm.

Quiche aux Légumes de Printemps. *Spring Vegetable Quiche*

A simple quiche that brings you spring's harvest at a reasonable cost. You can either follow the recipe as written, or take liberties and be creative with the freshest available produce at your local market. Knock yourself out... just not too hard! You might hurt yourself. Add a side salad and you have a complete meal.

Servings: 6

For 1-9 inch pie shell

Prep Time: 30 min

Oven Temp: 350F

Cost per person: $1.08

INGREDIENTS

Filling

- 4 oz broccoli florets
- 1 bell pepper, red, yellow or green, trimmed and sliced
- 1.5 oz baby spinach leaves
- 1-2 oz grated carrot
- ½ medium white onion, chopped
- 2 garlic cloves, minced
- Sea salt and pepper to taste
- 1 Tbsp olive oil

Quiche batter

- 1.5 cups (12 oz) whole milk, plain soy or almond milk

PROCEDURE

1. Preheat your oven at 350F.
2. Prebake your pie shell for about 8 minutes or until firm but not baked. Doing so will prevent the crust from being soggy later on.

Prepare the filling:

3. Put together in a bowl: cut broccoli florets, bell pepper slices, baby spinach leaves, grated carrot, chopped onion and garlic, and salt and pepper. Toss lightly together.
4. Sauté all your vegetables in olive oil until tender but still a little crunchy.
5. Pour into your prebaked pie shell.

For the quiche batter:

6. Measure/weigh all the ingredients for the quiche batter in your food blender bowl. Blend a low speed, do not allow to foam.
7. Pour the batter in slowly on one side, trying to keep the vegetables from floating to the surface.
8. Bake for about 30 minutes (turn once midway) until the batter is golden brown or is slightly firm to the touch.
9. Cool. Cut into 6 pieces per pie.

✓ Chef's Tip1: If you manage to eat only one

- 4 (8 oz) whole eggs
- ½ tsp sea salt
- ¼ tsp black pepper, ground

piece per person, you will have 2 slices leftover for tomorrow's lunch. It's very good at room temperature or warmed up at 350F for 5minutes.

✓ Chef's Tip 2: If you use a GF piecrust and replace the milk with plain soy or almond milk, you will end up with the perfect GFCF quiche.

SOUPES - SOUPS

Soupe de Santé Verte d'Alain. *Alain's Healthy Green Soup*

When I feel "barbouillé" or "pas dans mon assiette", like when I feel a cold or flu coming on, I take a large bowl of this soup, go to bed, sweat it out and I usually feel a lot better the next day. Since I always have these ingredients at hand, this soup is very easy to put together in a few minutes.

Servings: 2

Prep Time: 10 min

Cost per person: $1.81

INGREDIENTS

- 2 cups filtered or spring water
- 4 cups of mixed field greens, or any leafy greens you happen to have on hand
- 8 broccoli or cauliflower florets
- 1 carrot, sliced
- 2 garlic cloves, minced
- 1 tsp fresh ginger, sliced
- 1 Tbsp miso paste
- 1 tsp sea salt
- ½ tsp cayenne pepper
- 1tsp turmeric spice
- 1 Tbsp fish oil (optional)

PROCEDURE

1. Bring water to boil.
2. Meanwhile, put all the ingredients listed in your blender's jar. Be creative and add any fresh vegetables you have in your fridge. What appeals to you is probably what you need.
3. If you want it to be thicker, you can add 1 cup of cooked rice, a small cooked sweet potato, or even add a raw egg (at the end) for additional protein.
4. Pour hot water over the ingredients and start blending slowly, then at high speed until finely pureed.
5. Enjoy hot and go to bed to detox your body with a good sweating.

✓ Chef's Tip 1: This is a hot but raw soup. The water is boiled, but the vegetables are not cooked. All the vitamins, minerals and chlorophyll are fully active and ready to help you feel better.
✓ Chef's Tip 2: This recipe is GFCF.

Soupe à la Tomate et aux Pommes. *Tomato and Apple Soup*

I guess you could call this soup a French version of sweet and sour. The tomatoes, apples and red wine combined give this soup its delightful taste.

Servings: 4

Prep Time: 30 min

Cost per person: $2.03

INGREDIENTS

- 2 Tbsp butter
- 1 small (8 oz) white onion, finely chopped
- 1 tsp sea salt
- 2 medium (12 oz) tomatoes, diced or 1-15 oz can of crushed tomatoes
- 2 small (12 oz) Granny Smith apples, peeled, cored and diced
- 1 qt chicken stock or 1 qt water with 2 chicken bouillon cubes
- 1 cup (8 oz) red wine
- ½ tsp freshly ground black pepper
- a few chives (optional)
- ¼ cup sour cream (optional)

PROCEDURE

1. If using fresh tomatoes: To peel the tomatoes, place them in boiling water for about 1 minute; take them out with a slotted spoon and drop them in an iced water bath. The skins will peel off easily. Dice the tomatoes.

2. Peel and chop the onions; peel, core, and dice the apples.

3. Heat the butter at medium high heat in a large pot. Sauté the onions with salt until tender. Add the apples and tomatoes to the pot; continue to cook while stirring for a couple of minutes.

4. Pour the stock and the wine over them. Salt and pepper to taste. Bring to boil and simmer for 20 minutes or until the veggies are soft.

5. Puree the mixture. If you wish a smooth soup, strain with a fine sieve or Chinois to get rid of the tomato seeds. This soup should be completely smooth. Serve hot garnished with chives and a Tbsp of sour cream.

✓ Chef's Tip 1: This soup makes a tangy cold soup for summer nights as well.
✓ Chef's Tip 2: Without the sour cream, this soup is GFCF. Or use a CF soy cream.

Velouté de Carotte Coco. *Cream of Carrot and Coconut*

The classic combination of carrot and coconut milk is always a pleasant surprise to your taste buds. This very simple recipe is loaded with vitamin B and will please even the less adventurous! It can be enjoyed hot or cold.

Servings: 4

Prep Time: 25 min

Cost per person: $1.81

INGREDIENTS

- 2 lbs (about 6 large carrots)
- 1 orange, juiced and zested
- 1 can whole coconut milk (do not use shredded coconut).
- ½ tsp sea salt
- ¼ tsp cayenne pepper
- ¼ to ½ tsp turmeric or curry spice blend (optional)

PROCEDURE

1. Wash the carrots (no need to peel them if they are organic) and grate them (to cook faster) and place in your favorite pot.
2. Add the coconut milk and the orange juice.
3. Add hot water (or vegetable broth) up to one inch over the carrots' level. Season with salt, cayenne pepper and turmeric.
4. Cook over medium-high heat for about 20 minutes until carrots are tender. Taste the soup and adjust seasoning if necessary. When done cooking, add orange zest.
5. Mix it all in your blender to obtain a smooth soup. If needed, adjust consistency by adding a little more water. If you want to eat it cold, chill for a couple of hours.

✓ Chef's Tip 1: Serve with an Indian style meal and basmati rice.
✓ Chef's Tip 2: For my GFCF friends: no adjustments needed.

Soupe Rouge. *Red Soup*

Here is the perfect soup to please the hidden communist in you! It is light (if you omit the cream and cheese, but then again, why deprive yourself?). It can also be savored cold.

Servings: 4

Prep Time: 40 min

Cost per person: $2.32

INGREDIENTS

- 1 beet, peeled and cubed
- 2 stalks celery, sliced
- 2 medium tomatoes or 1-15 oz can of crushed tomatoes
- 1 bunch of radishes, cleaned and sliced
- 2 medium potatoes
- 1 qt chicken stock or 1 qt water and 2 chicken bouillon cubes
- Sea salt and black pepper to taste
- Butter or heavy cream to taste
- 2 oz grated Emmentaler or Swiss cheese

PROCEDURE

1. Peel and wash the vegetables carefully. Cut into coarse pieces.
2. Cover up with the broth (or water and bouillon cubes). Adjust salt and pepper to taste.
3. Cook until the vegetables are tender, about 30 minutes.
4. Reserve a pint of soup liquid. Blend the remaining vegetables and broth. Adjust consistency with reserved broth until you like the consistency.
5. Serve hot with a touch of butter or a teaspoon of heavy cream and a bit of Emmentaler.

✓ Chef's Tip: This recipe can easily be made CF (it's already GF) by replacing the cream with soy creamer and the cheese with your favorite CF grated cheese.

Soupe Pimentée aux Tomates et à la Roquette. *Spicy Soup with Tomatoes and Arugula*

I like the heat of the cayenne with the peppery arugula in this soup. It can also be savored cold; just replace the sour cream with plain yogurt.

Servings: 4

Prep Time: 35 min

Cost per person: $3.01

INGREDIENTS

- 2 Tbsp olive oil
- 1 medium onion, chopped
- 2 garlic cloves, sliced
- 6 medium tomatoes, cored and sliced
- 1 qt vegetable broth or water with 2 veggie bouillon cubes
- 2 handfuls (4 oz) of fresh arugula, saving a few leaves for decoration
- 1 Tbsp fresh oregano
- 4 bay leaves
- 1 tsp cayenne pepper
- Sea salt and pepper to taste
- 4 oz sour cream, plain yogurt or soy yogurt

PROCEDURE

1. In a large soup pot, heat the oil and sauté the onion and garlic with a touch of salt until soft and limp, about 5 minutes.
2. Add the sliced tomatoes and arugula. Stir well and cook another 5 minutes. Add the hot water or broth. Add herbs, cayenne, and salt. Bring to simmer and cook for 20 minutes.
3. At the last moment, remove the bay leaves and add the sour cream. Mix well. Adjust seasoning if needed.
4. Serve hot and add a few leaves of arugula for the presentation.

✓ Chef's Tip: This soup is GF. To make it CF, replace the sour cream with soy yogurt.

SALADES - SALADS

Vinaigrette de Santé d'Alain. *Alain's Healthy Salad Dressing*

This is not a magic potion, but pretty darn close. It's loaded with ingredients known to help keep your heart healthy. Plus, it's much cheaper to make your salad dressing at home.

Servings: 30

Prep Time: 15 min.

Cost per serving: $0.24 regular or $0.30 organic

INGREDIENTS

- 1 cup apple cider vinegar or fresh lemon or lime juice
- 4 cloves of fresh garlic, peeled and sliced
- 1-2" piece of fresh ginger, peeled and sliced
- 1 Tbsp Dijon mustard
- 1 tsp sea salt
- ½ tsp cayenne pepper
- ½ tsp turmeric spice
- 2 cups olive oil
- 2 Tbsp soy sauce or GF tamari sauce (optional)

PROCEDURE

1. Place the vinegar, garlic, ginger and spices in the blender. Blend at high speed until garlic and ginger are well processed.

2. Through the hole in the blender's lid, pour the olive oil slowly into the above mixture until it's fully absorbed.

3. If you want an additional burst of flavor, add soy sauce or GF tamari sauce.

4. Note: If you find this dressing a little too acidic (I personally love it that way), you can change the acid to oil proportions from 1:2 to 1:3. That is 1 cup of acid (vinegar or lemon juice) to 3 cups of oil.

✓ Chef's Tip 1: I prepare this size recipe and store it in the refrigerator in a squeeze bottle. That way, when I want to put together a quick salad, I just place some salad on a plate, shake the dressing and squeeze some of it on top of the salad. Voila!

✓ Chef's Tip 2: This recipe is GFCF.

Salade de Pommes de Terre au Yaourt et à la Menthe. *Potato Salad with Mint Yogurt*

This original potato salad reveals its entire flavor in one bite. The refreshing combination of plain, slightly sour yogurt and fresh mint will delight you. Give it a try: I guarantee you will love it or your money back!

Servings: 4

Prep Time: 30 min

Cost per person: $1.30

INGREDIENTS

- 2 lbs small potatoes with firm flesh: Yukon Gold or Baby Red
- 8 oz (1 cup) plain fresh yogurt
- 1.5 Tbsp apple cider vinegar
- 1 bunch fresh mint, chopped
- ½ tsp sea salt
- ¼ tsp freshly ground black pepper

PROCEDURE

1. Wash the potatoes, cut them into halves and cook them with the skins on in boiling salted water for about 20 minutes. Rinse them in cold water and drain. Let them cool.
2. In a salad bowl, mix the yogurt, vinegar, salt, pepper and chopped mint.
3. Add the cooled potatoes to the dressing and mix gently. Refrigerate an hour or two and serve chilled.

✓ Chef's Tip 1: To add protein to this salad you can add 4 oz of grilled or sautéed chicken breast ($1.80/serving) or a store-bought rotisserie chicken ($1.18/serving)

✓ Chef's Tip 2: For my GFCF Friends, all you have to do is replace the yogurt with plain soy yogurt and Voila!

Salade Colorée aux Epinards et sa Vinaigrette Crémeuse au Fromage Bleu.
Colorful Spinach Salad with Creamy Blue Cheese Dressing

Like many spinach salads, this one features chopped-up hard-boiled eggs. But that's not all; look out for the colorful and tasty beets and carrots. The creamy blue cheese dressing is a wonderfully tangy addition. Use your favorite blue cheese, the stronger the better. For me, only Roquefort cheese will do. It may not be as strong, but its flavor more than compensates for it.

Servings: 4

Prep Time: 20 min

Cost per person: $1.58

INGREDIENTS

Salad:

- 8 cups baby spinach (about 4 ounces)
- 1/2 cup creamy blue cheese dressing, divided (recipe follows)
- 4 large eggs, hard boiled, peeled and cubed
- 1 8-oz can beets, rinsed and sliced or 1 cooked beet, peeled and diced
- 2 carrots, shredded
- 2 Tbsp sunflower or pumpkin seeds, toasted

Dressing:

- 1/3 cup olive oil mayonnaise
- 1/3 cup plain yogurt
- 2 Tbsp apple cider or

PROCEDURE

1. Place eggs in a single layer in a saucepan; cover with water. Bring to a simmer over medium-high heat. Reduce heat to low, cover and cook at the lowest simmer for 10 minutes. Pour off the hot water and run cold water over the eggs until they are completely cooled. Peel and chop the eggs. Set aside.

2. Meanwhile, prepare the creamy blue cheese dressing. Whisk the mayonnaise, yogurt, vinegar, mustard, salt and pepper in a medium bowl until smooth. Add blue cheese and stir, mashing with a spoon until the cheese is incorporated.

3. Toss spinach and ¼ cup dressing in a large bowl. Divide between 4 plates. Top with chopped eggs, beets, carrots and seeds. Drizzle with the remaining ¼ cup dressing.

✓ Chef's Tip 1: To toast seeds: cook in a small dry skillet over medium-low heat, stirring constantly, until fragrant and lightly browned, 2 to 4 minutes.

✓ Chef's Tip 2: This recipe is GFCF.

tarragon vinegar
- 1 Tbsp Dijon mustard
- ½ tsp sea salt
- ½ tsp freshly ground pepper or to taste
- ¼ cup crumbled blue cheese, (about 1 ounce)

Salade de Printemps au Couscous et Lentilles et sa Vinaigrette. *Couscous, Lentil and Spring Greens Salad with Lemon-Dijon Vinaigrette*

This exotic combination of whole-wheat couscous and lentils perched atop a lightly dressed bed of spring greens makes a tasty vegetarian main-course salad. The lemony vinaigrette is especially refreshing and brings out the earthy notes of the lentils and couscous.

Servings: 4

Prep Time: 30 min

Cost per person: $2.18

INGREDIENTS

Lentils:

- 2-1/2 cups water
- 1 cup French green lentils, or brown lentils, rinsed

Couscous:

- 1-1/4 cups vegetable broth, or water
- 1 cup whole-wheat couscous

Vinaigrette:

- ½ cup olive oil
- ¼ cup lemon juice
- 1 Tbsp Dijon mustard
- 2 small cloves garlic, minced
- 1/2 tsp sea salt
- 1/4 tsp cayenne pepper

PROCEDURE

Lentils: Combine 2 1/2 cups water and lentils in a medium saucepan. Bring to a boil, reduce heat to a simmer, cover and cook until just tender, 15 to 25 minutes. (Caution: green lentils will be done faster than brown lentils.) Be careful not to overcook the lentils or they will fall apart in the salad. Drain the water, spread on a plate and let cool for about 10 minutes.

Couscous: Meanwhile, bring the vegetable broth (or water) to a boil in a small saucepan. Add couscous, stir well, and bring back to boil while stirring. When boiling, set aside covered and let stand until the liquid is absorbed, about 5 minutes. Fluff the couscous with a fork.

Vinaigrette: Combine oil, lemon juice, vinegar, mustard, garlic, salt and pepper in a blender or a medium size bowl. Blend or whisk until smooth. Adjust seasoning to your taste.

Salad: Toss Spring greens with 1/4 cup of the vinaigrette in a large bowl; divide among 4 large plates. In the same bowl, toss the couscous and lentils together with another 1/4 cup vinaigrette; divide the mixture among the plates. Top each salad with cucumber, tomatoes and feta and drizzle each with one

Salad:

- 4 cups mixed Spring salad greens
- 1 small cucumber, peeled, seeded and diced
- 2 Roma tomatoes, sliced
- 1/2 cup crumbled feta cheese

tablespoon vinaigrette.

✓ Chef's Tip 1: I like to serve this salad with sardines in oil ($2.00/serving) or canned tuna $0.70/serving) You can prepare the vinaigrette up to one week ahead, just keep it covered and refrigerated.

✓ Chef's Tip 2: This recipe can be made GFCF if using brown rice instead of couscous.

Salade de Radis Roses aux Herbes Fraîches. *Pink Radish Salad with Fresh Herbs*

Give a try to this simple and easily prepared salad. It's a different way to eat your radishes than with bread and salted butter. Radishes are part of the cruciferous family of vegetables and are loaded with vitamin A, carotenoids, vitamin C, folic acid, and fiber. Feel free to replace the sour cream with plain yogurt.

Servings: 4

Prep Time: 15 min.

Cost per person: $1.48

INGREDIENTS

- 2 radish bunches, washed and trimmed
- 4 Tbsp fresh herbs (chives, parsley, tarragon ...)
- 6 oz (3/4 cup) sour cream or plain natural yogurt
- 1 oz milk
- Sea salt and pepper to taste

PROCEDURE

1. Wash, trim and dry the radishes. Slice them thinly. Put them in a bowl.
2. Add the sour cream and milk (or yogurt). Chop fresh herbs of your choice and add them to radishes, stir.
3. Salt and pepper well. Mix again.

✓ Chef's Tip 1: This refreshing salad will go well with a quick-broiled or poached fish of your choice.
✓ Chef's Tip 2: For my GFCF friends, substitute the sour cream and milk with plain soy yogurt and soymilk.

POISSONS et FRUITS de MER - FISH AND SEAFOOD

Ma Façon Rapide de Préparer un Filet de Saumon. *Alain's Quick Way to Prepare Salmon Filet*

When I come back home from working all day in a professional kitchen and I want to eat my ration of fresh fish, this is the way I cook it. It is very tasty and very quick. Serve it with a composed salad and Voila! Dinner is served.

Servings: 4

Prep Time: 5 min.

Cooking Time: 3-4 min.

Cost per Person: $3.33

INGREDIENTS

- 4-4 oz salmon filets
- 2 oz of your favorite salad dressing as a marinade or...
- 2 tsp extra virgin olive oil with your favorite herbs or spice blend
- Sea salt and freshly ground black pepper
- Your favorite mixed green salad with your favorite salad dressing ($1.00)

PROCEDURE

1. Preheat your (toaster) oven to broil for 5 minutes. Place a Le Creuset enameled cast iron pan, cast iron pan or heavy stainless steel frying pan in your oven and allow to heat at least for 10 minutes.

2. Meanwhile, you can prepare your salmon (or any fish, really) one of two ways:

- Brush the filets with your favorite vinaigrette on both sides. Place in a plastic bag and let marinade for 10 minutes.

- Brush your filets with olive oil. Press them into your favorite herb blend. Let sit for 10 minutes.

3. When your pan is well heated, take it out of the oven with oven mittens and place your fish filets on the hot pan. Put back in the oven right away. Using a timer, cook for 3 minutes, or slightly more depending on your filets' thickness. It's ready!

✓ Chef's tip: Actually, if you don't mind the bones, I prefer to get a slice of the salmon tail and cook it this way. It's more fatty, thus more moist... and it costs less.

✓ Chef's Tip 2: This recipe is GFCF.

Salade de Crevettes Déesse Verte Française. *French Green Goddess Salad with Shrimp*

Why French Green Goddess? Because I like my goddess to be French. Don't you? This gorgeous salad combines fresh shrimp with fresh vegetables and homemade green goddess dressing. This beautiful green dressing is creamy, thanks to the avocado loaded with good-for-you fats. Plain yogurt and a dash of vinegar add tang.

Servings: 4

Prep Time: 30 min

Cost per person: $4.42

INGREDIENTS

Dressing:

- 1/2 cup plain yogurt
- 2 tsp apple cider or tarragon vinegar
- 2 Tbsp chopped fresh herbs, such as tarragon, chives or mint
- 1/2 tsp sea salt
- 1/4 tsp freshly white ground pepper
- 1 avocado, pitted, scooped out and cubed

Salad:

- 8 cups bite-size pieces green leaf lettuce (about 4 ounces) or mixed field greens
- 12 ounces peeled and deveined cooked shrimp, (35/40)
- 1 small cucumber, seeded and sliced

PROCEDURE

1. Dressing: Process yogurt, vinegar, herbs, spices and avocado in a blender until smooth.

2. Salad: Divide the lettuce among 4 plates. Top with cooked shrimp, cucumber, tomatoes, green peas, artichoke hearts and celery. Drizzle the dressing over the salads.

✓ Chef's Tip 1: Shrimp is usually sold by the number needed to make one pound. For example, "35/40 count" means there will be 35 to 40 shrimp in a pound. If possible, try to buy shrimp that have been raised or caught with sound environmental practices.

✓ Chef's Tip 2: This recipe is GFCF.

- 1/2 cup chopped celery (about 1 stalk)
- 2 Roma tomatoes, sliced
- 1 cup fresh (or frozen) green peas, rinsed (about 4 ounces)

Croquettes de Crabe à la Provençale. *Provencal Crab Cakes*

This may sound like an expensive dish, but you can find reasonably priced canned or previously frozen crabmeat. Plus, sometimes even fresh crabmeat is offered at a discount. It's a special treat and should be served with a nice arugula side salad drizzled with lemon juice and olive oil. Enjoy!

Servings: 4

Prep Time: 20 min plus 60 min cooling time

Cost per person: $4.95

INGREDIENTS

Croquettes:

- 1 lb crab meat, canned or frozen
- The zest of one lemon
- ½ bunch fresh basil, chopped
- 2 Tbsp capers
- 1 Tbsp Herbes de Provence
- 1 egg
- 2 Tbsp mayonnaise
- 4 slices whole wheat bread or GF bread, crumbled
- Sea salt and pepper to taste
- 2 Tbsp olive oil
- Dipping sauce:
- 8 oz mayonnaise
- ½ bunch fresh cilantro, chopped
- Salad:
- 4 oz arugula salad

PROCEDURE

1. Drain or defrost the crabmeat; crumble it. In a bowl, combine crab, egg, mayonnaise, bread, lemon zest, herbs, salt, pepper and basil.
2. Form small pucks of about 2 ounces each and 2 inches wide.
3. Refrigerate for 1 hour to firm them up.
4. Mix the mayonnaise and cilantro. Set aside.
5. Whisk together the salad dressing.
6. Fry both sides of the crab pucks at medium heat in olive oil.
7. Drizzle the arugula salad with the lemon dressing, top with crab cakes, and decorate with the cilantro mayonnaise.

✓ Chef's Tip: To make this recipe GF, replace the wheat bread with your favorite GF bread. Please note: you may have to add a little more GF bread as typically it does not absorb as much moisture as the regular bread.

- Juice of zested lemon
- 2 Tbsp olive oil
- Sea salt and pepper to
  taste

Flétan Cuit aux Herbes. *Baked Halibut with Herbs*

This quick and wonderful halibut dish will be on your table in no time at all! This recipe is a great way to add more omega-3 fatty acids to your meals. 4 ounces of halibut contains a quarter of your daily allowance of this essential fatty acid. It also gives you plenty of selenium.

Servings: 4

Prep and Cook Time: 30 minutes

Cost per serving: $4.66

INGREDIENTS

- 1 lb halibut fillet, about 1 inch thick, cut into 4 pieces
- ½ cup fish or vegetable stock
- 2 Tbsp lemon juice
- 3 garlic cloves, pressed
- 2 Tbsp capers
- Fresh parsley, a few springs, chopped
- 1 Tbsp fresh tarragon, chopped
- 1 Tbsp fresh chives, chopped
- Sea salt and pepper to taste

PROCEDURE

1. Preheat oven to 450F.
2. Press garlic and let sit for 5 minutes to bring out its antioxidants.
3. Place the fish in a baking dish just large enough to hold them, and add remaining ingredients. Cover and bake until done, about 15 minutes; don't overcook. Check for doneness by inserting the tip of a knife into the center of the fish. Halibut should flake easily when done, yet still be moist.
4. Serve at once, pouring the pan juices over the fish.

✓ Chef's Tip 1: Serve with whole wheat pasta ($0.50/serving) or sweet peas in butter ($0.40/serving.)
✓ Chef's Tip 2: Dried herbs will not work for this recipe.
✓ Chef's Tip 3: This recipe is GFCF.

VIANDES - MEAT

Pâtes Coudées à la Saucisse Italienne et à la Roquette. *Elbow Pasta with Italian Sausage and Arugula*

You'll like this spicy version of meat pasta. Make sure to pick a natural sausage without added chemicals. This is an updated version of a meal I used to enjoy as a child. The black pepper will add a piquant flavor to this quick pasta dish. If possible, use a high-quality cheese.

Servings: 4

Prep Time: 20 min

Cost per person: $2.00

INGREDIENTS

- 8 oz or 2 cups whole-wheat (or GF) elbow pasta, or shells or fusilli
- 1 lb hot Italian turkey sausage, removed from casing
- 4 cloves garlic, chopped
- 1 tsp freshly ground pepper
- ¼ tsp sea salt
- 4 cups arugula, or baby spinach
- 1 cup cherry tomatoes, halved
- 1 Tbsp extra-virgin olive oil
- ¼ cup finely shredded Pecorino Romano or Parmesan cheese

PROCEDURE

1. Bring a large pot of water to a boil. Cook pasta al dente for 10-12 minutes, or according to package directions.

2. Meanwhile, cook sausage in a large nonstick skillet over medium-high heat, breaking it into small pieces with a wooden spoon, until cooked through, about 4 minutes. Stir in garlic, spices, arugula (or spinach) and tomatoes. Cook, stirring often, until the greens wilt and the tomatoes begin to break down, about 1 to 2 minutes. Continue to cook another couple of minutes to reduce the tomato juice.

3. Drain the cooked pasta and toss with the olive oil to prevent sticking and add good quality fat. Top with the hot sausage-arugula sauce. Sprinkle with the grated Parmesan or Pecorino or allow everyone to help themselves to the grated cheese as they see fit.

✓ Chef's Tip: To make this recipe GFCF, use GF rice or quinoa pasta and replace the grated cheese by your favorite CF grated cheese.

Salade de Poulet de Printemps avec Sauce au Roquefort. *Spring Chicken and Roquefort Cheese Salad*

Obviously I'm not talking about myself, 'cause I'm no Spring chicken! This bluesy salad is a meal in itself. This chicken cooked in yogurt-tarragon sauce and mixed with creamy dressing will please your whole family. If you would like it sweeter, you can add honey or agave nectar.

Servings: 4

Prep Time: 20 min plus 40 min cooking time

Oven Temp: 350F

Cost per person: $4.46

INGREDIENTS

- 1 cup plain yogurt or plain soy yogurt
- 1 garlic clove, minced
- 2 Tbsp olive oil
- 2 Tbsp finely chopped fresh tarragon, or 1 tablespoon dried
- 1 pound boneless, skinless chicken breast, trimmed
- ¼ tsp sea salt
- ¼ tsp freshly ground pepper
- 1 head Romaine lettuce, cut in one inch pieces
- 1 cup baby arugula, baby spinach or mixed baby greens
- Roquefort Cheese Tarragon Dressing, (see below)
- ½ cup (1.5 oz) pecan

PROCEDURE

1. Preheat your oven to 350°F.
2. Combine yogurt, garlic, oil and tarragon in a large bowl. Season chicken with salt and pepper and add to the bowl; toss gently to coat. Place the chicken in a baking dish and cover completely with the yogurt mixture.
3. Bake until the chicken is cooked through and an instant-read thermometer inserted into the thickest part registers 165°F, about 40 minutes. Allow the chicken to cool, transfer it to a clean cutting board, and slice thinly.
4. Meanwhile, place the pecan pieces on a baking sheet and toast until fragrant, about 8 minutes.
5. In a large bowl, gently toss cut lettuce, radicchio and arugula (spinach or mixed greens) with the Roquefort dressing. Divide the greens among 4 plates and top with equal portions of the sliced chicken. Sprinkle with the toasted pecans.

Dressing

1. Mash the Roquefort cheese with the oil in a medium bowl with a fork. Add vinegar, tarragon and spices and whisk together until well combined. If you have any leftover, it can be saved for a few days in your refrigerator.

pieces, toasted and
chopped

Dressing:

- 2 oz Roquefort cheese
  or your favorite blue
  cheese
- 4 Tbsp extra-virgin
  olive oil
- 2 Tbsp apple cider
  vinegar
- 1 Tbsp fresh tarragon,
  finely chopped, or 1
  teaspoon dried
- 1-2 Tbsp organic
  plain yogurt
- ¼ tsp sea salt
- Freshly ground
  pepper, to taste

✓ <u>Chef's Tip 1</u>: If you prefer, you can replace
the plain yogurt with Greek-style yogurt.
It will make the chicken coating and the
dressing thicker.

✓ <u>Chef's Tip 2</u>: To make this recipe GFCF,
replace the yogurt with plain soy yogurt
and replace the blue cheese with your
favorite CF cheese.

Salade de Patates de Printemps au Poulet et sa Vinaigrette au Miel et Tahini. *Potato and Chicken Salad with Mixed Field Greens and Honey-Tahini Dressing*

In this salad, the chicken is tossed with spring ingredients — new red-skinned or Yukon gold potatoes and fresh peas — and placed atop spring greens and refreshing lemon tahini dressing. If you like it better that way, you can grill or broil the chicken.

Servings: 4

Prep Time: 35 min

Cost per person: $3.03

INGREDIENTS

- **Salad:**
- 1 pound baby red potatoes, quartered
- 1 pound chicken tenders
- 1/4 tsp plus pinch of sea salt, divided
- 1/4 tsp cayenne pepper
- 1 Tbsp coconut oil
- 1 small garlic clove, finely chopped
- 4 cups field greens (about 4 ounces)
- 1 cup shelled English peas, (about 1 1/2 pounds unshelled) or thawed frozen peas
- 1 Tbsp shallots, finely chopped
- **Dressing:**
- ½ cup extra-virgin olive oil
- ¼ cup lemon juice
- 3 Tbsp tahini

PROCEDURE

1. Potatoes: Place a steamer basket in a large saucepan, add 1 inch of water and bring to a boil. Put the quartered potatoes in the basket and steam covered until barely tender when pierced with the tip of a small knife, about 15 minutes, depending on size. Drain.

2. Chicken: Meanwhile, sprinkle the chicken with 1/4 teaspoon salt and pepper on both sides. Heat the oil in a large skillet over medium heat. Add the chicken and cook until golden brown and cooked through, about 4 minutes per side. Transfer to a clean cutting board to cool. Slice or cut into bite-size pieces.

3. Dressing: Combine oil, lemon juice, tahini, honey, mustard, minced garlic and spices in a blender or a medium bowl. Blend or whisk until smooth.

4. Finish the salad: When all the ingredients are cool, season a wooden salad bowl by rubbing with 1/2 clove garlic and sprinkle with a pinch of salt. Pour 1/2 cup dressing at the bottom of the bowl with the chopped garlic and shallots. Add the mixed field greens (or spinach), cooked potatoes, peas and cut chicken. Toss gently to coat all ingredients and serve.

✓ Chef's Tip 1: Tahini is nut butter made with ground sesame seeds. Look for it in

- 1 Tbsp honey
- 1 tsp Dijon mustard
- 2 garlic cloves
- ½ tsp sea salt
- Freshly ground pepper, to taste

your favorite store near the other nut butters. Feel free to substitute cashew, peanut or almond butter.

✓ Chef's Tip 2: This recipe is GFCF.

Burgers de Dinde Grillée Rapide avec Salade de Pommes de Terre Chaude. *Quick Broiled Turkey Burgers with Warm Potato Salad*

Instead of a typical beef burger we're going to make that a turkey burger. To avoid grilling it will be cooked with the quick-broil method (see cooking methods earlier). Instead of the classic French fries, we'll have a warm potato salad.

Servings: 4

Prep Time: 20 min

Cooking time: 20 min

Cost per person: $2.75

INGREDIENTS

Burgers:

- 1 lb ground turkey
- 4 oz ricotta cheese
- 2 tsp Worcestershire or steak sauce
- 2 tsp Dijon mustard
- ½ tsp sea salt
- ½ tsp ground black pepper

Potato Salad:

- 1 lb small red potatoes, halved
- ¼ cup olive oil
- 1 tsp grated lemon zest
- 2 Tbsp lemon juice
- 2 garlic cloves, minced
- 4 oz baby arugula greens (about 4 cups)
- 1 Tbsp black Niçoise

PROCEDURE

Burgers:

1. Preheat your oven to broil. Place a stainless steel or cast iron frying pan in it and heat.
2. In a large bowl, break up the ground turkey meat; add ricotta cheese, sauce, mustard, salt and pepper; mix well with your hands until all the ingredients are incorporated.
3. Divide meat into 4 equal portions and make patties.

Potato salad:

4. Cook your potatoes in large pot of boiling salted water until tender, about 15 minutes. Drain.
5. Meanwhile, prepare the dressing by mixing the oil, lemon zest, lemon juice, garlic, salt and pepper together in a medium bowl.
6. When the potatoes are ready add them to the dressing; add arugula and olives and toss gently.

To finish:

7. Place your turkey patties on the heated pan. Put them right back in the oven and cook for 2 minutes. Check that the internal

olives, sliced

temperature is 165F.

8. Serve on hot plate with the potato salad on the side.

✓ <u>Chef's Tip 1</u>: You will notice that no buns are included. They are not necessary to enjoy this dish. Too many carbs! Now if you have to have your buns served hot with meat, by all means…

✓ <u>Chef's Tip 2</u>: For my GFCF friends, replace the ricotta with soy cheese. Make sure the steak sauce you use is GF.

Filet de Porc Grillé et Salade de Cresson aux Abricots. *Broiled Pork Tenderloin and Watercress Apricot Salad*

This quick broiled pork dish offers a triple hit of apricots, with an apricot glaze for the tenderloin, plus a grilled apricot and watercress salad with apricot-spiked vinaigrette. This is a complete meal.

Servings: 4

Prep Time: 30 min

Oven Temp: Broil

Cost per person: $3.50

INGREDIENTS

- 1 pound pork tenderloin, trimmed
- 1 tsp coconut oil
- ¼ tsp sea salt
- ¼ tsp freshly ground pepper, plus more to taste
- 2 Tbsp olive oil
- 1 Tbsp apple cider vinegar
- ½ tsp Dijon mustard
- ¼ tsp sea salt
- ¼ tsp freshly ground black pepper
- 2 Tbsp apricot preserves, chopped
- 1 Tbsp shallot
- 4 ripe but firm fresh apricots, halved and pitted
- 1 – 4 ounce bag of watercress (8 cups)

PROCEDURE

1. Take the meat out of your fridge about 30 minutes before cooking.
2. Using the quick broil method, start your broiler, place the pan on the top rack and preheat for 10-15 minutes.
3. Brush the meat with coconut oil; sprinkle with 1/4 teaspoon each of salt and pepper or your favorite spice blend. Let sit for 5 minutes. Prepare the salad dressing.
4. Whisk together the oil, vinegar, mustard, salt and pepper, shallots and apricot preserves in a large salad bowl.
5. When the pan is very hot, take it out of the oven, place the pork loin on the heated pan and put it all back in the oven. Cook for 3-4 minutes depending on how thick the tenderloin is. If you wish to check the meat temperature, use an instant-read thermometer to read 145F.
6. Cut the fruits into wedges and coat with the dressing. Toss with the watercress (or arugula).
7. Thinly slice the pork. Serve the salad with the sliced pork on top.

✓ Chef's Tip 1: This is a complete meal by itself. Ne need for additional side dishes.
✓ Chef's Tip 2: This recipe is GFCF.

Poulet au Citron Vert et aux Epices. *Chicken with Lime and Spices*

This fragrant Mediterranean recipe flavored with lime and rosemary is a real treat for the taste buds. As a bonus, it is very light! Serve this chicken with brown rice, semolina or quinoa flavored with the marinade. Feel free to add sautéed red and yellow bell peppers as a side dish.

Servings: 4

Prep Time: 35 min

Oven Temp: 350F

Cost per person: $2.48

INGREDIENTS

- 1 lb chicken tenders cut in strips
- 2 limes, freshly squeezed (1 zested)
- 1 clove garlic, minced
- 1 Tbsp olive oil
- 1 tsp dried rosemary
- Sea salt and cayenne pepper to taste
- 1 medium red bell pepper
- 1 medium yellow bell pepper
- 1 Tbsp olive oil

PROCEDURE

1. In a bowl, mix together the olive oil, lime juice and the zest of one, minced garlic, rosemary, and spices.

2. Pour this marinade into a freezer bag, add the chicken strips; close and shake the bag well to coat the chicken with the marinade.

3. Marinate for 2 hours at room temperature (shake the bag once in a while) or overnight in the refrigerator.

4. Preheat your oven at 350F.

5. Drain the chicken and save the marinade; lay the strips in a baking dish and bake about 15 minutes, turning once midway.

6. Clean, core and cut the pepper into strips. Sauté in olive oil until tender with salt and pepper to taste.

✓ Chef's Tip 1: Serve with brown rice ($0.26/ser.) or semolina ($0.30/serv.). Add the reserved marinade to the cooking water of the grain.

✓ Chef's Tip 2: For my GFCF friends substitute the semolina with rice, quinoa ($0.42/serv.), millet or amaranth grains flavored and cook with the saved marinade.

ACOMPAGNEMENTS - SIDE DISHES

Sauce de Tomates Maison Facon Alain. *Alain's Homemade Tomato Sauce*

My easy-to-make tomato sauce. It's easy and cheap and you'll know exactly what is in it. No hidden sugar in this sauce!

Servings: 18

Prep Time: 20 min

Cost per 2 oz serving: $0.20

INGREDIENTS

- 1-28 oz crushed tomatoes
- 1 Tbsp olive oil
- 1 medium white onion
- 4 garlic cloves
- 1 Tbsp Herbes de Provence or frozen chopped herbs
- ½ tsp sea salt
- ¼ tsp cayenne pepper

PROCEDURE

1. In a large saucepan, sauté the onion in olive oil with the chopped garlic cloves and the sea salt. Cook until tender.
2. Add cayenne pepper and herbs; stir.
3. Pour in the can of tomatoes, juice and all, and simmer until the sauce thickens. If you wish, you can add additional flavor with a couple of pinches of the frozen herbs I mentioned before, or some homemade pesto sauce.
4. Voila! You have a perfectly good and cheap homemade tomato sauce in about 20 minutes, and you know exactly what's in it. Plus you can vary its taste according to your mood. If you feel French, add Herbes de Provence; if you feel Italian, use an Italian herb mix. If you feel bananas, add banana slices… NOT. Just checking to see if you're paying attention!

✓ Chef's Tip: This recipe is GFCF.

Haricots Verts à la Vapeur en Vinaigrette au Citron. *Steamed Haricots Verts with Lemon Vinaigrette*

This very simple and tasty recipe is also very healthy for you. If you can find them in season, haricots verts are smaller and more tender than regular green beans and well worth the additional cost. Otherwise, small green beans will do. You can easily adapt this recipe to many other vegetables like broccoli, asparagus, cauliflower and Brussels sprouts. Add variety according to season and cost.

Servings: 4

Prep Time: 15 min

Cost per person: $0.95 with green beans.

$1.39 with haricots verts.

INGREDIENTS

- 1 lb haricots verts or green beans
- 1 qt water
- 2 Tbsp sea salt
- 2 lemon juices
- 1 Tbsp Dijon mustard
- 1 tsp sea salt
- ½ tsp black pepper, ground
- 4 Tbsp olive oil

PROCEDURE

1   Place water in the bottom half of a steamer pan set. Bring to a boil.

2   If necessary, trim haricots verts/green beans. Place them in the top half of the steamer pan set and cover. Steam for 5 minutes or until al dente.

3   Whisk together lemon juice, mustard, salt and pepper. Whisk in olive oil. Toss haricots verts/green beans gently with the vinaigrette.

✓   Chef's Tip: This easy recipe is GFCF.

Gnocchis aux Rubans de Courgettes et Tomates. *Gnocchi with Zucchini Ribbons & Tomatoes*

To make your life easier, use premade potato gnocchi. Toss them with delicate ribbons of zucchini, shallots and cherry tomatoes sautéed in oil and butter and Voila! Dinner is ready.

Servings: 4

Prep Time: 20 min

Cost per person: $1.73

IINGREDIENTS

- 1 pound fresh or frozen gnocchi
- 1 Tbsp olive oil
- 1 Tbsp butter
- 2 medium shallots, chopped
- 2 small zucchini, (about 8 oz), very thinly sliced lengthwise
- 1 pint (8 oz) cherry tomatoes, halved
- ½ tsp sea salt
- ¼ tsp grated nutmeg
- Freshly ground pepper, to taste
- ½ cup (2 oz) grated Parmesan cheese
- ½ cup chopped fresh parsley

PROCEDURE

1. Bring a large saucepan of water to a boil. Cook gnocchi until they float, 3 to 5 minutes or according to package directions. Drain.
2. Chop the parsley. Cut the tomatoes in halves. Slice the zucchini into ribbons (see tip below).
3. Then melt the oil and butter in a large skillet over medium-high heat. Add shallots and zucchini and cook, stirring often, until softened, 2 to 3 minutes.
4. Add tomatoes, salt, nutmeg and pepper and continue cooking, stirring often, until the tomatoes are just starting to break down, about 2 minutes.
5. Stir in Parmesan and parsley. Add the gnocchi and toss to coat. Serve immediately.

✓ Chef's Tip 1: This recipe will go well with quick-broiled chicken ($1.80/serving)
✓ Chef's Tip 2: To make "ribbon-thin" zucchini, slice lengthwise with a vegetable peeler or a mandoline slicer.
✓ Chef's Tip 3: To make this recipe GFCF, replace the parmesan with your favorite CF grated cheese.

Légumes de Printemps Rôtis avec sa Sauce aux Epinards et Roquette.
Roasted Spring Vegetables with Arugula Spinach Pesto

These roasted vegetables tossed with arugula pesto are an easy side dish for a dinner party. Try serving them with a roasted pork tenderloin. If you can find beautiful, freshly harvested small carrots, they'll look and taste the best in this dish.

Servings: 6

Prep Time: 40 min

Oven Temp: 425F

Cost per person: $1.78

INGREDIENTS

Roasted Vegetables:

- 8 oz baby red or new potatoes, 1 to 2 inches in diameter, quartered
- 1 tsp fresh rosemary, chopped fine
- 1/4 tsp sea salt
- 1 tsp olive oil
- 8 oz peeled baby carrots
- 1/2 tsp dill seeds
- 1/4 tsp sea salt
- 1 tsp extra-virgin olive oil
- 1/2 bunch asparagus (about 8 oz), trimmed and cut into thirds
- 1 tsp extra-virgin olive oil
- 1/4 tsp sea salt
- 1/2 cup baby arugula for garnish

PROCEDURE

To prepare the vegetables:

1. Position rack in upper and lower thirds of oven; preheat to 425°F.
2. Toss potatoes with oil, rosemary and salt in a large bowl and spread on a large baking sheet. Roast in the lower third of the oven for 5 minutes.
3. Meanwhile, toss carrots with oil, dill and salt in the same bowl and spread on another large baking sheet. After the potatoes have roasted for 5 minutes, place the carrots in the upper third of the oven and roast potatoes and carrots for 15 minutes.
4. Toss asparagus with the remaining oil in the same bowl. At the 20 minute mark, take the roasting potatoes out of the oven, add in the bowl with the asparagus and toss together. Put back on the pan and return to the oven. Finish roasting until all the vegetables are tender and starting to brown, about 8 to 10 minutes more.

To prepare the pesto:

5. While the vegetables are roasting, place the arugula, spinach, garlic, cheese, pecans, oil and salt in a food processor's bowl. Pulse and then process these ingredients, scraping down the sides as necessary, until the mixture is a smooth

Arugula Spinach Pesto:

- 1 clove garlic, peeled and minced
- 2 cups baby arugula, chopped grossly
- 1 cup baby spinach
- 1/4 cup finely shredded Parmesan cheese
- 1/4 cup pecan pieces
- 1/4 cup extra-virgin olive oil
- 1/4 tsp sea salt

paste. Thin with additional oil if necessary.

6. Toss the roasted vegetables with 1/3 cup pesto and 1/2 teaspoon salt in the large bowl (reserve the remaining pesto for another use: refrigerate for up to 1 week or freeze). Transfer to a serving dish and garnish with arugula, if desired.

✓ Chef's Tip #1: You can prepare the pesto ahead of time. Place the amount needed in a tight-lidded container and store in your refrigerator for up to one week.

✓ Chef's Tip 2: This side dish would do very well with 4 oz per person ($2.50/serving) roasted pork tenderloin or oven-roasted chicken ($1.17/serving)

✓ Chef's Tip #3: This recipe is GFCF.

DESSERTS et GATEAUX - DESSERTS and CAKES

Yogourt Fait a la Maison. *Healthy Homemade Plain Yogurt*

Despite what you might have been told, you do not need to buy a yogurt machine if you're willing to prepare it the old-fashioned way. The result will be a wonderfully tangy fresh yogurt, full of live probiotics.

Servings: 8 8-ounce cups, or 2 32-ounce larger containers.

Prep Time: 20 min, plus 7 hours fermentation and 8 hours refrigeration

Cost per person: $0.46

EQUIPMENT

- 1 8-10 Qt stock pot
- 1 4-5 Qt pot with lid
- 1 slotted stainless steel or plastic silicone spoon
- 1 stainless steel hand whisk
- 1 thermometer with a range of 100 to 185F
- 1 heating pad (found in any drug store, Kmart, Walmart or Target store)

INGREDIENTS

- 1 half gallon of

PROCEDURE

Tips to get started

1. What you pour in is what you get. (1/2 gal milk = 1/2 gal yogurt). You can use your favorite milk: whole, reduced or no fat milk.
2. For your first batch, you will need to use plain yogurt with live, active cultures, like Dannon or Stoneyfield (all future batches you will use your own). Alternatively, you may use freeze-dried yogurt starter cultures.
3. The smaller pot needs to fit inside the larger one, creating a double-boiler or bain-marie. It's not required, but highly recommended to avoid scalding the milk which will ruin your yogurt.
4. Your spoon and whisk need to be plastic or metal, so they can be sterilized.
5. The thermometer you use can be a dial or instant-read digital thermometer with a range of at least 100°-185°F, and a clip to attach to your pot's rim.
6. If you wish, you may use your old reliable crock pot, but it will make the process a little more complicated.
7. Take your milk and 2-3 Tbsp of starter yogurt out and allow them to get to room temperature.

milk
- 2-3 Tbsp of plain yogurt (as a starter) or freeze-dried yogurt starter

Time to Get Started

1. Bring water to boil in the large pot. Sterilize the utensils and the smaller pot (placed upside down) in the boiling water. Cool down and wipe with a clean towel.
2. Add your milk to the smaller pot. Place smaller pot inside the larger pot. Make sure that the water level is halfway up the side of the smaller pot.
3. Clip your thermometer to the rim of the smaller pot.
4. Heat your milk to 185F. This prepares the proteins for the yogurt culture to thrive. Stir frequently while the milk is heating up. Do not let it go over 185F.
5. Meanwhile, fill your sink or another large pot with cold water and ice.
6. When your milk has reached 185F, remove the small pot from the hot water and set into the iced water. Make sure the cold water reaches the milk level inside the pot, but does not go inside.
7. Allow your milk to cool down to 110F while stirring once in a while. This is the perfect temperature for the live probiotics to start growing.
8. When it reaches 110F, add the 2-3 Tbsp of store-bought plain live yogurt to seed your first batch of homemade yogurt. Stir well with the stainless steel whisk. You can also use a good quality freeze-dried yogurt culture for the same results. Later on, you can use some of your own saved yogurt to seed every new batch.
9. Cover your yogurt mixture with a tight-fitting lid. In a quiet corner of your kitchen set the heating pad to medium, cover with a clean dish towel and keep warm for at least 7 hours (the longer it sits

nice and warm, the thicker and tangier it will be.) Please do not disturb this process.

10. A little explanation is in order: These friendly bacteria also called probiotics (usually lactobacillus bulgaricus or streptococcus thermophilus, or both) cause the milk to ferment. They like to do their work undisturbed or they will not do a good job for you. These live micro-organisms are alive in your yogurt starter. When you add them to the milk at 110°F, they feed on the sugar found in milk, called lactose. As a result, the milk curdles or thickens, and lactic acid is produced as a byproduct. This lactic acid gives your fresh yogurt its "tangy" taste, and preserves the milk from spoiling. Before refrigeration and pasteurization were invented, this was the only way to make milk last for long periods of time. The end result is a creamy, tangy, milk-based product, with millions of active bacteria cultures which aid your digestion and help populate your digestive system. Further, the fermentation process feeds on the lactose in the milk and allows people otherwise allergic to lactose to enjoy this dairy treat without annoying side effects. Seven hours at a warm temperature seems to produce a yogurt that is sufficiently thick, and just tangy enough. Prepare your first batch at exactly seven hours, and later adjust according to your taste preferences. I like mine tangier so 8 hours is better for me.

11. When the time is up, remove the pot from the heating pad and stir well with the clean stainless steel whisk to mix the curds with the liquid. If you're not used to it, it will look like cottage cheese but that is perfectly normal.

12. Pour the resulting mix in recycled (another way to save money) and cleaned yogurt or ricotta cheese containers. It may seem thin at this point but it will thicken further while cooling down.

13. Cover and place your containers in the coldest part of your refrigerator (usually at the back) and let chill overnight. Be sure to save some for your next batch.

✓ Chef's Tip: Open your newly-made fresh yogurt, add sugar-free fruit preserves, fresh fruit or any other form of natural sweetener (honey, maple syrup, turbinado sugar) and proudly enjoy your newest creation. Don't forget to enjoy the money savings as well. Bon Appétit!

Compote de Rhubarbe et Pommes. *Rhubarb and Apple Compote*

This recipe reminds me of Mamie. She used to grow rhubarb in her garden and would trade for a few apples at the market. Although she never gave me her recipe (I don't think she had one), this is the closest I could come from my memories of this dessert.

Servings: 8

Prep Time: 50 min

Cost per person: $0.80

INGREDIENTS

- 1 lb rhubarb
- 1 lb apples of your choice: Granny Smith, McIntosh, Gala, Braeburn
- 8 oz raw or turbinado sugar
- 1 lemon, zested
- 1 tbsp vanilla extract

PROCEDURE

1. Wash rhubarb, peel it and cut it into small even sections.
2. Peel, core and cube apples.
3. Put it in a saucepan with the sugar, zest, and vanilla.
4. Cover and cook over medium heat for about 40-45 minutes while stirring once in a while until it turns into a sauce.
5. Allow to cool, and enjoy.

✓ Chef's Tip 1: In France, we like this compote this way, but if you feel adventurous, add any combination of exotic spices: cinnamon, cardamom, ginger, allspice, etc.

✓ Chef's Tip 2: This compote is wonderful by itself but you can serve it over vanilla ice cream. There will be plenty of leftovers for lunch. Enjoy!

✓ Chef's Tip 3: This dessert is GFCF.

Gâteau au Chocolat Sans Farine. *Flourless Chocolate Cake*

This is the infamous cake a few ladies called me "the devil" for creating. Although it is not a Devil's Cake, it sure is tempting. Caution: although it appears to be a simple recipe, the execution is very delicate. I had to test multiple versions to get it right. Follow the directions carefully.

Servings: 12-16

Yield: One 9" Cake

Oven Temp: 325F

Prep Time: 20 min.

Baking Time: 60-70 min.

Cooling Time: Overnight

Cost per person:

Cake: $0.70 @ 16 slices

Cream and Strawberries: $0.40/serv.

INGREDIENTS

Step one:

- 1 lb Callebaut dark chocolate, coarsely chopped
- 8 oz (2 sticks) plus 1/2 tablespoon unsalted butter or non-hydrogenated soy margarine, cut into 1/2-inch cubes
- 2 oz Kahlua liquor (or 1 Tbsp of coffee

PROCEDURE

Cake

1. Preheat oven to 325F.
2. Using the 1/2 tablespoon of butter or margarine, grease a 9-inch spring form pan and line the bottom with a parchment round. Cover pan underneath and along sides with a single, large, continuous piece of aluminum foil (to keep the water out) and set in a roasting pan. Bring a medium saucepan of water to boil.
3. Combine the chocolate, butter (margarine), and Kahlua in a metal bowl set over simmering water, or in the top of a double boiler. Make sure no water gets into the chocolate mixture. Melt, stirring constantly, until smooth and creamy, about 5 minutes. Reserve. Do not warm too much, just to body temperature, or it will damage the fragile egg mousse.
4. Meanwhile weigh eggs, sugar, vanilla, and salt in your mixer's bowl. Using the whisk attachment, whip at high speed until frothy and almost doubled in volume, about 10 minutes.
5. Fold 1/3 of the egg mixture gently into the chocolate mixture using a rubber spatula. Repeat this process 2 more times – until all of egg mixture has been folded into chocolate mixture.
6. Pour the batter into the prepared spring form pan and place in the roasting pan. Pour enough boiling water into the

extract)

Step two:

- 1 lb large free range eggs (about 8)
- 6 oz turbinado sugar
- 1 tsp organic vanilla
- 1/2 teaspoon sea salt

Whipped cream for decoration (or use prepared Soy Whipped Cream)

- 1 pint heavy whipping cream
- 2 oz turbinado sugar
- ½ tsp vanilla extract
- 2 oz fresh strawberries or raspberries/slice

roasting pan to come about halfway up the sides.

7. Bake until the cake has risen slightly and the edges are just beginning to set, about 45-50 minutes. Let cool in the pan. Remove spring form pan from roasting pan and cool on wire rack to room temperature. Remove foil, cover, and refrigerate overnight.

8. Remove cake from refrigerator about 30 minutes before serving. Slide a paring knife blade carefully along the inside edge of the pan. Remove spring form pan sides, invert cake onto a large plate, and peel away parchment paper from bottom. Invert the cake back on a serving platter.

Whipped Cream

1. In a cold mixer bowl, whisk the whipping cream, sugar and vanilla until it reaches firm peaks. Do not overwhip or it will turn into butter. With a pastry bag fitted with a star tip, apply whipped cream scrolls around the edge and center of the cake. Or, decorate with soy whipped cream just before serving or at the table.

2. Add freshly cut fresh strawberries or raspberries. Bon Appétit!

✓ Chef's Tip : To make this cake CF, use non-hydrogenated oil spread instead of butter.

Crêpes à l'Orange et au Grand Marnier. *Orange Grand Marnier French Crepes*

This is a real treat for a special occasion. It's a winner at my yearly Mardi Gras crepe party. This is a modern version of a recipe Mamie taught me.

Servings: 6 (20 crepes)

Prep Time: 15 min.

Cooking Time: 20 min.

Cost per Person: $0.82

INGREDIENTS

- 2 cups whole milk or plain soy or almond milk
- 1 cup unbleached pastry flour
- 2 oz raw sugar
- 4 eggs
- 4 oz butter, melted (1 stick) or olive oil
- One orange, zested
- ¼ cup (2 oz) Grand Marnier or Cointreau liquor
- Adjust consistency with water

PROCEDURE

1. The reason I mentioned a modern version is because I prepare this recipe in my blender. Put the milk in the blender first. Add the flour, sugar, eggs, orange zest, Grand Marnier and melted butter at the end. Blend right away, first at low speed, then higher until it becomes smooth. If necessary, scrape the sides of the bowl with a rubber spatula.

2. Important: Pour in a mixing bowl. Cover with a kitchen towel. Let rest for at least 30 minutes at room temperature to allow the flour to absorb the liquid and thicken.

3. Heat an 8 or 9-inch frying pan, melt a little butter in it and spread thinly with a paper towel. Ladle 2 ounces of batter into your pan; rotate the batter quickly and evenly around the pan. Cook until the edges are turning light brown. With a metal spatula, pick up the crepe and flip carefully. If the batter is too thick, thin it down with water. Repeat until all the batter is used.

✓ Chef's Tip 1: My topping favorite is to sprinkle a little raw sugar and a little lemon juice and fold it. Miam!
✓ Chef's Tip 2: This recipe can be made CF. to make it GF, use your favorite GF mix.

SUMMER SEASON

SUMMER FOOD CALENDAR

- Anise Hyssop **
- Apples **
- Apricots (Ryland, Rival, Perfection)
- Apriums **
- Asian pears (20th Century, Hosui, Ichiban, Kosui, Yakuma, Tojuro) **
- Arugula *
- Artichokes **
- Asparagus **
- Basil, purple, cinnamon * and **
- Beans (Romano, Yellow Wax, Haricot Vert, Blue Lake, Italian, Dragon Tongue, Conseca, Japanese Long, shelled Flageolet beans) **
- Beets, golden, red & chioggia * and **
  Blackberries * and **
- Blueberries **
- Braising greens (Pea Vines, Kairan (rare Japanese variety) **
- Bok Choy **
- Broccoli **
- Broccoli Rabe **
- Cabbage **
- Cabbage, Napa **
- Carrots, maroon & golden **
- Carrots (Thumbelina, Maroon,

- Marjoram **
- Melons (Bittermelon, Butterscotch, Cantaloupe, Charentais, Charlynn, Crenshaw, Honeydew, Japanese, Watermelon (orange fleshed and seedless), Ice Box Watermelon, Yellow Doll Watermelon) * and **
- Mint *
- Mibuna Hanana **
- Mizuna **
- Mushrooms, chanterelles **
- Nectarines **
- Onions (Walla Walla, Cipollini, Sweet Onion, Red Torpedo) * and **
  Okra * and **
- Oregano **
- Pac Choi **
- Parsley, Flat Leaf **
- Pea Vines **
- Peaches * and **
- Peanuts **
- Pears **
- Peppers, sweet and hot * and **
- Peppermint **
- Plums (Burbank, Duarte, Italian Prunes, Shiro, Sun, Small "Wild" varieties) **

- Yellow, Orange) **
- Cauliflower, lilac and golden **
- Cauliflower, Romanesco **
- Celeriac **
- Cherries (Attika, Skeena, Summit, Bings, Rainiers, Vans, Baliton, Montmorency) **
- Cherries, ground **
- Chicory **
- Chinese Broccoli **
- Chinese Mustard Greens **
- Chives **
- Cilantro Root * and **
- Collards **
- Coriander **
- Corn * and **
- Cucumbers (Pickling, Su Yu Long, English, Lemon) * and **
- Dandelion Greens **
- Dewberries *
- Dill **
- Edamame **
- Eggplant (Japanese, Purple, Lilac, White, Green Striped) * and **
- Epazote * and **
- Fava beans **
- Fennel **
- Figs *
- French turnips **
- Garlic *
- Garlic tops **
- Garlic Chives **
- Green Beans *
- Greens in September (Mache, Squash Vines, Chicory,

- Pole beans (Blue Lake, Green, Haricot Verts, Romano, Yellow Wax) **
- Pluots **
- Potatoes * and **
- Potatoes, Ozette **
- Pumpkins * and ** (September)
- Radishes **
- Radicchio **
- Raspberries **
- Raspberries, golden **
- Red gooseberries **
- Red Mustard Greens **
- Rhubarb **
- Rosemary * and **
- Sage **
- Scallions **
- Shallots * and **
- Shelling beans **
- Shelling peas **
- Shinguko **
- Shiso **
- Squash * and **
- Squash blossoms **
- Sorrel **
- Spearmint **
- Spinach **
- Spinach, Chinese **
- Strawberries **
- Sugar snap peas **
- Summer squashes (Pattypan squash (Scallop squash), Yellow crookneck squash, Yellow summer squash, Zucchini (courgette) * and **
- Summer Savory **

Purslane, Chinese Spinach,
Chinese Broccoli, Red Russian
Kale, Lacinato Kale, Tatsoi,
Sorrel, Mizuna, Broccoli Rabe,
Spinach, Chinese Mustard, Red
Mustard, Collards, Arugula,
Bok Choy, Swiss, White &
Rainbow Chard)
- Haricot verts **
- Hazelnuts **
- Huckleberries **
- Marionberries **
- Kale, Lacinato **
- Kale, Red Russian **
- Kohlrabi **
- Loganberries **
- Leeks **
- Lemon Balm **
- Lemon Basil **
- Lemon Verbena **
- Lettuces in July and August
(Wildman's Green, Prizehead,
Romaine, Galisse, Red Oak,
Sierra, Black Seeded Simpson,
Jericho, Red Riding Hood,
Merlot, Bronze Arrow,
Esmeralda, Capitain, Cardinale,
Redina, Red Rumple, Iceberg)
**
- Lettuces in September Speckled
Amish Butterhead, Cherokee
Red Crisphead, Wildman's
Green, Prizehead, Romaine,
Galisse, Red Oak, Sierra, Black
Seeded Simpson, Jericho, Red
Riding Hood, Merlot, Bronze

- Sunchokes **
- Sweet corn **
- Swiss and Rainbow Chard **
- Tarragon **
- Tatsoi **
- Tayberries **
- Thyme **
- Tomatillos **
- Tomatoes *
- Tomatoes, heirloom * and **
- Tomatoes (hothouse) **
- Turnips, read and whites **
- Turnips, baby **
- Wild black berries **
- Winter squash **
- Zucchini * and **
- And many more…

Also available: Artisan breads and baked goods, pastries, confections, pasture-raised meats (pork, beef, lamb, goat, poultry, sausages, jerky), coffees and teas, eggs, dairy products, fresh pasta, gourmet cheeses, fresh seafood from the Gulf, oysters, shrimp, clams **, mussels **, geoduck **, tuna **, wild salmon **, shellfish, honey, ciders **, hard ciders **, dried fruits, dried herbs, dried wild mushrooms, pickles and preserves, jams and jellies, sauces and salsas, spreads, syrups **, seasonal cut flowers, soups stocks **, tacos and wines **.

Arrow, Esmeralda, Stem
Lettuce, Capitain, Cardinale,
Redina, Red Rumple, Iceberg)
**

Please note:

* = TX and other southern states.

** = All other states.

SUMMER MENUS and COSTING

<u>Monday</u>: Breakfast $1.50; Lunch $2.65; Dinner: Soup: **Cream of Chilled Heirloom Cucumbers** $1.42. Entrée: **Crab Salad with Tomato Vinaigrette** $3.62. **Fruit and chocolate** $0.90. Total day: ~**$10.09** per person.

<u>Tuesday</u>: Breakfast $1.50; Lunch $2.65; Dinner: Entrée: **Refreshing Tabbouleh with Dates and Cherry Tomatoes** $2.02 ; **Grilled Pork Chops in Mustard and Sage** $3.60. **Fruit and chocolate** $0.90. Total day: ~**$10.67per** person.

<u>Wednesday</u>: Breakfast $1.50; Lunch $2.65; Dinner: Entrée: **Chicken, Melon, and Pecan Salad** $2.82. **Side salad** $1.00. **Fruit and chocolate $0.90.** Total day: ~**$8.87** per person.

<u>Thursday</u>: Breakfast $1.50; Lunch $2.65; Dinner: Entrée: **Ratatouille** $2.83 with wide pasta $0.26; Mixed Greens Salad $1.00. Fruit and chocolate $0.90. Total day: ~**$8.14** per person.

<u>Friday</u>: Breakfast $1.50; Lunch $2.65; Dinner: Soup: Gazpacho Soup $2.18. Entrée: **Sirloin Steak and New Red Potato Salad** $4.29. Fruit and chocolate $0.90. Total day: ~**$11.52** per person.

<u>Saturday</u>: Breakfast $1.50; Lunch $2.65; Dinner: Entrée: **Barramundi with Niçoises Olives, Tomatoes & Garlic** 3.50. **Side salad** $1.00. Dessert: **Frozen Strawberry Lollipops without an Ice Cream Machine** $0.54. Total day: ~**$9.19** per person.

<u>Sunday</u>: Brunch: $3.75; Dinner: Entrée: Chicken Provencal $3.26. Side: **Oven-roasted Rosemary New Potatoes** $0.72 Dessert: **Almond Panna Cotta with Berries** $1.36. Total day: ~**$9.09** per person.

<u>Total for the week</u>: ~**$67.57** or ~**$9.65** average per day per person.

SUMMER RECIPES
PETIT DEJEUNER et BRUNCH - BREAKFAST and BRUNCH

Petits Gâteaux à la Poêle aux Bleuets et Noix de Pecan. *Blueberry Pecan Pancakes*

This is not really a French recipe, but if you'll allow me, we'll call it a French Canadian recipe. I wanted to include it to give you a recipe with nut fiber and oil, as well as blueberry fiber and antioxidants.

Servings: 4

Prep Time: 35 min

Cost per person: $1.03

INGREDIENTS

- 2 cups organic whole wheat pastry flour or GF pancake flour mix
- ¼ tsp sea salt
- 2 ½ tsp baking powder
- ½ cup pecan pieces
- 1 cup milk or unsweetened soy/almond/hemp milk
- 1 Tbsp apple cider vinegar
- ½ cup water
- 2 tsp olive oil, for the pancake batter
- 1 cup blueberries, fresh or frozen
- 3 Tbsp melted butter

PROCEDURE

1. Mix all the dry ingredients, including the pecan pieces, together in a large bowl.
2. In a separate bowl, combine the milk or alternative milk, vinegar and olive oil. Allow to set for 10 minutes, turning it into buttermilk. Combine the water with the rest of the liquids.
3. Whisk the wet ingredients in with the dry.
4. Fold in the blueberries carefully.
5. Heat and butter a pancake griddle or cast iron skillet.
6. Ladle 1/3 to 1/2 cup batter for each pancake onto the griddle.
7. Fry until golden at the edges and the top starts to form bubbles.
8. Flip over and fry until golden.
9. Remove and place on a serving plate.
10. Repeat until all batter is used.
11. Serve with butter and pure maple syrup, unsweetened applesauce, or sugar-free fruit preserves.

Omelette Grecque. *Greek Omelet*

Another tasty Mediterranean egg dish. This easy omelet is just right for a light dinner or brunch. If you use frozen leaf spinach, it makes it even faster.

Servings: 4

Prep Time: 20 min

Oven: Broiler

Cost per person: $1.81

IINGREDIENTS

Spinach:

- 4 cups spinach (1 bunch) or 1 package frozen
- 2 Tbsp butter
- 4 scallions, thinly sliced
- ½ tsp ground nutmeg
- Sea salt and pepper to taste

Omelet:

- 8 large eggs
- ½ tsp sea salt
- ½ tsp freshly ground black pepper
- 1 cup crumbled feta cheese, (4 ounces)
- 2 Tbsp fresh dill, chopped
- Freshly ground pepper, to taste
- 1 Tbsp olive oil

PROCEDURE

1. Preheat your oven's broiler.
2. <u>Fresh spinach</u>: Rinse and dry spinach. Chop in wide strips. Heat a large frying pan, melt the butter; sauté the scallions until tender; add the spinach and cook until it wilts; add the nutmeg and salt and pepper. Cook until the juices are almost evaporated. Set aside.
3. <u>Frozen spinach</u>: Thaw spinach and squeeze to remove excess water. Sauté with butter, scallions, nutmeg, salt and pepper. Set aside.
4. Whip eggs with a fork with salt and pepper in a medium bowl. Add feta, dill, spinach, salt and pepper; mix gently with a rubber spatula.
5. Heat oil in a 10-inch nonstick skillet over medium heat. Pour in the egg mixture and tilt to distribute evenly. Reduce the heat to medium-low and cook until the bottom is light golden, lifting the edges to allow uncooked egg to flow underneath. Place the pan under the broiler and cook until the top is set, 1 to 2 minutes.
6. Slide the omelet onto a platter and cut into wedges.

✓ <u>Chef's Tip</u>: This recipe is GFCF.

Petits Gâteaux aux Bluets et Citron. *Blueberry Lemon Muffins*

My version of an old time favorite.

Yield: 12 medium muffins

Oven Temp: 350F

Cost each: $0.46

INGREDIENTS

Dry ingredients

- 12 oz unbleached pastry flour or GF pastry flour mix
- ½ tsp xanthan gum
- 2 tsp GF baking powder
- ½ tsp baking soda
- ½ tsp sea salt

Wet ingredients

- 4 oz milk or plain soy, almond or other alternative milk, warm
- 6 oz local honey or agave nectar
- 4 oz olive oil
- 2 eggs (4 oz)
- The zest of a lemon
- The juice of a lemon
- 8 oz blueberries, fresh or frozen
- 1 Tbsp unbleached pastry flour or GF pastry flour mix

PROCEDURE

1. Preheat your oven at 350F.
2. Spray your muffin pans with olive oil spray. Place paper inserts in the pan.
3. In your mixer's bowl, weigh all the dry ingredients. Using the whisk attachment, mix together at slow speed until well blended.
4. In small pan, weigh the milk. Warm it up to body temperature over low heat. Add the additional wet ingredients and whisk together.
5. While your mixer is going at low speed, add the wet ingredients into dry ingredients. Mix well but gently.
6. In a separate bowl, toss the fresh or frozen blueberries with flour; add to mix and mix gently by hand with a rubber spatula.
7. Scoop into paper cups.
8. Bake on middle rack for 18-20 minutes until done.

✓ Chef's Tip: This recipe can be GF if you use GF pastry flour.

SOUPES – SOUPS

Soupe de Carottes au Fenouil et au Yaourt Epicé. *Chilled Carrot-Fennel Soup with Spiced Yogurt*

This cool orange soup is loaded with vitamins. I like the way the anise-like flavor of the fennel contrasts with the carrot's sweetness, while the orange lends a brightening touch. Enjoy!

Servings: 4

Prep Time: 30 min plus cooling time

Cost per person: $3.09

INGREDIENTS

- 2 Tbsp olive oil
- ½ white onion, chopped
- 1 small fennel bulb, cored and chopped
- 1 lb large carrots, peeled, cut into 1/2-inch dice (2 cups)
- 1-inch piece of fresh ginger, peeled and grated
- 2 ½ cups vegetable stock
- 1 Tbsp local honey
- 1 orange, zested and juiced (save the zest for garnish in a separate bowl)
- Sea salt and pepper
- ½ cup plain yogurt
- 1 tsp ground allspice
- Orange zest
- 2 Tbs. fresh mint

PROCEDURE

1. Heat olive oil in large saucepan over medium-high heat. Add onion and fennel, cook 2 minutes. Add carrots and the ginger. Add broth.

2. Bring to boil. Reduce heat, cover, and simmer until carrots are very tender, about 20 minutes.

3. Remove your soup from the heat and allow it to cool. Purée in batches in your blender until smooth. Adjust thickness with stock or water. Stir in honey, orange juice and zest. Adjust seasoning. Transfer to a pitcher. Keep chilled until ready to serve.

4. When ready to serve, pour soup into glasses or small bowls. Drop a tablespoon of yogurt over the soup and sprinkle with allspice, orange zest and mint.

✓ <u>Chef's Tip</u>: This soup is GFCF.

Cream of Chilled Heirloom Cucumber Soup with Fresh Dill

By Amanda Love, "The Barefoot Cook", Austin, TX

This cool summertime soup is simple and delicious and really hits the spot when the weather is hot. If you have a garden going, you are probably harvesting more cucumbers than you know what to do with. Simply puree them with the other ingredients in this soup and in no time you will have a creamy savory treat. The humble and prolific cucumber has some very worthy benefits - the main one being to cool us off! Along with being cooling and hydrating, cucumbers are also rich in alkalizing minerals, which help to neutralize over-acidity in the blood. They are rich in the minerals potassium and silicon, which help to regulate blood pressure and calcium absorption. Cucumbers are also natural diuretics and facilitate excretion of wastes through the kidneys including excess uric acid accumulations.

The heirloom varieties are best. I especially like English cucumbers because their skins are soft. Regular cukes have tough skins, which can be eaten, but take longer to chew. I usually peel them. Fiber is only good if you can digest it, and tough cucumber fiber is hard to digest. Definitely peel the skins if they have been waxed. The yogurt in this soup will give your beneficial gut bacteria a boost as well.

Servings: 4

Prep Time: 15 min

Cost per person: $1.42

INGREDIENTS

- 2 medium size heirloom or organic cucumbers – peeled, seeded and sliced into big chunks
- 1 medium avocado
- 1/8 cup fresh minced dill
- 2-4 scallions, sliced
- ½ cup plain, organic, whole yogurt (homemade or White Mountain brand is

PROCEDURE

1. Set aside small amount of cubed cucumber, avocado and dill for garnish.
2. Place remaining ingredients in blender and puree until smooth. Thin with more water if you desire a thinner consistency.
3. Chill for 15 minutes. Pour into bowls and garnish with small slices of cucumber, avocado, minded dill and fresh cracked pepper.

✓ Chef's Tip: This recipe is GF. To make it CF, use plain soy yogurt instead of regular yogurt.

excellent)
- 1 cup water
- 1 tsp sea salt
- ½ tsp fresh cracked pepper
- 2 Tbsp fresh lemon juice

Soupe de Lentilles à la Tomate et aux Épinards. *Lentil Tomato Soup with Spinach*

I love lentils. This is a vegetarian version of a traditional lentil soup. If you wish, you can add cubed ham to make it more of a meal.

Servings: 4

Prep Time: 15 min

Cooking Time: 30 min

Cost per person: $2.01

INGREDIENTS

- 1 Tbsp olive oil
- ½ medium white onion, chopped
- 2 garlic cloves, minced
- 1 celery stalk
- 1 tsp sea salt
- 1 tsp dried oregano
- 1 tsp dried basil
- 1 dried bay leaf
- ½ tsp black pepper, ground
- 1 cup (4 oz) dry green lentils
- 2 large tomatoes or 1 can (15 oz) of crushed tomatoes
- 2 carrots, diced
- 1 quart organic vegetable broth
- ½ cup baby spinach, sliced

PROCEDURE

1. In a large soup pot, heat oil over medium heat.

2. Add onions, garlic, celery and salt; cook until all vegetables are tender.

3. Stir in the bay leaf, oregano, and basil; cook for 2 minutes.

4. Add in vegetable broth, lentils, carrots, and tomatoes. Bring to a boil.

5. Reduce heat, and simmer for at least 30 minutes.

6. When ready to serve, stir in sliced spinach and finish cooking until the spinach wilts but still is green (about a minute). Enjoy!

✓ Chef's Tip 1: I personally like to keep this soup as is, but if you wish, you can puree half of it to make it smoother.
✓ Chef's Tip 2: This soup is GFCF.

SALADES - SALADS

Salade de Roquette, Epinards et de Fraises. *Arugula, Spinach and Strawberry Salad*

Arugula is a rich source of iron and vitamins A and C, but some people don't care for its flavor. Let's balance it with equal amount of baby spinach and add a little sweetness with strawberries. Balsamic vinegar will add tartness and walnuts some much needed omega-3 fatty acids. I love this salad.

Servings: 4

Prep Time: 25 min

Cost per person: $1.25

INGREDIENTS

- 1/2 cup (2 oz) pecan pieces
- 2 cups (2 oz) baby arugula
- 2 cups (2 oz) baby spinach
- 2 cups (4 oz) strawberries, sliced
- ½ cup (2 oz) Parmesan cheese, shaved and crumbled into small pieces

PROCEDURE

1. Toast pecan pieces in a small dry skillet over medium-low heat, stirring frequently, until lightly browned and aromatic, 3 to 5 minutes. Transfer to a salad bowl; let cool.
2. Prepare the vinaigrette at the bottom of a salad bowl. Add arugula, spinach, strawberries and Parmesan; toss gently.
3. To serve, divide onto 4 plates and sprinkle with toasted pecan pieces.

✓ **Chef's Tip 1: If you want to intensify the** balsamic vinegar flavor, double the amount and boil it over high heat in a small skillet until it begins to thicken and become syrupy, about 2 to 3 minutes.

✓ Chef's Tip 2: This recipe is GFCF.

Salade du Chef avec sa Sauce Crémeuse à l'Aneth. *Chef's Salad with Creamy Dill Dressing*

This lighter and more colorful version of the traditional Chef's Salad is a whole summer meal in itself. The cottage cheese may surprise you here, but you'll see. It makes for a wonderfully creamy dressing. If you're in the mood for it, top it off with some homemade garlic croutons.

Servings: 4

Prep Time: 20 min

Cost per person: $3.75

INGREDIENTS

For the salad:

- 8 cups mixed salad greens (about 4 ounces)
- 1 cup carrots (about 2 carrots), shredded
- 1/2 red onion, peeled and sliced thin
- 1 yellow bell pepper, cut in half, seeded and sliced
- 10 cherry tomatoes, cut in halves
- 4 slices natural oven-roasted turkey breast, cut up (about 4 ounces)
- 4 slices natural Swiss cheese, cut up (about 2 ounces)

For the dressing:

- 3 Tbsp olive oil
- 1 Tbsp apple cider

PROCEDURE

1. Salad: Toss greens, carrots, onion, bell pepper and half of the dressing in a large bowl until coated. Divide between plates. Arrange tomatoes, turkey and cheese on top of the salad. Drizzle with more dressing.
2. Dressing: In your blender's bowl, place all the ingredients in proper order. Blend well until smooth. If needed, adjust consistency with additional buttermilk.

✓ Chef's Tip 1: To prepare homemade croutons, first preheat your oven at 350F. Trim 2 slices of whole wheat bread; cut into cubes. Mix together 1 Tbsp extra virgin olive oil, 1 clove fresh garlic (crushed and chopped), Italian seasoning and a touch of sea salt. Toss the bread cubes with the flavored olive oil. Spread the bread on a baking sheet pan bake for about 8-10 minutes or until gold and crunchy. Let cool. These croutons can be stored in a tight-lidded container for a few days.

✓ Chef's Tip 2: To make this recipe GF, replace the regular croutons with GF croutons. To make it CF, replace the buttermilk with plain soy creamer with ½ lemon juice and the cottage cheese with your favorite soy cottage cheese.

vinegar
- 1/2 cup cottage cheese
- 1/4 cup mayonnaise
- 2 Tbsp buttermilk
- 1 small shallot, peeled and chopped
- 1 Tbsp fresh dill, chopped (or 1 tsp dried dill seeds)
- 1/4 tsp sea salt
- 1/4 tsp freshly ground pepper

Salade de Pâtes aux Epinards avec sa Vinaigrette au Yogourt et aux Tomates. *Baby Spinach Pasta Salad with Yogurt and Tomato Dressing*

I like this salad for its tart combination of fresh greens, goat cheese and bacon. If you feel adventurous or if your budget permits it, feel free to substitute the baby spinach with dandelion or arugula greens.

Servings: 4

Prep Time: 35 min

Cost per person: $2.15

INGREDIENTS

Pasta:

- 8 ounces small pasta shells, preferably whole-wheat or GF
- 2 qt hot water
- 2 Tbsp sea salt

Salad:

- 2 slices natural bacon
- 1 Tbsp extra-virgin olive oil
- 1 medium red onion, cut in half and thinly sliced
- 4 cups baby spinach or arugula or dandelion greens, coarsely chopped, OR...
- 2 cups each baby spinach and arugula or dandelion greens
- 1/4 cup goat cheese, crumbled

PROCEDURE

1. Pasta: Bring a large saucepan of salted water to a boil. Add pasta and cook until done. Drain, rinse with cold water, toss with a teaspoon of olive oil and set aside.

2. Cook the bacon in a large skillet over medium heat until crisp, about 4 minutes. Drain on a paper towel. Crumble when cool. If you wish to keep the bacon flavor in, do not wipe out the pan. Heat the pan on medium heat; add 2 teaspoons of olive oil and the sliced onions. Cook, stirring once in a while, until soft, about 5 minutes. Let cool.

3. Dressing: Combine olive oil, vinegar, spices and yogurt in a blender or food processor and blend until combined. Cut tomatoes in half, squeeze and scrape the seeds out and chop coarsely. Add to dressing and continue to blend until smooth. Stir in the chopped tarragon. Set aside until needed.

4. Salad: When the bacon and onion are cool, toss them in a large bowl with baby spinach or a mix of spinach and arugula or dandelion greens. Mix gently with about ¾ cup dressing. Mix in the pasta.

5. To serve: Drizzle more dressing over each serving, if desired, and decorate with the crumbled goat cheese or grated Parmesan cheese.

✓ Chef's Tip 1: The dressing can be made up to 3 days ahead and stored, covered in

Dressing:

- 1/4 cup olive oil
- 2 Tbsp apple cider vinegar
- 1/2 tsp sea salt
- 1/8 tsp cayenne pepper, or to taste
- 1/4 cup plain (or soy) yogurt
- 2 Roma or plum tomatoes, seeded and chopped
- 1 Tbsp fresh tarragon, chopped

your refrigerator.

✓ Chef's Tip 2: This recipe is GFCF when using rice or quinoa pasta.

Taboulé Frais aux Dattes et aux Tomates Cerise. *Refreshing Tabbouleh with Dates and Cherry Tomatoes*

The best way to feel satisfied is to emphasize flavor and not quantity. This sweet and savory tabbouleh fits the bill. I also like it with raisins (lower cost) or dried cranberries (a little more). This can be a complete meal given the protein provided by the almonds.

Servings: 4

Prep Time: 20 min

Cost per person: $2.02

INGREDIENTS

- 1 pt vegetable broth OR...
- 1 pt water with 1 vegetable bouillon cube
- 2 cups couscous
- 3 tablespoons olive oil
- 2 lemon juices
- A few sprigs of fresh parsley, chopped
- A few fresh mint leaves, chopped
- Sea salt and pepper
- 1 small cucumber, diced
- 2 tomatoes, diced
- 1 small red onion, peeled and chopped
- 8 dates, pitted and cubed, or 4 oz raisins
- 8 cherry tomatoes

PROCEDURE

1. Bring the broth to a boil. Sprinkle in the couscous. Bring back to boil while stirring. Take off the heat and cover. Let sit for 10 minutes.
2. When ready, pour into a large bowl and fluff up with a fork to loosen the grains.
3. In a separate bowl, mix the olive oil, lemon juice, chopped herbs, salt and pepper; mix with the grains.
4. Add the diced cucumber and tomatoes, chopped onion, chopped dates and finally the whole cherry tomatoes.
5. Cover with plastic wrap and refrigerate for several hours, stir occasionally and serve chilled.

✓ Chef's Tip: For my GFCF friends, substitute couscous with quinoa, millet or amaranth.

POISSONS et FRUITS de MER - FISH and SEAFOOD

Salade de Crabe en Vinaigrette de Tomate. *Crab Salad with Tomato Vinaigrette*

Delicious crab without the mess? Dreams do come true! If you can afford it, by all means, use real crabmeat. Otherwise a good imitation crab will do just as well. This light salad wins the prize.

Servings: 4

PROCEDURE

Prep Time: 20 min

Cost per person: $3.62

INGREDIENTS

- 2 medium tomatoes, diced
- 12 oz crab meat or imitation crab
- 2 green onions, sliced thin
- 1 Tbsp chopped fresh dill
- 2 Tbsp mayonnaise
- ½ lemon juice
- 2 Tbsp olive oil
- 1 Tbsp apple cider vinegar
- Sea salt and pepper to taste
- 4 oz (4 cups) of "mesclun" or mixed field greens

1. Cut the tomatoes into small cubes. Sauté in a little olive oil with salt and pepper, just long enough for them to release their juice. Set aside to cool.

2. Break up your crabmeat in a large ceramic or glass bowl. Add sliced green onions and chopped dill; stir in the mayonnaise and lemon juice. Set aside.

3. Wash and dry the "mesclun" or mixed greens leaves. Set aside.

4. Prepare the vinaigrette with the cooked diced tomatoes, olive oil, vinegar, salt and pepper, either by whisking (for a lumpy texture) or blending (for smooth).

5. Arrange the mixed greens on each plate. Drizzle with the tomato vinaigrette. Top with the crab salad and decorate with a few sprigs of dill.

✓ Chef's Tip 1: This is a light but complete summer meal.

✓ Chef's Tip 2: For my GFCF Friends, no changes needed.

Barramundi avec Olives Niçoises, Tomates et Ail. *Barramundi with Niçoises Olives, Tomatoes & Garlic*

Barramundi is the Australian trade name for the Asian Sea Bass. According to the Monterey Bay Aquarium, it is farmed in the U.S. in an environmentally sound way, making it a Best Choice. The same fish coming from Australia is rated a Good Choice. You prepare it and cook it the same way as you would sea bass. The good news is it is cheap to buy, yet has a good amount of omega-3 fatty acids (unlike catfish). Here's my simple version of this French meal.

Servings: 4

Prep Time: 40 min

Oven Temp: 400F

Cost per person: $3.50

INGREDIENTS

- 4 – 4 oz barramundi fillets, skinned and deboned
- ¼ cup (2 oz) Niçoises olives, pitted and chopped
- 2 medium tomatoes, cubed
- 6 cloves garlic, minced
- 3 sprigs fresh thyme
- 1 tablespoon olive oil
- Sea salt and pepper to taste

PROCEDURE

1. Preheat your oven at 400F.
2. Combine chopped olives, tomatoes, garlic, thyme and olive oil in medium bowl. Season with salt and pepper.
3. Lightly salt and pepper the barramundi on both sides. Put olive mixture in a baking dish; add the fish on top of the mixture.
4. Bake for 30 min or until flesh just begins to flake when touched with tip of sharp knife. Remove to warm platter, pour over the sauce, and serve.

✓ Chef's Tip 1: I would serve this with pasta or rice (to soak up the sauce) and a side salad of your choice.

✓ Chef's Tip 2: This recipe is GFCF.

Poisson Cru Mariné Lait de Coco et Citron Vert. *Raw Fish Marinated in Coconut Milk and Lime*

Don't be afraid of tasting a strong "fishy" flavor with this recipe. Like in ceviche, the fish is "cooked" and flavored with the lime juice and spices. The coconut milk brings sweetness to add another layer of flavor. A refreshing recipe for the hot days of summer. Serve with homegrown tomatoes and cucumbers.

Servings: 4

Prep Time: 10 min plus marinating time.

Cost per person: $3.90

INGREDIENTS

- 1 lb fresh boneless fish fillets with a firm flesh: perch or bream, or tilapia in the South
- The juice and pulp of 4 limes
- 1 can coconut milk
- 2 stalk green onion, sliced thinly
- 1 tsp Thai chili sauce (hot pepper sauce, garlicky and slightly sweet)
- 1 fresh red chili, chopped finely (use as much as you wish)
- Sea salt to taste
- 2 medium ripe tomatoes, sliced half moon
- 2 cucumbers, sliced

PROCEDURE

1. Cut the fish into bite-size pieces.
2. Mix the lemon juice, chili sauce and some of the fresh pepper to taste. Salt lightly. Mix with the fish and marinate overnight in your fridge in a clean and tight container. The acidity of the lime and spices will "cook" the fish.
3. The next day, 20 minutes before serving, add the coconut milk and chopped green onions. Adjust salt if necessary.
4. Serve cold on top of a salad of tomatoes and cucumbers.

✓ Chef's Tip 1: Make sure to wear rubber gloves when you handle the red chili, or if you can't find them, wash your hands thoroughly afterward and do not rub your eyes.

✓ Chef's Tip 2: For my GFCF friends, no substitution needed.

Crevettes au Gingembre et au Citron Vert. *Shrimp with Ginger and Lime*

Wake up these sleepy shrimp with a touch of fresh ginger, fresh lime juice and cayenne pepper. With less than a tablespoon of oil per serving, feel free to enjoy this exotic recipe at home.

Servings: 4

Prep Time: 15 min plus 2 hours marinating time

Cost per person: $3.06

INGREDIENTS

- 1 lb of fresh medium shrimp without shells, OR…
- A little more with shells
- 1 oz (2 inches) fresh ginger, peeled cut into thin strips
- 2 Tbsp olive oil
- 1 Tbsp coconut oil for sautéing
- 4 Tbsp fresh lime juice
- 1 Tbsp GF soy sauce
- 2 Tbsp fresh cilantro, chopped
- A touch of cayenne pepper to taste

PROCEDURE

1. Wash the shrimp under running water, drain and dry.
2. In a shallow dish, combine 2 Tbsp of the lemon juice with the olive oil. Add ginger, soy sauce and pepper. Mix gently and marinate the shrimp for 2 hours in the mixture.
3. Drain the shrimp, reserving the marinade. Sauté shrimp in skillet over high heat for 2 minutes. Add the marinade back and the remaining lemon juice. Bring to a boil and cook for 30 seconds.
4. Sprinkle with the chopped cilantro just before serving.

✓ Chef's Tip 1: Serve over cooked whole wheat pasta or brown rice.
✓ Chef's Tip 2: For my GFCF friends, no changes.

VIANDES - MEAT

Salade de Poulet au Melon et Pecans. *Chicken, Melon and Pecan Salad*

A light and refreshing summertime meal full of vitamins. If you wish, switch the melon for any other summer fruit you like. A summer favorite.

Servings: 4

Prep Time: 20 min

Cost per person: $2.82

INGREDIENTS

- 1 lb quick-broiled chicken breast, sliced
- 1/4 cup (2 oz) sour cream
- 3 Tbsp apple cider vinegar
- 1-1/2 tsp poppy seeds
- 1/4 tsp sea salt
- Freshly ground pepper, to taste
- 8 cups (about 4 oz) mixed greens salad
- 2 cups (8 oz) cantaloupe or honeydew melon, cubed
- 1/4 cup (1 oz) chopped pecan pieces, toasted
- 1/4 cup goat cheese, crumbled (optional)

PROCEDURE

1. <u>Chicken</u>: Cook your chicken breast using the quick-broil method (see healthy cooking methods). Season each breast with your favorite spice blend or herbs. Broil for about 3 minutes. Set aside to cool.

2. <u>Dressing</u>: In a large salad bowl, whisk sour cream, vinegar, poppy seeds, salt and pepper until smooth. Reserve 1/4 cup of the dressing in a separate cup.

3. <u>Finish</u>: Add the mixed greens to the same bowl and toss to coat. Divide among 4 plates and top with the sliced chicken, melon, pecans and cheese. Drizzle each portion with 1 tablespoon of the reserved dressing. Top with toasted pecan pieces and goat cheese (optional).

✓ <u>Chef's Tip 1</u>: If you're on a diet, replace the sour cream with natural unsweetened yogurt and reduce the vinegar by 1 Tbsp.

✓ <u>Chef's Tip 2</u>: To toast nuts, heat a small dry skillet over medium-low heat. Add nuts and cook while stirring until lightly browned and fragrant, 2 to 3 minutes.

✓ <u>Chef's Tip 3</u>: To make this recipe CF, replace the sour cream by plain soy or coconut yogurt.

Poulet Epicé au Basilic. *Spicy Chicken with Basil*

No need to call your favorite take-out restaurant to order this dish. You can do it easily at home with this simple recipe. It can be made with either Thai or Italian basil.

Servings: 4

Prep Time: 30 min

Cost per person: $2.56

INGREDIENTS

- 4 green or red serrano or jalapeno peppers, stemmed, cleaned and chopped
- 1 cup fresh basil leaves, tightly packed
- 2 garlic cloves, chopped
- 1 Tbsp GF soy sauce
- 1 tsp apple or rice vinegar
- Sea salt to taste
- Cayenne pepper to taste
- 1 lb boneless, skinless chicken breasts, trimmed and cut into 1 inch pieces
- 2 Tbsp olive or sesame oil
- 2 shallots, minced

PROCEDURE

1. Wash peppers, take the stems off, cut into halves and scrape out the seeds. Chop finely.
2. Place the washed and packed basil in a food processor. Add basil, garlic, soy sauce, vinegar and salt and pepper. Pulse to chop a few times until the basil is finely chopped. Set aside.
3. Wash, dry and cut your chicken into 1 inch pieces. In two batches, place your cut chicken back in food processor (no need to wash in between) and chop coarsely.
4. Heat a frying pan. Add the oil and shallots and sauté until fragrant. Add the basil mix and cook for 2-3 minutes.
5. Add the chicken and cook for another 5-6 minutes while separating the pieces with a wooden spoon until it's not pink anymore. Serve hot.

Chef's Tip 1: Serve this dish over cooked brown rice ($0.26/serving) or pasta ($0.18/serving)

Chef's Tip 2: For my GFCF friends, this recipe is safe for you as long as you use GF soy or tamari sauce.

Côtes de Porc Grillées à la Moutarde et Sauge. *Grilled Pork Chops in Mustard and Sage*

This aromatic recipe is very easy to prepare. This is the French way of flavoring your pork chops. I use a Le Creuset cast iron grilling pan; that way I avoid the bad side effects of grilling over charcoal.

Servings: 4

Prep Time: 20 min

Cost per person: $3.60

INGREDIENTS

- 4 pork chops
- 4 tsp Dijon mustard
- Sea salt to taste
- Freshly ground black pepper to taste
- Fresh sage leaves, chopped
- Coconut oil

PROCEDURE

1. The day before, using a brush, spread mustard on both sides of your pork chops.
2. Salt and pepper them to your taste; sprinkle fresh chopped sage leaves all over the chops, pressing them in lightly.
3. Place your chops on a plate; drizzle them all over with coconut oil. Wrap them in plastic film and store them in your refrigerator overnight.
4. The next day, take your pork chops out of the refrigerator at least one hour before cooking to allow them to come back up to room temperature.
5. Preheat your cast-iron grilling pan at medium temperature on the stovetop and cook your chops the way you like them best.

✓ Chef's tip 1: I also like my chops sprinkled with fresh rosemary, a very aromatic and healing herb.
✓ Chef's Tip 2: For my GFCF friends, no changes needed.

Poulet à la Provençale. *Chicken Provencal*

Here's a tasty and simple family meal coming from Provence. Add a nice side salad to it and you have a good meal.

Servings: 4

Prep Time: 45 min

Cost per person: $3.26

INGREDIENTS

- 4 chicken thighs or legs
- ½ cup all purpose flour or GF flour
- 1 tsp sea salt
- ½ tsp freshly ground pepper
- 3 Tbsp olive oil
- 1 onion, chopped
- 1 cup white wine
- 2 medium tomatoes, diced
- 1 clove garlic, minced
- 2 Tbsp chopped fresh parsley
- 1 Tbsp lemon juice
- ½ cup (4 oz) black olives, sliced
- Fresh parsley leaves to decorate

PROCEDURE

1. Combine the flour, salt and pepper in a plastic bag. Put the chicken thighs inside, seal the bag and shake well. Remove thighs from the bag and tap to remove excess flour.
2. Heat olive oil in a frying pan and fry the chicken until golden brown and thoroughly cooked, about 5 minutes per side. Set aside and keep warm in a serving dish.
3. In the same fat, brown the chopped onion and garlic until cooked. Pour the white wine and bring to a boil, stirring well with a spatula to loosen the scraps from the bottom of the pan. Add the chopped tomato and simmer to thicken.
4. Add chopped parsley, lemon juice and olives. Pour over chicken. Garnish with parsley leaves to decorate.

✓ Chef's Tip: For my GFCF friends, substitute the flour with your favorite GF flour mix.

Pépites de Poulet en Croute de Semoule de Maïs à la Moutarde aux Mûres.

Cornmeal-Crusted Chicken Nuggets with Blackberry Mustard

These chicken tenders coated with cornmeal will give you the crunchiness you crave without deep-frying. Blackberries (or raspberries, if you prefer) combined with whole-grain mustard make for a sweet-and-savory dipping sauce. Serve with steamed broccoli and carrots drizzled with olive oil and lemon juice.

Servings: 4

Prep Time: 20 min

Oven Temp: 400F

Cost per person: $2.08

INGREDIENTS

- 1 cup fresh blackberries or raspberries, mashed
- 2 Tbsp whole-grain mustard
- 1 pound chicken tenders, cut in half crosswise
- ½ tsp sea salt
- ¼ tsp freshly ground pepper
- 3 Tbsp cornmeal

PROCEDURE

1. Preheat your oven at 400F. Place a baking pan in the oven to heat.
2. Mash blackberries (or raspberries) and mustard in a small bowl until it looks like a chunky sauce.
3. Sprinkle chicken tenders with salt and pepper on both sides.
4. Place cornmeal in a medium bowl and press chicken into it one at a time. Discard any leftover cornmeal.
5. Take the pan out of the oven. Place the chicken tenders on the pan in one layer. Put back in the oven. Cook the chicken, turning once, until browned and just cooked through, 6 to 8 minutes total. <u>Caution</u>: the thinner nuggets will cook faster than the thicker ones.
6. Serve the chicken nuggets with the berry mustard dip.

✓ <u>Chef's Tip 1</u>: When fresh berries are out of season, you can use berry preserves thinned down with lemon juice. Just add the mustard to it.

✓ <u>Chef's Tip 2</u>: I would also suggest you serve this fun dish with one of the summer salads.

✓ <u>Chef's Tip 3</u>: This recipe is GFCF.

ACOMPAGNEMENTS - SIDE DISHES

Cannellonis au Maïs. *Corn Cannelloni*

This summer dish is lighter than the traditional meat-filled cannelloni. For a change of pace, they are filled with cottage cheese and corn. Feel free to use fresh corn in season or defrost organic corn. I like this dish served with a mixed green salad to make a whole meal.

Servings: 4

Prep Time: 40 min

Oven Temp: 400F

Cost per person: $1.96

INGREDIENTS

- 1 qt water with 2 chicken bouillon cubes
- 8 sheets of lasagna
- 8 oz frozen corn, defrosted
- 1 lemon, squeezed and zested
- 1 shallot, chopped
- 8 oz cottage cheese
- 3 Tbsp olive oil
- Sea salt and pepper to taste
- 1 pinch ground nutmeg
- 4 oz mixed field greens
- House dressing

PROCEDURE

1. Bring chicken broth to boil. Cook the lasagna sheets 4 at a time for 12 minutes. Drain and spread them on a clean cloth.
2. Preheat your oven at 400F.
3. Meanwhile, grate and squeeze the lemon. Peel and chop the shallot. Mix the two ingredients in a bowl with the olive oil.
4. In a separate bowl, mix the cottage cheese, corn, lemon zest, salt, pepper and nutmeg.
5. Stuff the lasagna sheets with the cheese mix. Roll them, making sure the seal sits at the bottom.
6. Place them in a baking dish. Sprinkle with grated Parmesan or Swiss cheese. Bake for 10-12 minutes or until the cheese is golden brown.
7. Coat with the lemon sauce and serve with a mixed green salad ($1.00/serv.)

✓ Chef's Tip 1: If you want the filling to be firmer, drain the cottage cheese in a cheesecloth or sifter for two hours in your refrigerator.

✓ Chef's Tip 2: For my GFCF friends, substitute the cottage cheese with soy cottage cheese and top with grated soy cheese.

Gratin d'Aubergines. *Eggplant au Gratin*

This simple meal from the South of France is bursting with seasonal goodness. If you decide to do it out of tomato season, I have found that good quality canned crushed tomatoes will substitute wonderfully.

Servings: 4

Prep Time: 60 min

Oven Temp: 400F

Cost per person: $2.21

INGREDIENTS

* 2 lbs eggplant
* 2 lbs fresh tomatoes in season, OR ...
* 1-28 oz can of crushed tomatoes
* 2 Tbsp olive oil, split
* 1 onion, chopped
* 2 garlic cloves, minced
* 1 Tbsp Herbes de Provence
* 1 tsp sea salt
* ½ tsp black pepper
* 4 oz grated Swiss cheese or other favorite cheese

PROCEDURE

1. Peel the eggplants. Cut into thin slices. Sprinkle with salt and allow to drain for 1 hour.

2. Meanwhile, prepare the tomato sauce: Dip your tomatoes for 1 minute in boiling water. Pick up with a slotted spoon and drop gently into a bath of iced water. This will allow you to peel the tomatoes easily. Drain, peel and chop coarsely. Then fry them gently with 1 Tbsp olive oil with chopped onion and a clove of garlic. Simmer for 30 minutes. Set aside.

3. Preheat your oven at 400F.

4. When the eggplants have disgorged their water, dry them on paper towels. Fry them in the olive oil in a large skillet over medium heat until tender. Since they may not fit all at once, repeat cooking several times (that's what takes the most time in this recipe). Set aside on paper towels.

5. Prepare the gratin: place a layer of eggplant at the bottom, add a layer of tomato sauce and a layer of grated cheese. Repeat about 3 times making sure to save some of the cheese for the top.

6. Bake at 400F for 20 minutes.

✓ Chef's Tip: For my GFCF friends, replace the grated cheese with your favorite CF cheese alternative.

Patates Nouvelles Rôties aux Romarin. *Oven-roasted Rosemary New Potatoes*

I honestly don't remember where I learned this recipe, but I absolutely love it. It is a simple dish, full of the aromas of my Provence. The potatoes are melt-in-your-mouth tender, yet slightly crunchy from the sea salt.

Servings: 4

Prep Time: 10 min

Cooking Time: 30 min

Cost per person: $0.72

INGREDIENTS

- 1 lb baby Yukon Gold potatoes or red potatoes
- 2 Tbsp extra virgin olive oil
- 2 Tbsp melted butter
- 4 sprigs fresh rosemary, leaves separated from the branch
- 2 tsp coarse sea salt
- 1 tsp coarse black pepper

PROCEDURE

1. Preheat your oven to 400°F.
2. In a large bowl, mix together the olive oil, melted butter, fresh rosemary leaves, sea salt and black pepper.
3. Cut your potatoes in halves or quarters depending on their size.
4. Toss the potatoes in the flavored oil/butter mix.
5. Place in one layer on a baking pan.
6. Bake for 30-40 minutes (depending on p size) or until the edges of the potatoes are turning golden brown.

✓ Chef's tip 1: Don't even think about using dried rosemary. There is no comparison in flavor. If you do, I will take you out of my will. This simple side dish is wonderful with lamb, roasted chicken or really any meat.

✓ Chef's Tip 2: This recipe is GFCF if you prepare it with olive oil only.

Pâtes à la Crème de Courgettes. *Pasta with Cream of Zucchini*

This recipe is a good way to sneak in zucchini without your kids knowing it. I personally like it with a touch of chili powder, but if you feel exotic, feel free to substitute curry powder or just "Herbes de Provence". A light sprinkle of grated parmesan will add an extra zest.

Servings: 4

Prep Time: 25 min

Cost per person: $1.81

INGREDIENTS

Sauce:

* 4 small zucchini, sliced
* 2 cups of water with 2 cubes of vegetable stock, OR …
* 2 cups of vegetable broth
* 4 Tbsp heavy cream
* 1 tsp of chili powder or curry powder

Pasta:

* 4 qt water
* 1 Tbsp sea salt
* 8 oz spaghetti
* Sea salt and pepper to taste

Finish:

* 1 oz grated Parmesan 4 sprigs of fresh parsley, chopped

PROCEDURE

1. Cook the zucchini in the vegetable stock for 10 minutes or until tender. Drain, reserving the cooking liquid.
2. In a separate pan, mash zucchini with a fork (or a masher) until chunky. Add the heavy cream and the spices, salt and pepper and continue to mix until you have a nice sauce. Add cooking liquid as needed to adjust the consistency. Warm until it reaches boiling point.
3. Meanwhile, cook the spaghetti for 10-12 minutes or until al dente. Drain. Add the pasta to the sauce, mix well.
4. Sprinkle with grated parmesan and chopped parley for additional color and chlorophyll.

✓ Chef's Tip: For my GFCF friends, replace the heavy cream with soy creamer and the parmesan with non-dairy cheese.

Soufflé Léger au Chou-Fleur. *Light Cauliflower Soufflé*

For a change from the classic "soufflé au fromage" (cheese soufflé), try this one with a vegetable: cauliflower. For a lighter touch, you can substitute the sour cream with cottage cheese. The grated Swiss will provide additional flavor. It is a great side dish with fish or meat and makes sublime leftovers for tomorrow's lunch.

Servings: 4

Prep Time: 50 min

Oven Temp: 350F

Cost per person: $1.83

INGREDIENTS

- 1 lb 4 oz cauliflower cleaned and cut into florets
- 8 oz sour cream
- 2 oz grated Swiss cheese
- 2 eggs
- Freshly grated nutmeg to taste
- Sea salt and freshly ground white pepper to taste

PROCEDURE

1. Preheat your oven to 350F.
2. Meanwhile, steam the florets for 10 minutes or until very tender.
3. Separate eggs whites from yolks.
4. Mash or blend the cooked cauliflower with the sour cream, 1.5 oz of the grated Swiss cheese, 2 eggs yolks, salt, pepper and nutmeg.
5. Whisk the egg whites with a pinch of salt until they make soft peaks (firm enough to stand up, but not stiff, or they will break down). Gently fold into the cauliflower mixture.
6. Pour into a greased baking dish or 4 individual soufflé dishes and top with remaining Swiss cheese.
7. Bake at 350F between 25 and 30 minutes. Be careful not to open your oven while cooking or it will deflate. If you can see through the oven window, look for the top and sides of your soufflé to be a golden color.

✓ Chef's Tip: for my GFCF friends, try replacing the sour cream with soy cream and the grated cheese with cheese substitute.

DESSERTS et GATEAUX - DESSERTS and CAKES

Soufflé aux Framboises Léger Comme un Nuage. *Light as a Cloud Raspberry Soufflé*

This is a very healthy, very light, melt-in-the-mouth version of the traditional soufflé recipe. Unlike the traditional recipe, it does not contain any flour, just a touch of corn starch. I learned this recipe at a famous French health spa.

Servings: 4

Prep Time: 30 min

Oven Temp: 400F

Cost per person: $2.73

INGREDIENTS

- 4 - 3 3/4 " (7 3/4 fl oz) ceramic ramekins
- 4 oz raspberries fresh or frozen (about 1 full cup)
- ½ tsp fresh lemon juice
- ¼ cup powdered sugar
- ½ tsp corn starch
- 2 egg yolks
- 4 egg whites
- 1 pinch sea salt
- 2 Tbsp granulated sugar
- 2 Tbsp butter or Earth Balance margarine, at room temperature
- 2 Tbsp granulated sugar

Raspberry Sauce :

- ½ cup raspberries,

PROCEDURE

1. Preheat your oven at 400°F standard or 350°F convection.
2. With a pastry brush, brush the inside of the ramekins with the softened butter or margarine. Sprinkle with granulated sugar. Turn the ramekins around to allow the sugar to stick evenly. Tap out the excess sugar gently.
3. In a food processor or blender, blend the raspberries, sugar, cornstarch and lemon juice together. If you don't mind the raspberry seeds, leave this mix alone. Otherwise, strain the seeds out.
4. Add the egg yolks to the fruit mixture. Blend well. Pour into a large mixing bowl.
5. In a grease-free stand mixer bowl, start whisking the egg whites with the salt and sugar at medium speed, allowing them to fluff up gently. When all your ingredients are ready, increase the speed until they form soft peaks. (Do NOT over whip, or the whites will form lumps while mixing.)
6. Add 1/3rd of the whipped egg whites into the fruit mixture. Mix in gently with a hand whisk to lighten the mix. Add the rest of the egg whites and fold gently with a rubber spatula. With a spoon, carefully fill your prepared ramekins with the soufflé mixture. Level the tops carefully with a spatula or the back of a knife. With your right thumb, clean the inside edge of

fresh or frozen
- ¼ cup powdered sugar
- ½ tsp fresh lemon juice

each ramekin to allow your soufflé to rise straight up.

7. Bake at 400°F (350°F convection) for about 12 minutes or until the sides are light brown and firm to the touch.

8. Sprinkle the top with powdered sugar and serve with the raspberry sauce (optional.)

9. Raspberry Sauce: process all ingredients in a food processor or blender. Strain through a fine mesh strainer or chinois. Refrigerate. Serve in a sauceboat with your hot soufflés. Pour sauce over soufflés just before eating. Bon Appétit!

✓ Chef's Tip 1: You can replace the granulated sugar with finely processed turbinado sugar.

✓ Chef's Tip 2: The thin layer of butter/margarine spread inside the ramekins will allow the soufflé mixture to rise without sticking to the edge. The sprinkled sugar will bring an additional crunchiness to your soufflés. Be very careful not to allow your fingers to touch the inside of your ramekins once they have been prepared or your soufflé will stick and rise sideways.

✓ Chef's Tip 3: This recipe is GF. To make it CF, use Earth Balance margarine instead of butter.

Esquimaux à la Fraise Express sans Sorbetière. Frozen Strawberry Lollipops without Ice Cream Machine

Want to please your whole family in no time? Prepare these frozen lollipops and see those smiles flourish. And you will know it's made from fresh ingredients. A real summer treat.

Servings: 12

Prep Time: 15 min plus freezing time

Cost per person: $0.54

INGREDIENTS

- For 12 molds or about 1 qt…
- 1 lb ripe strawberries
- 4 Tbsp raw sugar
- 1 lemon juice
- 2 Tbsp strawberry syrup (Monin) or 1 tsp strawberry extract
- 1 small can (12 oz) of evaporated milk

PROCEDURE

1. Equipment: a blender or plunging blender, a fine mesh or Chinese hat strainer, a flexible spatula, a 1 qt airtight container or 12 individual lollipops molds and wooden sticks (found in a hobby shop.)
2. Wash and hull strawberries and place in blender (or in a tall bowl if using a plunging blender). Add sugar. Mix to obtain a thick sauce. Filter through a chinois or fine mesh strainer to remove seeds, pushing pulp through with your flexible spatula.
3. Rinse the blender or bowl and pour back to the cleaned blender. Add the strawberry syrup and condensed milk. Blend again until you obtain a foamy, smooth and thick liquid. Correct sugar to your taste by adding a bit of strawberry syrup.
4. Pour into an airtight 1-quart container or 12 lollipops molds; place a stick in the center of each (the texture is thick enough, the sticks should stand up).
5. Store in your freezer for 12 hours. To unmold the lollipops, dip the molds briefly hot water and turn them slightly. Serve immediately! Or if you want to store them, wrap them in plastic film and

in a Ziploc bag until needed... if you can resist.

✓ <u>Chef's Tip 1</u>: You can have fun with all the fruits your imagination can come with. Bear in mind that you will need at least 12 oz of fruit puree. You can have additional fun by dipping them in melted chocolate. Play with your food!

✓ <u>Chef's Tip 2</u>: For my GFCF friends, replace the condensed milk with soy cream or silken tofu.

Panna Cotta aux Amandes et Fruits Rouges. *Almond Panna Cotta with Berries*

Here is a light version of a very simple (yet always impressive) panna cotta. This light cream tastes sweet, and can be eaten plain or accompanied by a strawberry or raspberry sauce.

Servings: 4

Prep Time: 20 min plus cooling time

Cost per person: $1.36

INGREDIENTS

- 3 sheets of gelatin
- 1 pt (16 ounces) half and half cream
- 2 Tbsp honey
- 1 tsp almond extract
- 1 pint (8 oz) red berries: strawberries or raspberries
- 3 oz raw sugar
- ½ lemon juice

PROCEDURE

1. Soften the gelatin for 10 minutes in a bowl of cold water.
2. Mix the cream, honey and almond extract in a saucepan. Heat gently to scalding, but not boiling.
3. Squeeze the water out of the gelatin. Place the gelatin in the scalding milk and mix with a whisk thoroughly to dissolve.
4. Divide the cream into 4 ramekins or glasses. Let them cool, then cover with plastic wrap before placing in the refrigerator at least 4 hours.
5. Meanwhile, prepare the coulis or berry sauce. Clean the berries. Dry gently with a paper towel. Reserve four beauties for decoration. Place the rest in a food blender, add sugar and lemon juice and blend well. If you don't care for the seeds, strain your sauce.
6. When cold, if you used ramekins, unmold them onto dessert plates after running hot water over them. Cover with the fruit coulis. Decorate with the reserved berries and a mint leaf.
7. If you used glasses, pour the sauce over the top of the panna cotta in the glasses to create a beautiful top red layer. Decorate with the reserve berries and a mint leaf.

✓ <u>Chef's Tip</u>: For my GFCF friends, replace the half and half with soy creamer. Make sure to not burn it. It's very sensitive to heat.

Gâteau Leger au Champagne et Cointreau. *Champagne-Cointreau Chiffon Cake*

I created this cake while at the Barr Mansion in Austin. This is the GF version. In case you are worried about giving this cake to children, the alcohol in the Champagne and Cointreau evaporates during baking. Only the flavors stay.

Yield: Two 9" cake layers or 12 serv.

Prep Time: 20 min.

Baking time: 45-50 min.

Freezing time: 1-2 hours

Oven Temp: 350F

Cost per person: $1.19

INGREDIENTS

Step 1:

- 8 oz pastry flour or GF pastry flour mix
- 8 oz turbinado sugar
- 1 Tbsp baking powder
- ½ tsp sea salt

Step 2:

- 4 oz dry champagne
- 2 oz Cointreau liquor
- 2 oz concentrated orange juice
- 3 oz olive oil
- 4 oz egg yolks (about 6)

Step 3:

- 8 oz egg whites

PROCEDURE

1. Preheat your oven to 350F.
2. Prepare your pans. Grease them with soft coconut oil or olive oil spray. Sprinkle them with white rice flour. Tap out the excess. Or, cut 2 pieces of baking paper to the size of the pan bottom. Spray, stick and spray again.
3. Weigh and sift all ingredients in Step 1 into a large mixing bowl.
4. Weigh all wet ingredients in Step 2 into a large measuring cup.
5. Weigh egg whites, salt, cream of tartar and sugar into your mixer's bowl. Start whipping them with the whisk attachment at medium speed.
6. Meanwhile mix the wet ingredients into the large bowl of dry ingredients with a hand whisk. Make sure there are no lumps left.
7. When the egg whites are light and foamy, increase the mixer's speed to high until your meringue is at the soft peak point. Turn mixer off.
8. Fold half of the meringue into the batter in the large bowl gently with a rubber spatula to lighten the mix. Add the rest of the meringue and fold carefully.
9. Spread evenly into the two prepared pans. Bake right away on the middle rack for about 45-50 minutes or until s small knife's blade come out clean.
10. Cool down. De-pan and freeze the cake

(about 6)
- ¼ tsp sea salt
- 1 knife tip cream of tartar
- 2 oz turbinado sugar

layers. The reason for freezing it is that it is a very soft sponge cake and it will be too difficult to ice if it's only refrigerated.

Glaçage a l'Orange. *Orange Frosting*

Yield: This recipe is enough to ice this size cake.

This recipe is **GFCF**

INGREDIENTS

- 14 to 16 oz powdered sugar, sifted if clumpy
- 4 oz cold coconut oil cut in small pieces
- 4 oz cold non-hydrogenated margarine cut in small pieces
- 2 oz orange juice concentrate
- ½ tsp orange extract
- Candied Orange slices (optional)

PROCEDURE

1. Weigh the sifted powdered sugar into your mixer's bowl. Cut the cold coconut oil and margarine in small pieces.
2. With the paddle attachment on, start the mixer on slow speed and mix until the frosting gets together. Switch to medium speed and cream well. Add the concentrated orange juice and extract a little at a time until you reach the desired consistency.
3. Switch tool to a whisk and whip well on high speed until light and fluffy. If frosting is getting too soft, place it in your refrigerator until it firms up.
4. Ice your cake as you usually would. Decorate with candied orange slices.

FALL SEASON

FALL FOOD CALENDAR

- Apples (Ashmead's Kernel, Belle de Boskoop, Braeburn, Cameo, Cox's, Egremont, Egremont Russet, Galas, Gingergolds, Golden Russet, Fujis, Jonagold, Jonathan, Honey Crisp, Macintosh, Melrose, Newton Pippin, Orange Pippin, King, King David, Rome, Russet, Smokehouse, Spitzenburg, Stayman, Winesap)* and **
- Artichoke **
- Arugula *
- Basil *
- Beans, dried (Cannolini, Black Turtle, Peas) **
- Beets * and **
- Bok Choy *
- Braising greens (Arugula, Beet Greens, Bok Choy, Black Italian Collards, Chard, Collards, Endive, Kale, Mizuna, Mustards, Rapini (broccoli rabe), Radicchio, Sorrel, Spinach) * and **
- Broccoli * and **
- Brussels sprouts **
- Cabbage * and **
- Cabbage, baby **
- Carrots * and **

- Kiwis, hardy **
- Kohlrabi * and **
- Okra *
- Onions **
- Onions, green *
- Melons **
- Mint *
- Nectarines **
- Parsley *
- Parsnips *
- Peaches **
- Peas **
- Pears (20th Century, Bartlett, Bosc, Bronze Beauty, D'Anjou, Ichiban, Kosui (Honey), Moonglow, Red Bartletts, Yakumo)* and **
- Pecans *
- Peppers, Sweet *
- Peppers, Hot *
- Plums **
- Pluots **
- Pole beans **
- Potatoes, all kinds * and **
- Pumpkins Squash (Fairy Tale, Sugar Pie, French Rouge) * and **
- Quince **
- Radishes * and **
- Raspberries, ever-bearing (red & golden) **

- Cauliflower * and **
- Celery * and **
- Celery root **
- Celeriac **
- Chestnuts **
- Corn, sweet **
- Cilantro *
- Cucumbers * and **
- Dill *
- Edamame **
- Eggplant * and **
- Fava beans **
- Figs *
- Fresh herbs **
- Garlic **
- Garlic, green *
- Garlic: Elephant and Spanish Roja **
- Green Beans *
- Greens, Chard *
- Greens, Collard *
- Greens, Kale *
- Greens, Lettuce Mix *
- Greens, Head *
- Greens, Mustard *
- Horseradish root **
- Jerusalem artichokes **
- Kohlrabi **
- Lettuces **

Please note:

* = TX and other southern states.

** = All other states.

- Rutabagas *
- Scallion **
- Shallots **
- Shelling beans (Black Turtle, Cannolini,
- Cranberry, Dixie Speckled Butter Peas, Flageolet, Panda) **
- Spinach *
- Squash, Summer *
- Squash, Hard *
- Sweet Potatoes *
- Tomatoes (field and hothouse) * and **
- Turnips * and **
- Wild mushrooms (Chanterelles, Porcini, Lobster, Matsutake) **
- Wild mushrooms **
- Winter Squashes (Acorn, Amber Cup, Butternut, Carnival, Cinderella, Delicata, Galeux d' Eysines, Golden Nugget, Honey Boat, Hubbard, Kabocha, Kuri, Loofah, Sweet Dumpling, Sugar Loaf, Spaghetti, Sweet Dumpling, Turk's Turban **
- And many more...

Also available: Artisan breads and baked goods, pastries, confections, pasture-raised meats (pork, beef, lamb, goat, poultry, sausages, jerky), coffees and teas, eggs, dairy products, fresh pasta, gourmet cheeses, fresh seafood from the Gulf, oysters, shrimp, clams **, mussels **, geoduck **, tuna **, wild salmon **, shellfish, honey, ciders

	**, hard ciders **, dried fruits, dried herbs, dried wild mushrooms, pickles and preserves, jams and jellies, chutneys **, chocolates, sauces and salsas, spreads, syrups **, seasonal cut flowers, flowers bulbs **, soups stocks **, tacos * and wines **. Holiday wreathes and bouquets **.

FALL MENUS and COSTING

<u>Monday</u>: Breakfast $1.50; Lunch $2.65; Dinner: Soup: **Butternut Squash Vichissoise Soup** $1.67. Entrée: **Crab Salad with Celery and Fresh Mango** $3.44. **Fruit and chocolate** $0.90. Total day: ~**$10.16** per person.

<u>Tuesday</u>: Breakfast $1.50; Lunch $2.65; Dinner: Entrée: **Lemon Butter Barramundi** $2.99 **with brown rice** $0.30. **Side salad** $1.00. **Fruit and chocolate** $0.90. Total day: ~**$9.34** per person.

<u>Wednesday</u>: Breakfast $1.50; Lunch $2.65; Dinner: Soup: **Fire Roasted Tomato Soup** $1.61.Entrée: **Meat Loaf Niçois** $1.34 with **Mashed Potatoes with Garlic and Olive Oil** $0.78. **Fruit and chocolate** $0.90. Total day: ~**$8.79** per person.

<u>Thursday</u>: Breakfast $1.50; Lunch $2.65; Dinner: Entrée: **Orange Marmalade Chicken** $1.91 **with pasta** $0.26. **Side salad** $1.00. **Fruit and chocolate** $0.90. Total day: ~**$8.22** per person.

<u>Friday</u>: Breakfast $1.50; Lunch $2.65; Dinner: Soup: **Chestnut and Mushroom Soup** $2.37.Entrée: **Shrimp Salad with Cabbage and Pear** $3.04. **Fruit and chocolate** $0.90. Total day: ~**$10.46** per person.

<u>Saturday</u>: Breakfast $1.50; Lunch $2.65; Dinner: Entrée: **Mediterranean-Style Tilapia** $3.29 with **Butternut Squash Orzo** $0.86. Dessert: **Pear Tiramisu Mousse** $0.97. Total day: ~**$9.27** per person.

<u>Sunday</u>: Brunch: $3.75; Dinner: Entrée: **Crispy Salmon and Curried Leek Wraps** $4.06 ; **Side salad** $1.00. Dessert: **Pumpkin Cheese Cake** $1.34. Total day: ~**$10.15** per person.

<u>Total for the week</u>: ~**$66.39** or ~**$9.48** average per day per person.

FALL RECIPES
PETIT DEJEUNER et BRUNCH - BREAKFAST and BRUNCH

Galettes aux Patates Douces. *Sweet Potato Pancakes*

Here's another simple but tasty recipe for breakfast... and it's loaded with vitamins. Please notice I kept the sugar amount to a minimum, since the sweet potatoes are already what they are: sweet.

Servings: 4

Prep Time: 25 min

Cost per person: $0.82

INGREDIENTS

In the first bowl:

- ¾ cup unbleached all purpose flour or GF flour
- 1 Tbsp raw sugar
- 1 Tbsp baking powder
- ½ tsp sea salt
- 1/4 tsp pumpkin pie spice
- 1/8 tsp nutmeg
- 1/4 tsp cinnamon

In another bowl:

- ¾ cup milk or alternative milk
- 1 egg
- ¼ tsp vanilla extract
- 1 cup sweet potato puree, fresh or canned

PROCEDURE

1. For fresh sweet potatoes: Peel and cube one large or two small sweet potatoes; cook in boiling salted water until tender; mash with a fork until smooth. For canned: simply measure it out.

2. Mix all the dry ingredients in a bowl. Mix all the wet ingredients in another bowl. Pour the wet ingredients into the dry ingredients while stirring.

3. Heat up your skillet to medium and add 1 tbsp butter to the skillet.

4. When it sizzles, add ¼ cup batter to the skillet and cook about 2 minutes on each side. Be careful they don't burn--sweet potatoes burn easily.

✓ Chef's Tip 1: For my GFCF friends, use your favorite GF flour blend instead of regular flour. Replace butter with oil.

✓ Chef's Tip 2: This is a good use of leftover baked sweet potatoes. Just scoop the flesh out of the skins and mash.

To cook:

- 1 Tbsp butter or oil
- Top with maple syrup

Gâteaux Légers aux Pommes. *Light Apple Muffins*

Ready to bring in your lunch bag, backpack or even your pockets, these light and easy-to-make muffins can be the perfect breakfast or snack for the whole family. One for mom, one for dad, one each for the kids and a couple of extra for lunch. It's also perfect for Saturday or Sunday's brunch.

Servings: 6

Prep Time: 35 min

Oven Temp: 400F

Cost per person: $0.66

INGREDIENTS

- 3 medium apples (I like granny Smith), peeled, cored and diced
- 3 Tbsp whole wheat pastry flour (or 2 Tbsp whole wheat flour and 1 Tbsp pastry flour OR 3 Tbsp GF flour mix
- 1 Tbsp raw sugar, honey or agave nectar
- 2 tsp baking powder
- ½ tsp ground cinnamon
- 2 eggs (4 oz)

PROCEDURE

1. Preheat oven to 400F.
2. In a bowl, mix flour, sugar, and baking powder together; add the eggs and whisk to avoid lumps; add the diced apples; fold gently (Please note: there is very little dough compared to the quantity of apple).
3. Spray muffin pan with olive oil. Scoop the mix evenly into each muffin cup.
4. Bake at 400F for about 20 minutes or until a knife's tip comes out clean.

✓ Chef's Tip: For my GFCF friends, make an easy substitution with an all-purpose GF blend.

Omelette aux Fines Herbes et Fromage de Chèvre. *Fines Herbs Omelet with Goat Cheese*

This is a lively omelet filled with the flavor of fresh herbs and the slight saltiness of goat cheese. A lovely dish for a family weekend brunch.

Servings: 4

Prep Time: 20 min

Cost per person: $1.84

INGREDIENTS

- 8 large eggs
- 1 Tbsp fresh chives, chopped fine
- 1 Tbsp fresh parsley, chopped fine
- 1 Tbsp fresh chervil, chopped fine
- 1 Tbsp fresh rosemary, chopped fine
- ½ tsp sea salt
- ½ tsp cayenne pepper
- 2 Tbsp extra virgin olive oil or coconut oil
- 2 Tbsp butter
- 8 Tbsp (4 oz) fresh goat cheese, crumbled

PROCEDURE

1. Remember, all ingredients must be at room temperature.
2. Chop your fresh herbs. Beat the eggs; add the herbs, salt and cayenne. Mix well. Let sit for 5 minutes to allow the salt to soften the eggs.
3. Heat your frying pan at medium high heat; melt the butter and oil; when the butter fizzles, pour your eggs in the pan. Stir gently with a heat-proof rubber spatula.
4. When it barely starts to set, crumble the goat cheese all over it and fold in half. Slide on the serving platter immediately.

✓ Chef's Tip: This recipe if GF. To make it CF, replace the goat cheese with your favorite CF cheese.

SOUPES - SOUPS

Soupe de Châtaignes et Champignons des Bois. *Chestnut and Mushroom Soup*

Talk about memories! This recipe takes me way back to my youth in Normandy. Usually, we had to peel (a tough job. Believe me, I know!) and poach the chestnuts in water to prepare this soup. To make your life easier, we'll use chestnut puree. Mamie used to send us in the forest to find mushrooms but again, I'll make your life easier by sending you to your farmer's market. Feel free to use a variety of mushrooms.

Servings: 6

Prep Time: 55 min

Cost per person: $2.37

INGREDIENTS

- 4 oz whole wheat or GF twist or rotini pasta
- 2 Tbsp butter
- 2 shallots, minced
- 10 oz of fresh mushrooms of your choice, cleaned and sliced
- 1 Tbsp fresh thyme, split
- Sea salt and pepper to taste
- 1 qt vegetable or chicken broth
- 1-14 oz can chestnut purée
- 1 cup heavy cream

PROCEDURE

1. Cook your pasta al dente in a large pot of salted water, about 12 minutes. Drain.
2. Sauté the shallots 3 minutes in a soup pot with the butter without browning. Add mushrooms, salt, pepper and half the thyme. Sauté until they render their water.
3. Add the broth and the chestnut puree and bring to a gentle simmer. Simmer about 20 minutes to allow the flavors to blend.
4. Blend your soup with the heavy cream in two batches.
5. Serve hot and sprinkle the remaining thyme on each plate.

✓ Chef's Tip 1: I like to serve this soup with herbed croutons.
✓ Chef's Tip 2: To make this soup GF, use GF pasta. To make it CF, use soy or coconut creamer.

Soupe de Tomates Rôties au Feu. *Fire-Roasted Tomato Soup*

This is a simple but tasty soup I created for my customers at Peoples Pharmacy. They love it and always come back for more.

Servings: 4

Prep Time: 30 min

Cost per person: $1.61

INGREDIENTS

- 1 Tbsp olive oil
- ½ medium white onion, chopped
- 2 garlic cloves, chopped finely
- 1 tsp sea salt
- 1 ½ qt hot water, plus
- 3 vegetable bouillon cubes
- 1 can (28 oz) fire-roasted tomatoes
- ½ can (3 oz) tomato paste
- 1 tsp dried basil
- 1 tsp dried cilantro
- 2 Tbsp agave nectar or honey
- ½ tsp cayenne pepper
- 1 cup heavy whipping cream

PROCEDURE

1. Heat olive oil over medium heat in your favorite soup pot.
2. Add chopped onion and garlic. Sprinkle salt over it. Sauté 2 to 3 minutes, stirring constantly, until the onions are tender.
3. Add broth, stir in tomatoes, tomato paste, basil, agave nectar or honey and cayenne pepper.
4. Bring to boil. Reduce heat to medium heat; Cover and simmer for 20 minutes.
5. Remove from heat; uncover and cool slightly, about 5 minutes.
6. Place half of the mixture in blender. Cover and blend with whipped cream until pureed. Blend the other half.

✓ Chef's Tip 1: Serve with croutons and shredded white cheddar cheese.
✓ Chef's Tip 2: To make this soup GFCF, replace the cream with plain soy creamer; replace croutons with GF croutons and cheddar with CF cheddar substitute.

Cream of Delicatta Squash Soup

By Amanda Love, "The Barefoot Cook", Austin, TX

I love so many soups, but this is my favorite! It represents the beginning of the cool weather season and the availability of wonderful winter veggies. Many people just use winter squash as Thanksgiving table decorations, but did you know they are also edible? They are one of my favorites and are loaded with good nutrition. If I could only take one food to outer space, winter squash would definitely be the one. The skin is a good source of fiber, the flesh is loaded with beta-carotene and potassium, and the seeds are a great source of zinc, protein and good fat. This recipe is best with Delicatta Squash – my favorite of all the winter squashes, but is also good with Butternut, Acorn, Gold Table, Hubbards, Kabocha or Turban squash. As with all of my recipes, adjust seasonings to your own liking. Each squash tastes different and may need more or less spice to bring out the flavor.

Servings: 6

Prep Time: 15 min

Cook Time: 90 min

Total Time: 120 min

Cost per person: $2.08

INGREDIENTS

- 1 medium to large size Delicatta or other variety winter squash (about 2 lbs)
- 1 qt organic chicken or vegetable broth (homemade broth is best, but store bought is second best if organic)
- 1 can organic coconut milk or 1 cup raw cream, raw milk, or goat milk

PROCEDURE

1. Heat oven to 400 degrees and place squash in oven on baking dish. Bake for about1 hour or until tender.
2. While squash is baking, chop onion coarsely and sauté in a medium size pot with 1 tablespoon butter on medium low heat until onion is caramelized. Add broth and heat till just simmering. Then add spices and ginger.
3. Once squash is tender, remove from oven and cool; slice in half and remove seeds.
4. Cut squash into large chunks and place in pot (including the skin). Add wine (optional) and simmer for a couple of minutes.
5. Puree soup in blender or with an immersion blender (worth the investment!) until smooth. Add coconut milk or dairy of choice. Add salt and spice to taste. Keep warm but do not bring to simmer once coconut milk or dairy is added. Garnish with pumpkin or baked squash seeds. Enjoy!

- 1 organic yellow onion
- 1 Tbsp organic butter
- 1 tsp ground coriander
- 1 tsp white pepper
- 1 tsp ground nutmeg
- ¼ tsp ground cloves
- ¼ tsp cayenne pepper (optional)
- ¼ tsp ground ginger or 2 Tbsp fresh minced ginger
- ¼ tsp ground cinnamon
- 1-2 tsp of good sea salt (Celtic sea salt or Real salt)
- ½ cup organic white wine (optional)

✓ Chef's Tip: This soup is GFCF if you use coconut milk.

Soupe Vichyssoise a la Citrouille. *Butternut Squash Vichyssoise*

Traditionally, a Vichyssoise soup is a cold soup made with leeks and potatoes. To give you more vitamin B, I created this version with Butternut squash to savor on a warm Fall evening.

Servings: 4

Prep Time: 10 min.

Cooking Time: 25 min.

Cost per person: $1.67

INGREDIENTS

- 4 Tbsp butter
- 1 white onion, peeled and chopped
- 4 celery stalks, sliced
- 4 leeks, white part only, sliced
- 1 medium Butternut squash (about 1 lb)
- 1 sprig of fresh thyme
- 1 Tbsp sea salt
- 1 tsp black pepper, ground
- 1 quart chicken or vegetable broth
- Additional water to cover the veggies, if necessary
- 4 Tbsp heavy cream
- 1 tsp of Gomasio per soup bowl (optional)
- Or a few thin slices of fresh chives

PROCEDURE

1. Wash, peel and slice all the vegetables. Peel the butternut squash, cut in halves and take the seeds out.

2. Chef's tip: If they are very tender, I keep the skin on and process it with my blender. More vitamin B for the taking!

3. In a large pot, melt the butter. Add the sliced onion and sauté while stirring for about 2 minutes.

4. Add the celery and leeks and sweat for another 3 minutes.

5. Add the cubed squash and thyme; cover with the broth and additional water.

6. Bring to boil and simmer for another 20 minutes, until the squash pieces are melting.

7. Take the thyme sprig out, and puree the soup with the heavy cream.

8. Cool down for at least 2 hours; serve with a generous sprinkle of Gomasio, or, if you cannot find it, a generous pinch of finely sliced fresh chives.

✓ Chef's Tip 1: Gomasio is made of toasted sesame seeds ground in a mortar with sea salt. A very tasty and aromatic condiment.

✓ Chef's Tip 2: For my GFCF friends, replace the butter with olive oil and the cream with soy half-and-half.

SALADES - SALADS

Salade de Crabe au Céleri et à la Mangue Fraîche. *Crab Salad with Celery and Fresh Mango*

Here is a whole new way to serve crab! Green apple and lime add their own acidity and freshness, while the mango softens it all with its deliciously sweet tropical juices. This is another whole meal when you add a mixed green salad on the side.

Servings: 4

Prep Time: 15 min

Cost per person: $3.44

INGREDIENTS

- 12 oz crab meat or imitation crab meat, drained
- 1 Granny Smith or other apple
- 2 stalks celery
- 1 fresh mango
- The juice of 1 lime
- 1 Tbsp mayonnaise
- 1 Tbsp olive oil
- The juice of 1 lemon
- Sea salt and pepper to taste

PROCEDURE

1. In a bowl, mix the limejuice with the mayonnaise. Add salt and pepper, set aside.
2. Add the drained crabmeat and mix well.
3. Trim and cut the celery into small cubes. Peel, core and cube the apple. Peel and cube the mango.
4. Arrange the cubed celery, apple, and mango in bowls or on a green salad drizzled with olive oil and lemon. Top with the crab salad.

✓ Chef's Tip 1: You can sprinkle your salad with shredded coconut for a touch of sweetness.

✓ Chef's Tip 2: For my GFCF friends, no changes needed.

Salade de Thon, Artichauts et Raisins Secs. *Artichoke and Raisin Tuna Salad*

An easy salad with a flavorful combination of ingredients; serve this salad with sliced tomatoes on a bed of baby lettuce.

Servings: 4

Prep Time: 15 min

Cost per person: $3.76

INGREDIENTS

- 2-6 oz cans chunk light tuna, drained and flaked
- 1-14 oz can of canned artichoke hearts in juice, drained and sliced
- 1/4 cup (2 oz) raisins
- 1/2 cup (4 oz) mayonnaise
- 1 Tbsp fresh lemon juice
- 1 1/2 tsp chopped fresh oregano, or 1/2 teaspoon dried
- 1/4 tsp sea salt
- Freshly ground pepper to taste
- Lettuce leaves
- 2 tomatoes, sliced

PROCEDURE

1. Drain and squeeze the tuna well. Flake between your fingers.
2. Drain and cut the artichoke hearts.
3. At the bottom of a large salad bowl, mix the mayonnaise, lemon juice, oregano, salt and pepper. Whisk well.
4. Add the flaked tuna, artichoke and raisins. Toss well together.
5. Serve on top of a few leaves of lettuce, a few tomato slices and top with a few black olives.

✓ Chef's Tip 1: Chunk light tuna, which comes from the smaller skipjack or yellowfin, has less mercury than canned white albacore tuna.

✓ Chef's Tip 2: This recipe is GFCF.

Salade de Quinoa aux Pois Chiches et Tomates. *Quinoa Salad with Chickpeas and Tomatoes*

Want to surprise your taste buds? Here's an original cold salad that blends the earthy flavors of quinoa, chickpeas and tomatoes. Serve chilled with quick-broiled chicken or fish.

Servings: 4

Prep Time: 25 min

Cost per person: $1.90

INGREDIENTS

- 8 oz (1 cup) quinoa
- 2 large tomatoes, cleaned and diced
- 2 shallots, minced
- 12 oz cooked chickpeas, drained (or canned)
- 4 Tbsp olive oil
- 2 Tbsp balsamic vinegar
- Sea salt and pepper to taste
- Chopped parsley

PROCEDURE

1. Rinse the quinoa grain well to get rid of the saponins that can make it taste soapy.
2. Cook the rinsed quinoa in twice its volume of water or vegetable broth. Start cooking in cold water, bring to boil and cover. Cook for 12 minutes. Leave covered for 5 minutes. Remove from heat and rinse with cold water.
3. In a large bowl mix the quinoa with the chickpeas, diced tomatoes, and minced shallots. Drizzle with oil and vinegar. Salt and pepper to taste.
4. Mix and refrigerate several hours.
5. When serving, sprinkle with freshly chopped parsley.

✓ Chef's Tip 1: With this nice salad I recommend 4 oz per person of oven roasted turkey ($1.48/serving) or oven roasted chicken ($1.17/serving)

✓ Chef's Tip 2: This recipe is GFCF.

POISSONS et FRUITS de MER - FISH and SEAFOOD

Salade de Crevettes au Chou et Poire. *Shrimp Salad with Cabbage and Pear*

Make way for this ingenious salad! It combines flavors that you may not have thought to associate, and it is a success. Give it a try. This is a whole meal and provides you with plenty of protein and all the goodness contained in the cruciferous family of vegetables.

Servings: 4

Prep Time: 20 min.

Cost per person: $3.04

INGREDIENTS

- ½ White or Chinese cabbage
- 1 pear, Bartlett, Bosc or other variety
- 1 avocado, ripe
- 8 oz shrimp, cooked and peeled
- 2 oz bean sprouts
- A few crisp lettuce leaves
- a few pine nuts

For the sauce:

- 1 oz Roquefort or your favorite blue cheese
- 1 Tbsp apple cider vinegar
- 1 Tbsp mayonnaise
- 2 Tbsp olive oil
- Sea salt and pepper

PROCEDURE

1. Prepare the sauce: In a bowl, mash the blue cheese with a fork into the vinegar to make a paste. Add the mayonnaise, oil, salt and pepper. Emulsify well with a whisk.
2. Cut the cabbage into thin strips with a knife; add to sauce and mix.
3. Peel and take the pit out of the avocado. Slice or cut in small pieces. Toss with the lemon juice.
4. Peel (only if the skin is tough) and core the pear and cut into small slices.
5. Tear lettuce leaves into thirds.
6. Mix cabbage with sauce, shrimp, bean sprouts and salad leaves. Then at the end, add the fragile ingredients - pears and avocados - with care. Serve. Sprinkle with pine nuts (optional).

✓ Chef's Tip 1: Be careful not too salt too much because blue cheese is usually quite salty.

✓ Chef's Tip 2: For my GFCF friends, replace the blue cheese with your favorite soy or rice cheese.

Croustillants de Saumon et Poireaux au Curry. *Crispy Salmon and Curried Leek Wraps*

There's nothing like fish for a light meal, especially salmon! Wrapped in crispy phyllo pastry dough and well seasoned, it's a pure joy.

Servings: 4

Prep Time: 50 min

Oven Temp: 350F

Cost per person: $4.06

INGREDIENTS

- 1 Tbsp butter
- 1 medium onion, peeled and chopped
- 1 lb leeks, cleaned and sliced
- 2 oz (1/4 cup) dry white wine (optional) or vegetable broth
- Sea salt and pepper to taste
- 1 lb salmon filets
- ¼ tsp curry powder
- 8 phyllo sheets (defrosted)
- Olive oil to brush

PROCEDURE

1. Peel and mince the onion. Wash and slice the leeks.
2. Melt the butter in a frying pan; add onion and leeks. Sautee over low heat; then add the white wine, salt, pepper and curry. Cook until liquid has evaporated. Remove from heat and let cool.
3. Cut the salmon filets into small pieces. Mix with the leek-onion curry.
4. Preheat your oven to 350F.
5. Prepare 4 bricks. Brush a layer of the phyllo dough with a little olive oil. Add another layer on top for added strength and crispiness. Bush the edges of the dough with more olive oil. Divide leek-salmon mixture into 4 parts and place one part at the center of each brick. Fold dough over to close.
6. Place the bricks on a baking sheet lined with parchment paper. Slide into the oven and bake for 20-25 minutes.

✓ Chef's Tip 1: Feel free to replace salmon with cod or another oily fish if you're on a tight budget or consider it a treat for a special occasion.
✓ Chef's Tip 2: For my GFCF friends: replace the phyllo dough with rice paper.

Barramundi au Beurre Citronné. *Lemon Butter Barramundi*

Barramundi (Asian Sea Bass) is a fish imported from the coastal waters of Australia. I find this fish to be not only versatile, but a healthy fish to cook with. The sweet, mild taste of this fish works very well with this recipe.

Servings: 4

Prep Time: 20 min

Cost per person: $2.99

INGREDIENTS

- 4 – 4 oz barramundi fillets (skin on or off)
- 1 Tbsp olive oil
- Salt and pepper

Sauce:
- 2 Tbsp butter
- 1 garlic clove, minced
- ½ tsp sea salt
- 2 lemon juices
- 4-6 leaves of fresh basil, minced

PROCEDURE

1. Thaw, rinse fillets and pat dry with paper towel. Rub with olive oil. Salt and pepper to taste.
2. Sauté the fillets on high heat for three minutes (skin side up). Flip and cook for one more minute.
3. Transfer to serving dish.

Make the sauce:
4. Gently sauté the garlic in butter for two minutes. Stir in salt, lemon juice and basil.
5. Remove from heat and spoon over fillets immediately before serving.

✓ Chef's Tip 1: Serve over rice or steamed vegetables and enjoy!
✓ Chef's Tip2: This recipe is GF. To make it CF, use olive oil through the whole recipe.

Tilapia a la Façon Méditerranéenne. *Mediterranean-Style Tilapia*

I like this dish because it is simple, yet full of Mediterranean flavor. Feel free to replace the tilapia with your favorite white fish at the best local price.

Servings: 4

Prep Time: 30 min

Oven Temp: 400F

Cost per person: $3.29

INGREDIENTS

- 2-8 oz tilapia filets, cut in 4 halves
- 1-15 oz canned diced tomatoes
- 1 tsp Herbes de Provence
- Sea salt and pepper
- 1 oz red wine
- 4 oz vegetable broth or ½ cup water and 1 vegetable bouillon cube
- ½ white medium onion, diced
- 2 garlic cloves
- 1 red bell pepper, diced
- 1 Tbsp fresh basil, chopped
- 1 Tbsp fresh parsley, chopped or 1 tsp dried
- 1 tsp sea salt
- ½ tsp black pepper

PROCEDURE

1. Preheat your oven at 400F.
2. Toss the diced tomatoes with wine, herbs and spices in a bowl.
3. Pour the vegetable broth into a large sauté pan. Sauté the onions, garlic, bell pepper, and fresh herbs until tender (about 5 minutes)
4. Add the macerated tomatoes/wine/honey/herbs and spices. Cook uncovered until all the veggies are tender, about 5 more minutes.
5. Season with salt and pepper.
6. Take an oven dish and spread the cooked veggies at the bottom.
7. Place the tilapia filets on top of the veggies. Cover with aluminum foil; poke holes into it.
8. Bake for 12-15 minutes or until the fish is steamed through with the vegetable aroma.

✓ Chef's Tip 1: You can serve this dish with pecans, quinoa, or steamed veggies in lemon vinaigrette. Feel free to replace the tilapia with sole filets, cod or any other white fish.

✓ Chef's Tip 2: This dish is GFCF.

234 | Healthy French Cuisine for Less Than $10/Day

VIANDES - MEAT

Pain de Viande Niçois. *Meatloaf Niçois*

This recipe yields a flavorful and moist meatloaf. You can also make meatballs out of it and size them small (1 oz ea) or larger (2 oz each) and bake them. Just keep in mind that 4 ounces of protein per meal is enough.

Servings: 8

Prep Time: 80 min

Cost per person: $1.34

INGREDIENTS

- 4 natural bacon strips
- 1 Tbsp olive oil
- 1 medium white onion, finely sliced
- 2 garlic cloves, finely chopped
- 4 oz cremini mushrooms, sliced
- 1 lb grass-fed ground beef
- 1 large egg
- 2 oz breads crumbs or GF bread crumbs
- 2 tsp Worcestershire sauce
- 4 chives or green onions, sliced thin or 2 tsp dried
- 1 tsp sea salt
- ½ tsp dried sage
- ½ tsp dried basil
- ½ dried thyme

PROCEDURE

1. Preheat your oven to 350F.
2. Fry your bacon until crispy; drain on paper towel and crumble. Set aside.
3. Sauté the onion and garlic with a pinch of salt in olive oil until soft; add sliced mushrooms and cook gently until almost all the liquid is evaporated. Set aside.
4. Combine beef, breadcrumbs, egg, bacon, and cooked mushrooms with juice, all herbs and spices in a large bowl. Mix well with your hands.
5. Place that mix in a loaf pan sprayed with olive oil.
6. Bake for about 60 minutes or until internal temperature reaches 160F.
7. 15 minutes before the meatloaf is ready, warm the tomato sauce with salt and pepper to taste, or warm 8 ounces of Alain's tomato sauce recipe. Simmer gently.
8. Allow meatloaf to cool and settle for 5 minutes before slicing and serving.
9. To serve, cut the loaf in 8 slices. Spoon 2 ounces of tomato sauce on top of each slice.
10. Please note: this recipe yields 8 servings at 4 ounces meat each. There should be

- ½ tsp black pepper, ground
- 1-15 oz can crushed tomatoes
- Sea salt and tomato to taste

plenty for leftovers.

✓ Chef's Tip 1: Serve with haricots verts in lemon vinaigrette or mashed potatoes.

✓ Chef's Tip 2: This recipe is GFCF when using GF bread crumbs.

Poulet a la Marmelade d'Orange. *Orange Marmalade Chicken*

These delicious chicken tenders come alive with the orange marmalade and freshly grated orange zest. I like them with brown rice or wide ribbon whole wheat pasta.

Servings: 4

Prep Time: 20 min

Cost per person: $1.91

IINGREDIENTS

Sauce:

- 1 tsp cornstarch
- 1 cup chicken broth
- 2 Tbsp apple cider vinegar
- 2 Tbsp orange marmalade
- 1 tsp freshly grated orange zest
- 1 tsp Dijon mustard

Chicken:

- 1 pound chicken tenders, or chicken breast sliced thin
- ½ tsp sea salt
- ¼ tsp freshly ground pepper
- 2 Tbsp olive oil

To finish:

- 1 Tbsp olive oil
- 2 large shallots, minced

PROCEDURE

1. Sauce: Place the cornstarch in a medium bowl. Whisk in progressively the broth until smooth; add the vinegar, marmalade, orange zest and mustard.

2. Chicken: Sprinkle chicken with salt and pepper. Heat the oil in a large skillet over medium-high heat. Add the chicken and cook until golden, about 2 minutes per side. Transfer to a plate and keep warm.

3. To finish: Add the remaining oil and shallots to the pan and cook, stirring often, until they begin to brown. Whisk the sauce mixture and add it to the pan. Bring to a simmer, scraping up any browned bits. Reduce heat to maintain a simmer; cook until the sauce is slightly reduced and thickened.

4. Add the chicken; return to a simmer. Cook, turning once, until the chicken is heated through, about 1 minute. Remove from the heat.

✓ Chef's Tip 1: These tender and sweet chicken pieces with go well with brown rice or pasta. Make sure to toss some of the sauce with it.

✓ Chef's Tip 2: This recipe is GFCF.

Médaillons de Porc avec sa Sauce au Sirop d'Érable et Chili. *Maple-Chili Glazed Pork Medallions*

These pork medallions are quick and easy to prepare, and the maple-chili glaze gives them that special flavor you yearn for. Pour the extra sauce on garlic mashed potatoes, or sauté a veggie medley with it. Yum!

Servings: 4

Prep Time: 20 min

Cost per person: $2.14

IINGREDIENTS

- 1 teaspoon chili powder
- ½ tsp sea salt
- 1/8 tsp ground chipotle pepper
- 1 pound pork tenderloin, trimmed and cut crosswise into 1-inch-thick medallions
- 1 Tbsp olive oil
- ¼ cup apple cider
- 1 Tbsp maple syrup or honey
- 1 tsp apple cider vinegar

PROCEDURE

1. Mix chili powder, salt and ground chipotle in a small bowl. Sprinkle over both sides of pork.
2. Heat oil in a large skillet over medium-high heat. Add the pork and cook until golden, about 2 minutes per side. Set aside and keep warm.
3. Add apple cider, maple syrup and vinegar to the pan. Bring to a boil, scraping up any browned bits. Reduce the heat to medium and cook the sauce until it is reduced to a thick glaze, 1 to 3 minutes. Serve the pork drizzled with the glaze.

✓ Chef's Tip 1: If you have time, prepare garlic mashed potatoes (see recipe); set the medallions on top and drizzle the sauce over. Tasty! If you're short on time, sauté a (frozen) veggie medley in the sauce and serve with the medallions.

✓ Chef's Tip 2: This recipe is GFCF.

Roulade de Poulet Vapeur, Pesto et Tomates Séchées. *Chicken Roulade with Pesto and Dried Tomatoes*

Find the Southern French flavors of sundried tomatoes and pesto in this chicken wrap recipe. It is steamed to avoid the addition of extra fat. If you wish, you can oven-bake it at 350F for 20 minutes. This is a very simple yet tasty recipe to prepare for your family for next to nothing!

Servings: 4

Prep Time: 30 min

Cost per person: $3.72

INGREDIENTS

- 2 chicken breasts cut into halves
- 4 tsp pesto sauce
- 2 oz (4 ea) sundried tomatoes in olive oil
- Sea salt and pepper to taste
- 4 oz canned crushed tomatoes with basil, heated

PROCEDURE

1. Bring your steamer to boil gently.
2. Drain the sundried tomatoes and chop finely.
3. Pound the chicken breasts until they are thin, or ask your friendly butcher to do it for you. Season with salt and pepper.
4. Spread the pesto then the chopped tomatoes on each cutlet. Roll them tightly and hold them with one or two small wooden skewers or toothpicks.
5. Place in your steamer's basket and cook for 15-20 minutes.
6. Serve immediately. Top the rolls with heated crushed tomatoes with basil.

✓ Chef's Tip 1: I suggest you serve this dish with whole wheat pasta ($0.26/serv.) or a mixed field salad with Italian dressing and a sprinkle of goat cheese ($1.20/serv.)
✓ Chef's Tip 2: For my GFCF friends, no substitutions are needed.

ACOMPAGNEMENTS - SIDE DISHES

Recette Facile d'Alain de Riz et Haricots a la Tomate. *Alain's Easy Tomato, Rice and Bean Recipe*

This one-pot side dish is a simple recipe I put together when I need a side dish full of helpful fiber. You get it from the rice and the beans and, to make it tasty, I added the tomatoes and herbs. The kombu adds goodness from the sea.

Servings: 6

Prep Time: 40 min

Cost per person: $0.86

INGREDIENTS

- 1 cup long-grain brown rice
- 3 cups filtered water
- 1 inch kombu seaweed (optional), soaked and cut in small pieces
- 1-15 oz can Amy's Organics Vegetarian Chili
- 1-15 oz can Muir Glen crushed tomatoes with basil
- 2 Tbsp olive oil
- 1 Tbsp Herbes de Provence mix
- 1 tsp sea salt
- ½ tsp cayenne pepper

PROCEDURE

1. If you choose to use the kombu – which I recommend – break off a one inch piece and soak for a few minutes to soften. Drain and cut in small pieces.

2. Place your rice in a bowl full of water. Swirl around to wash it. Drain in a colander and run cold water over it to rinse it some more. Place in a 2-quart saucepan. Add 3 cups of filtered water. Add the kombu pieces and bring to a boil. Lower the heat to a gentle simmer and cook, covered, for about 20 minutes. Do not overcook. Keep your rice al dente. Let sit covered for another 10 minutes.

3. While your rice is cooking, mix together the vegetarian chili, crushed tomatoes, olive oil, salt and pepper in a separate pot. Bing to boil, turn down the heat, and simmer for as long as the rice.

4. When the rice has rested, mix the rice into the tomato and bean mixture. Adjust seasoning and enjoy.

✓ Chef's Tip: This recipe is GFCF.

Purée de Patates a l'Ail et Huile d'Olive. *Mashed Potatoes with Garlic and Olive Oil*

This mashed potato recipe may surprise you with its garlic and olive oil. It's a recipe I came up with for my gluten-free clients and they love it. I prefer to leave the skins on: that's where all the goodness is. You could peel them, take out the garlic and replace the oil with butter, but where would be the fun in that? Give it a try... you might actually like them better this way.

Servings: 4

Prep Time: 30 min

Cost per person: $0.78

INGREDIENTS

- 4 medium Yukon Gold potatoes
- 4 oz olive oil
- 4 oz milk, plain soy or almond milk, unsweetened
- 4 garlic cloves, minced
- 4 scallions, sliced thin
- 2 tsp sea salt
- 1 tsp black pepper, ground

PROCEDURE

1. Fill the bottom of the steamer with 1 inch of lightly salted hot water.
2. While the water is heating, mince the garlic and let sit for a few minutes.
3. Wash and cut potatoes into 1/2-inch cubes with the skin on. Add them to the steamer basket. Cover.
4. Steam for 12-14 minutes, depending on the size of your potato cubes, until tender.
5. Mash potatoes with olive oil, garlic, and milk.
6. Add scallions; salt and pepper to taste. Mix well.

✓ Chef's Tip 1: This side dish can be served with the meatloaf Niçois or any other meat dish.

✓ Chef's Tip 2: This dish is GFCF.

Courge « Butternut » avec Pâtes **Orzo.** *Butternut Squash Orzo*

I like this side dish for its ease of execution. Nothing fancy, just good nutrition. A perfect dish for the Fall.

Servings: 6

Prep Time: 20 min

Cost per person: $0.86

IINGREDIENTS

- 2 cups vegetable broth, or water with 1 bouillon cube
- 1 cup (4 oz) orzo pasta or any inexpensive pasta
- 1 Tbsp olive oil
- 1 shallot, chopped
- 1 clove garlic, minced
- 1 medium (1 lb) butternut squash, peeled and deseeded, chopped into 1-inch cubes
- Sea salt and pepper to taste
- 1/4 cup parmesan cheese, grated

PROCEDURE

1. Bring the broth to boil in a large pot. Cook orzo pasta until al dente - about 8 minutes.
2. Meanwhile, add olive oil to a large skillet and sauté garlic and shallot until fragrant, about 2 minutes.
3. Add the butternut squash and sauté until cooked through. Salt and pepper to taste.
4. Add the butternut squash to the cooked orzo and allow to simmer until all the flavors mesh. It should be creamy.
5. Serve immediately. Top with parmesan cheese or cheese of choice.

✓ Chef's Tip 1: This simple yet healthy dish is a wonderful foil to a fish dish ($3.33/serv.)

✓ Chef's Tip 2: For my GFCF friends, replace parmesan with your favorite CF grated cheese.

Quinoa aux Noix de Pecan. *Pecan Nut Quinoa*

This side dish offers you a gluten-free alternative to cracked wheat. It is loaded with vegetable protein and has a delightful nutty flavor. Just make sure to rinse it well. It goes well with the Mediterranean tilapia.

Servings: 4

Prep Time: 8 min

Oven Temp: 350F

Cost per person: $0.68

INGREDIENTS

- 2 oz pecan pieces
- 4 oz quinoa grain, well rinsed
- 12 oz hot water and 2 vegetable bouillon cubes or…12 oz vegetable broth
- ½ tsp sea salt
- ¼ tsp black pepper, ground

PROCEDURE

1. Preheat oven at 350F.
2. Toast the nuts for about 5 min or until fragrant. Set aside.
3. Rinse the quinoa well in cold running water while stirring to eliminate all the saponins that sometimes give it a soapy flavor. Drain.
4. Place the drained quinoa in an oven dish. Pour vegetable broth over it.
5. Cover with aluminum foil and cook for about 30 minutes or until all the broth has been absorbed and the grain pops open. Uncover.
6. Mix in the toasted nuts and serve.

✓ Chef's Tip 1: If you do not wish to heat your oven, you can sauté the nuts in a frying pan and cook the quinoa in a covered saucepan.
✓ Chef's Tip 2: This recipe is GFCF.

DESSERTS et GATEAUX - DESSERTS and CAKES

Tartelettes Fines aux Pommes et à la Cannelle. *Fine Apple Tart*

This simple yet fanciful dessert is composed solely of puff pastry, apples and a little brown sugar. To add a spicy touch, you can sprinkle a little cinnamon over the apples if you like. If you want to treat yourself, add a scoop of vanilla ice cream or dairy-free coconut "ice cream" and serve it "a la mode".

Servings: 4

Prep Time: 40 min

Oven Temp: 350F

Cost per person: $1.62

INGREDIENTS

- A roll (8 oz) of defrosted puff pastry
- 4 Granny Smith apples
- 2 oz brown sugar
- 1 lemon juice
- 2 oz butter
- 1 tsp cinnamon (optional)

PROCEDURE

1. Preheat your oven to 350F.
2. Unroll the puff pastry carefully. Divide into 4 equal portions. Place on baking paper on a baking sheet
3. Peel, core and slice the apples into very thin half moons. Place them in a round "flower petal" pattern on each piece of dough.
4. Sprinkle with brown sugar. Drizzle with lemon juice. Drop a few butter pieces here and there. Sprinkle with cinnamon if desired.
5. Bake them at 350F for 15 to 20 minutes on a baking sheet or until golden brown.

✓ Chef's Tip: If you feel rich and decadent, add a scoop of vanilla ice cream or, for my GFCF friends, a scoop of frozen coconut "ice cream."

Douceur de Poire Façon Tiramisu. *Pear Tiramisu Mousse*

I like the sweetness of the pear against the crunchiness of the cookie and the lightness of the mousse. A light and delicious dessert for a simple family meal. You could also serve this with a dollop of whipped cream. Enjoy!

Servings: 8

Prep Time: 25 min

Cooling Time: 1 hour

Cost per person: $0.97

INGREDIENTS

- 1 gelatin leaf or one packet gelatin
- 1 can of pears in syrup, drained and sliced
- 1 Tbsp butter
- 2 tablespoons brown sugar

Mousse:

- 4 egg yolks
- 2 oz powdered sugar
- 8 oz mascarpone cheese or sour cream
- 1 oz Port wine
- 4 egg whites
- Pinch of sea salt
- 2 oz powdered sugar

Finish:

- 16 Speculoos cookies (spicy Belgian cookies) or short

PROCEDURE

1. Take the mascarpone out an hour before preparing the recipe. Allow it to come to room temperature.
2. Soak the gelatin leaf in cold water. If you're using gelatin powder, sprinkle it over 1 Tbsp of cold water.
3. Sauté your pears with the butter and brown sugar until they slightly caramelize. Allow to cool.
4. Whisk the egg yolks with the powdered sugar until light and foamy. Add the Port wine.
5. If you used the gelatin leaf, squeeze out the water, place in a small pan and melt at low temperature over a bain-marie until just melted, not hot. Whisk gently into the eggs/sugar mix. Carefully add the mascarpone.
6. Beat the egg whites with salt and sugar until soft peaks form. Fold the yolk mixture gently into the whites.
7. In each straight sided glass, place a layer of pears, a layer of crumbled cookies Speculoos (2 per glass) and a layer of mousse.
8. Allow to cool for at least an hour before serving. When serving, sprinkle with cocoa powder.

✓ Chef's Tip: To make this dessert GF, use

bread cookies

GF cookies. To make it CF, you can replace the mascarpone with soft soy cheese or soy yogurt and use soy whipped cream.

Gâteau au Fromage et à la Citrouille. *Pumpkin Cheese Cake*

I once brought this cheesecake to my church for the Thanksgiving brunch. They've been raving about it ever since and request it every year. Of course, it is prideful of me to be happy about this, but who said I was a saint? I like to serve each slice with a dollop of heavy whipped cream.

Servings: 12

Cake size: 9 inch

Prep Time: 20 min

Cooking Time: 2 ½ hours

Oven Temp: 250F

Cost per person: $1.34

INGREDIENTS

Crust:

- 10 oz graham crackers or GF version
- 4 oz (1 stick) butter, melted

Cheese cake filling:

- 1.5 lbs cream cheese
- 12 oz sour cream
- ½ cup (4 oz) raw sugar
- 2 Tbsp cornstarch
- 2 tsp ground cinnamon
- 1.5 tsp ground ginger
- ½ tsp ground nutmeg
- 1 lb 4 oz canned

PROCEDURE

1. Preheat your oven at 250°F.
2. Wrap a piece of aluminum foil around the outside of the bottom and sides of a spring-form pan, in such a way that it will keep water out.
3. Grind the graham cookies with the melted butter in a food processor fitted with a metal blade.
4. Press into the bottom of the spring-form pan. Bake at 250°F for 8 minutes; turn around, bake for another 8 minutes. Cool.
5. Whisk sugar, cornstarch and spices together.
6. Wash the food processor's bowl. Fit with the metal blade again. Add cream cheese. Cream with the sugar, cornstarch and spice mix until smooth.
7. Blend in the sour cream.
8. Add pumpkin puree. Blend in.
9. Add sea salt and vanilla to the eggs. Whisk together.
10. Add eggs/salt/vanilla to cheesecake; mix a little at a time at low speed.
11. Pour mix into the pan. Place the cake pan in an oven dish. Pour hot water around cake pan. Place in the oven.
12. Bake at 250°F for 1.5 hour – turn around – then 1 hour at 200°F. Let cool overnight.

pumpkin puree
- 4 whole eggs, beaten
- ¼ tsp sea salt
- 2 tsp vanilla extract

Turn out of the pan and serve cold.

✓ Chef's Tip: This cheese cake can be made GF by using GF crackers. Sorry! This recipe cannot be made CF.

Compote de Pruneaux au Vin Rouge et Cannelle. *Red Wine and Cinnamon Prune Compote*

I used to prepare this recipe as part of a compote cart at a few of the 4-star hotels where I used to work. Not only it is good for your digestive system, but it makes you slightly drunk. What's not to like?

Servings: 4

Prep Time: 40 min

Cost per person: $1.76

INGREDIENTS

- 1 lb pitted prunes
- 1 cup red wine
- 1 cup filtered water
- 8 oz local honey or raw agave nectar
- 1 tsp vanilla extract
- 1 cinnamon stick

PROCEDURE

1. The day before, soak the prunes in the red wine and water in a saucepan. Cover with a kitchen towel and let sit overnight.
2. The next day, add the honey or agave nectar, vanilla bean and cinnamon stick.
3. Bring to boil, reduce the heat and let simmer for 30 minutes. Let cool to room temperature.
4. Serve in glass coupes so you can see the prunes floating in the red wine. Enjoy and be regular.

✓ Chef's Tip 1: If you feel like indulging, place two scoops of vanilla ice cream in a bowl. Add you prunes in wine, and yum, yum and triple-yum!
✓ Chef's Tip 2: This recipe is GF. You can make it CF if you use soy or coconut ice cream.

WINTER SEASON

WINTER FOOD CALENDAR

- Apples **	- Greens, Chard *
- Arugula *	- Greens, Collards *
- Asian pears **	- Greens, Kale *
- Beets *	- Greens, Mustard *
- Broccoli *	- Leeks *
- Brussels Sprouts *	- Lettuce, head / leaf *
- Cabbage *	- Onions **
- Carrots *	- Pears **
- Cauliflower *	- Potatoes *
- Celeriac *	- Radicchio *
- Chervil *	- Radishes *
- Cilantro *	- Rutabagas **
- Dandelion Greens *	- Salad greens **
- Dill *	- Spinach *
- Dried shelling beans **	- Spring Onions *
- Endive Frisée *	- Squash, hard *
- Escarole *	- Turnips *
- Fennel *	- Wild greens **
- French Sorrel *	- Wild mushrooms **
- Fresh herbs **	- Winter greens and lettuces **
- Garlic **	- Winter squashes **
- Kohlrabi *	
- Parsley *	And many more…
- Parsnips **	
- Garlic, Green *	Also available: Artisan breads and baked goods, confections, pasture-raised meats (pork, beef, lamb, goat, poultry, sausages, jerky), coffees and teas, eggs, dairy products, gourmet cheeses, fresh seafood from the Gulf, salmon, shellfish, honey, ciders, hard ciders, dried fruits, dried herbs, dried wild
- Green Onions *	
Please note:	
* = TX and other southern states.	
** = All other states.	

	mushrooms, pickles and preserves, and tacos.

WINTER MENUS and COSTING

<u>Monday</u>: Breakfast $1.50; Lunch $2.65; Dinner: **Creamy Pumpkin Soup** $1.20. **Mushroom and Spinach Crepes** $1.34. **Side Salad** $1.00; **Fruit and chocolate** $0.90. Total day: ~**$8.59** per person.

<u>Tuesday</u>: Breakfast $1.50; Lunch $2.65; Dinner: **4 oz Pan Fried Grass-fed Ground Beef Patty** $1.50. **Gratin Dauphinois** $1.18. **Side Salad:** $1.00. **Fruit and chocolate** $0.90. Total day: ~**$8.73** per person.

<u>Wednesday</u>: Breakfast $1.50; Lunch $2.65; Dinner: **Baked Barramundi with Spinach** $4.25. **Cool Season Steamed Greens** $1.01. **Fruit and chocolate** $0.90. Total day: ~**$10.31** per person.

<u>Thursday</u>: Breakfast $1.50; Lunch $2.65; Dinner: **Red Wine Onion Soup** $2.84. **Chicken with Sugar Snap Peas and Herbs** $3.16; **Fruit and chocolate** $0.90. Total day: ~**$11.05** per person.

<u>Friday</u>: Breakfast $1.50; Lunch $2.65; Dinner: **Chicken Noodle Soup** $1.90. **Alain's Way of making a Potato Omelet** $1.08. **Red Lentil Coconut Curry** $1.15. **Fruit and chocolate** $0.90. Total day: ~**$9.18** per person.

<u>Saturday</u>: Breakfast $1.50; Lunch $2.65; Dinner: **Daube Provençale** $3.66. **Lemony Carrot Salad with Raisins** $0.87. **Rhubarb and Apple Compote** $0.80. Total day: ~**$9.48** per person.

<u>Sunday</u>: Brunch: $3.75; Dinner: **Lentil and Tomato Soup with Spinach** $2.01. **Old Fashion Turkey Roll** $1.51. **Side Salad** $1.00. **Exotic Carrot Cake** $1.83. Total day: ~**$10.10** per person.

<u>Total for the week</u>: ~**$67.44** or ~**$9.63** average per day per person.

WINTER RECIPES
PETIT DEJEUNER et BRUNCH. BREAKFAST and BRUNCH

Crêpes Petit Déjeuner au Quinoa. *Quinoa Pancakes*

This is a tasty alternative to your regular pancakes and so much healthier for you. Enjoy them with your favorite topping.

Servings: 6. About 12 pancakes depending on size.

Cost per person: $0.68

INGREDIENTS

- 4 oz white rice flour
- 2 oz quinoa flour
- 1 tsp baking powder
- 1 Tbsp turbinado sugar
- 8 oz eggs (about 4)
- 10-12 oz Milk or soy or almond milk
- Coconut oil for cooking

PROCEDURE

1. Weigh the flours, baking powder and sugar in your mixer's bowl. With the whisk attachment, start mixing at low speed.
2. Add the eggs and the soy milk progressively until there are no lumps. Switch to medium speed and whisk for another minute until the batter is smooth. Let rest for at least 30 minutes.
3. Heat your frying pan. When hot, pour about 2 oz of batter into the pan. Cook until colored on one side. Flip over and finish cooking.

✓ Chef's Tips: This will make fluffy and nutty pancakes filled with fiber and protein. Top them with your favorite topping. I personally like to make a cake with them, alternating butter (or margarine) and fruit preserves in between.

Omelette aux Pommes de Terre à la Manière d'Alain. *Alain's Way of making a Potato Omelet*

In France, we do not add milk or cream to our eggs when making an omelet. We also like our omelets "baveuses" (runny). I know, gross! But that's the way they taste the best! Give it a try; you might like it.

Servings: 4

Prep Time: 15 min

Cost per person: $1.08

INGREDIENTS

- 2 Tbsp extra virgin olive oil
- 2 Tbsp butter
- 2 large Yukon Gold potatoes, sliced thin
- 8 eggs
- 1 Tbsp Herbes de Provence
- ½ tsp sea salt
- ¼ tsp cayenne pepper
- Fresh parsley chopped for decoration

PROCEDURE

1. The secret of a good omelet is that all your ingredients must be at room temperature, especially your eggs.

2. Beat your eggs with the sea salt and cayenne (once in a while, I like to add some Provencal herbs to it for added flavor). The salt will break down the eggs albumin and make the omelet creamier (without adding cream).

3. Slice your potatoes thin but not too thin (about 1/8th of an inch for the engineers out there).

4. In a large frying pan on medium heat, melt the butter with olive or coconut oil. When the fat is hot but not smoking, place your potato slices carefully at the bottom of the pan. Cook on each side until golden.

5. Just at the time your potatoes are done, turn off the heat and pour the eggs all over the potatoes. With a heat-proof rubber spatula, stir your omelet carefully until it's almost set. Transfer immediately to the serving platter.

✓ Chef's Tip: This recipe is GFCF.

Quiche Lorraine. *Quiche Lorraine*

I love quiches. They're easy to prepare and have an endless variety... and they're pretty cheap to make. Here my version of a classic from the Northeastern part of France, Alsace-Lorraine. Add a side salad and you have a complete meal.

Servings: 6

For 1-9 inch pie shell

Prep Time: 30 min

Oven Temp: 350F

Cost per person: $1.12

INGREDIENTS

Filling

- ½ oz (2 slices) natural bacon, cooked
- 3 oz natural oven-baked ham
- 1 oz white sharp cheddar cheese

Quiche batter

- 1 cup (8 oz) whole milk or plain soy or almond milk
- ½ cup (4 oz) heavy cream or plain soy creamer
- 4 ea (8 oz) whole eggs
- ½ tsp sea salt
- ¼ tsp black pepper, ground

PROCEDURE

10. Preheat your oven at 350F.
11. Prebake your pie shell for about 8 minutes or until firm but not baked. Doing so will prevent the crust from being soggy later on.

Prepare the filling:

12. Either bake the bacon on 2 stacked sheets of paper towel until crispy, about 10 min or sauté in a frying pan until ready. Set on paper towels to absorb the excess fat. Allow to cool. Cut in small pieces or crumble.
13. Cube the ham. Toss together with the cut bacon. Place at the bottom of the prebaked pie shell. Top off with the cheddar.

For the quiche batter:

14. Measure/weigh all the ingredients for the quiche batter in your food blender bowl. Blend a low speed, do not allow to foam.
15. Pour the batter slowly on one side, trying to keep the cheddar dry.
16. Bake for about 30 minutes (turn once midway) until the cheese is golden brown or the batter is slightly firm to the touch.
17. Cool down. Cut into 6 pieces per pie.

✓ Chef's Tip1: If you manage to eat only one

piece per person, you will have 2 slices leftover for tomorrow's lunch. It's very good at room temperature or warmed up at 350F for five minutes.

✓ <u>Chef's Tip 2</u>: If you use a GF pie crust and replace the milk/cream with soy creamer, and replace the cheese with your favorite CF cheese, you will end up with the perfect GFCF quiche.

SOUPES - SOUPS

Soupe Crémeuse de Citrouille. *Creamy Pumpkin Soup*

This amazing soup reminds me of Mamie. She used to make the best pumpkin soups, probably because her pumpkins where fresh from her garden. The orange coloring of the pumpkin tells us that it's loaded with the cancer-fighting antioxidant beta-carotene while pumpkin seeds are loaded with zinc, which is known for supporting prostate health.

Servings: 6

Prep Time: 1 hour

Cost per person: $1.20

IINGREDIENTS

- 1 small cooking pumpkin, cut and seeded (about 2 pounds)
- 1 Tbsp olive oil
- 1 large onion, diced
- 2 cups vegetable broth
- 2 cups half and half or soy or almond milk
- 1 tsp sea salt
- 1 tsp ginger
- ½ tsp ground nutmeg
- ½ tsp ground cinnamon
- ½ tsp freshly cracked pepper
- Fresh pumpkin seeds

PROCEDURE

1. Preheat your oven at 400F.
2. Cut your pumpkin in half; remove seeds with a spoon. Set aside.
3. Roast the pumpkin with the skin on, cut side up, for about 30 minutes, or until a fork easily punctures the meat all the way through to the skin. Allow to cool for a while.
4. While your pumpkin is roasting, wash and dry the seeds. Toast or roast them for additional crunchiness and flavor.
5. When cooked, cut and add the pumpkin to a blender and blend continuously until smooth. You may need to add some broth to thin down the puree a little.
6. Sauté onion in olive oil until softened a bit. Add in pumpkin puree, broth, milk, and all the spices. Cook for another 15 minutes.
7. Pour the soup back in your used blender and blend until smooth and creamy. If you want to make sure there are no lumps left, push it through a fine sieve or Chinois. I actually like a little bit of chunks in my soup.

8. Garnish with pumpkin seeds.

✓ Chef's Tip 1: Personally, if the pumpkin is young, I use the skin in the puree but you can just scoop out the cooked meat if the skin is too tough.

✓ Chef's Tip 2: To make this wonderful soup CF, use soy or almond milk instead of half and half.

Poule au Pot aux Pâtes. *Chicken Noodle Soup*

This is the French version of the healing chicken soup you all know about. I made it as easy as possible for you to prepare but there is still some work involved. I do believe strongly that the whole chicken should be cooked in the broth so you get all the benefits from the meat and bones.

Servings: 6-8

Prep Time: 75 min.

Cost per person: $1.90

INGREDIENTS

- 1 small natural chicken (about 2 lbs)
- 2 gallons hot water
- 8 ea chicken bouillon cubes
- 1 medium white onion, sliced
- 4 garlic cloves, minced
- 2 celery stalks, chopped
- 2 medium carrots, sliced
- 1 Tbsp sea salt
- 1 tsp dried basil
- 1 tsp dried marjoram
- 1 tsp dried thyme
- 1 tsp black pepper
- 2 ea bay leaves
- 8 oz small bow tie or GF pasta
- 1 bag (1 lb) frozen small peas

PROCEDURE

1. Place your chicken in a large pot. Cover with cold water at least one inch above the chicken. Add bouillon cubes, all cut vegetables, herbs and spices. Bring to boil. Cover and lower the heat down. Simmer for about an hour or until meat falls of the bones.

2. Take the chicken out of the broth gently and let cool. Save the broth. When cool enough to handle, take all the meat apart from the bones. Note: watch out for the small bones.

3. If you wish, skim the fat from the top of the broth, place the chicken meat back into the soup, stir and bring back to simmer.

4. Add the peas and cook for another 5 minutes.

5. Meanwhile, cook the pasta al dente for about 10 minutes in salted water. Drain and add to the soup. Serve hot.

✓ Chef's Tip: This soup is GFCF when you use GF pasta. That's what I do at PeoplesRx and my customers love it.

Soupe Aigre-Piquante aux Champignons et Chou et Riz. *Hot and Sour Mushroom, Cabbage, and Rice Soup*

This sweet and sour recipe is reminiscent of a Vietnamese soup, but with Western ingredients. If you have extra money, you can spend it on shiitake mushrooms and take advantage of their healing benefits.

Servings: 6

Prep Time: 35 min

Cost per person: $1.77

IINGREDIENTS

- 1 Tbsp olive oil
- 2 (or more) jalapeno peppers, seeded and diced
- 1 medium onion, chopped
- 3 cloves garlic, minced
- 1 inch lump ginger, grated
- 1 1/2 cups (4 oz) cremini mushrooms, washed and sliced
- 1 qt vegetable or chicken broth
- 1 lime, zest and juice
- 1 Tbsp GF soy sauce
- Chili garlic to taste
- 1/2 cup jasmine rice
- 1/2 head green cabbage, cut in half and shaved thin

PROCEDURE

1. Heat the oil in a large heavy pot or Dutch oven over medium heat. Add the onion, garlic, diced peppers, and ginger and cook for about five minutes or until fragrant and slightly softened.
2. Add the mushrooms and cook for another five minutes over medium heat, or until mushrooms are browned.
3. Add the broth with the lime zest and juice, soy sauce and hot sauce; bring to a simmer.
4. Add the rice, cover, and simmer for about 20 minutes or until the rice is just barely soft. Add water to adjust if necessary. Add the shaved cabbage and simmer for another few minutes or until cabbage is hot.

✓ Chef's Tip 1: Any type of mushroom, cabbage and even rice will work as well.
✓ Chef's Tip 2: This recipe is GFCF.

Soupe de Pois Cassés au Lard et Ratte. *Split Pea Soup with Bacon and French Fingerlings*

This warming dish makes a very substantial main course for dinner. I like to use French fingerling potatoes for this recipe, but if they are difficult to find in your region please substitute with young red potatoes or Yukon Gold potatoes.

Servings: 4

Prep Time: 50 min

Cost per person: $1.35

INGREDIENTS

- 1 lb dried split peas
- 2 Tbsp pork fat
- 4 slices thick bacon or Canadian bacon
- 4 French fingerling potatoes, sliced
- Salt and freshly ground pepper 4 slices of whole wheat bread or rye bread
- Heavy cream (optional)

PROCEDURE

1. Start cooking the peas in 2 quarts of lightly salted cold water. Bring to a boil and simmer for about 20 minutes, skimming regularly. They are cooked when they crush easily between your fingers.

2. 15 minutes before serving, cut the bacon into small squares and cook in a heavy pan without fat on both sides. Take out and reserve.

3. Slice the potatoes into thin slices and cook in the same fat, turning over halfway through cooking.

4. Blend the peas in a blender with the cooking water. Adjust consistency and seasoning. Pour soup into hot plates; give a turn of pepper mill on each.

5. Arrange the potato slices and bacon on top of the soup. Serve with a slice of toasted bread.

✓ Chef's Tip 1: This is what we call a "soupe de paysan" in France. Cheap and filling. If you want to go upscale, add a tablespoon of heavy cream to the soup.

✓ Chef's Tip 2: This recipe is GFCF without the bread or your can substitute with your favorite GF bread.

Soupe du Chalet. *Mountain Cabin Soup*

This is a very good and thick winter soup. For once, don't worry about the calorie! It's a classic soup served in the mountains when a snowstorm is howling just outside your windows.

Servings: 4

Prep Time: 70 min

Cost per person: $2.09

INGREDIENTS

- 2 oz butter
- 4 oz smoked bacon, cut into pieces
- 1 large onion, chopped
- 1 lb fresh spinach or frozen leaf spinach
- 4 medium baking potatoes
- 1 pt whole milk or alternative milk
- 1 pt water
- Sea salt and pepper to taste
- 4 oz macaroni (or rice macaroni)
- 4 oz heavy cream or sour cream
- 2 oz grated cheese (Gruyere or better yet, Emmentaler)

PROCEDURE

1. Peel the potatoes; cut them into pieces. Rinse spinach and remove stems. Peel and chop onions.
2. In a large skillet, melt butter and add the bacon and onions. Sautee for 5 minutes.
3. Add the potatoes and cook for 10 minutes over medium low heat.
4. Meanwhile, boil the milk and the water together in a saucepan. Add to the onions and potatoes, and salt and pepper to taste. Cover and simmer for 40 minutes.
5. Add the spinach (don't worry about the volume, spinach melts quickly).
6. 10 minutes before the end of cooking, add the macaroni and cook for 10 minutes. Remove from heat, add sour cream and grated cheese. Adjust seasoning and serve hot. Bon appétit!

✓ Chef's Tip 1: This is a whole meal in itself. If you want some fresh greens, add a small side salad.

✓ Chef's Tip 2: To make this recipe CF (it is GF already), replace the butter with olive oil, the milk with plain soy or almond milk, the heavy cream with plain soy creamer and the grated cheese with your favorite CF alternative cheese.

SALADES - SALADS

Salade de Carottes au Citron et Raisins Secs. *Lemony Carrot Salad with Raisins*

Tangy lemon and fresh dill make a bright dressing for shredded carrots. Raisins add a touch of sweetness. A great way for you to get your daily allowance of vitamin B.

Servings: 4

Prep Time: 15 min

Cost per person: $0.87

INGREDIENTS

- 2 cups shredded carrots (about 1 lb)
- 1 1/2 Tbsp chopped fresh dill
- 1 Tbsp chopped scallion
- 2 Tbsp fresh lemon juice
- 1 tsp Dijon mustard
- 1 garlic clove, minced
- ¼ tsp sea salt
- Freshly ground pepper, to taste
- 2 Tbsp olive oil

PROCEDURE

1. Place your grated carrots, chopped dill and scallions in a salad bowl.
2. Whisk lemon juice, garlic, mustard, salt and pepper to taste in a small bowl.
3. Pour on prepared veggies and toss gently to coat.

✓ Chef's Tip: This recipe is GFCF.

Salade de Pousses de Choux de Bruxelles et Pommes. *Raw Brussels Sprout Salad with Apples*

The combination of flavors in this very refreshing salad will surprise you. Be adventurous and give it a try! It's loaded with powerful antioxidants.

Servings: 4

Prep Time: 20 min

Cost per person: $1.90

IINGREDIENTS

- 1 lb Brussels sprouts, thinly sliced
- ½ large purple onion, thinly sliced
- ¼ cup apple cider vinegar
- 1 medium Granny Smith apple, peeled, cored then sliced thinly
- ½ cup pecan pieces
- ¼ cup grated pecorino or parmesan

Dressing:

- 3 Tbsp olive oil
- 1 lemon juice
- Sea salt and pepper to taste

PROCEDURE

1. Add sliced onions to a small bowl and top with vinegar. Let stand for 15 minutes.
2. Meanwhile, slice the Brussels sprouts and place into a large bowl. Add apple, pecan and cheese. Toss together.
3. Remove onions from the vinegar. Add to salad.
4. Prepare the vinaigrette by whisking together oil, lemon juice, and vinegar from the onion, salt and pepper.
5. Add vinaigrette to the salad and toss with your hands.
6. Cover and let set for 1 hour at room temperature before serving to allow the flavors to meld.

✓ Chef's Tip 1: This recipe works well with all sorts of sprouts.
✓ Chef's Tip 2: For my GFCF friends, this recipe works well without the cheese but feel free to add your favorite alternative grated cheese.

POISSONS et FRUITS de MER - FISH and SEAFOOD

Ma Façon Rapide de Préparer des Crevettes ou Coquilles de St. Jacques.
Alain's Quick Way to Prepare Poached Shrimp or Scallops

When I come back home tired from working all day in my professional kitchen, I don't want to spend a lot of time "slaving over a hot stove". I came up with this quick and tasty way to poach shrimp and scallops. Give it a try, it's really easy. Serve your shrimp or scallops on top of GF pasta or with a salad and Voila! Dinner is served in no time at all.

Servings: 4

Prep Time: 10 min

Cost per person: $3.33

INGREDIENTS

- 1 lb peeled shrimp or scallops
- 1 Tbsp Extra virgin olive oil and 1 Tbsp Coconut oil OR 2 oz veggie broth
- 1 tsp of your favorite spice blend: Herbes de Provence, Cajun mix, or Chili mix
- 1-2 pinches of Sea salt depending on your spice blend choice

PROCEDURE

1. Heat an enameled cast iron pan like Le Creuset, a cast iron pan or heavy stainless steel frying pan on your stove over medium heat.
2. Add the oils (or broth) to the pan. Allow to heat gently, but not to smoke. Add the spice blend of your choice and salt, let it all to warm up to develop the flavors.
3. When the spices sizzle, add your peeled shrimp or scallops and poach gently (do not fry) over medium-low heat. They will render their juices and create a wonderful sauce. Flip shrimp or scallops over; finish cooking.
4. You can either toss the cooked seafood with cooked pasta ($0.18/serv.) or add them on top a mixed green salad ($0.75/serv.) and drizzle the sauce over it.

✓ Chef's tip 1: A "healthier" way to prepare them is to poach them in veggie broth using the same spices and principle.
✓ Chef's Tip 2: This dish is GFCF with a serving of GF pasta.

Barramundi aux Epinards Cuit au Four. *Baked Barramundi with Spinach*

I like this simple and healthy dish. It's loaded with vitamins, chlorophyll, iron and omega-3 fatty acids. What's not to like? Use the juice to flavor the steamed red potatoes.

Servings: 4

Prep Time: 35 min

Oven Temp: 375F

Cost per person: $4.25

INGREDIENTS

- 4– 4 oz barramundi fillets, thawed
- Sea salt and pepper to taste
- 2 Tbsp. olive oil
- ½ cup dry white wine
- 3 garlic cloves, minced
- 2 fresh chiles, cleaned and chopped
- ½ cup fresh parsley, chopped
- ½ cup fresh shallots, minced
- 1 lemon, juiced
- One bunch (8 oz) spinach leaves, chopped or frozen, defrosted
- 1 lb baby red potatoes, steamed

PROCEDURE

1. Preheat your oven at 375F.
2. In a baking dish, place a sheet of baking parchment on top of a large piece of aluminum foil.
3. Cover the paper/foil with a bed of baby spinach or defrosted spinach.
4. Rinse and pat the fish dry. Salt and pepper on both sides. Lay it on top of the spinach.
5. Cover with olive oil and white wine.
6. Spread minced garlic, finely chopped chili, chopped parsley and shallots on and around the fillet.
7. Squeeze the lemon juice over the barramundi and add a few twists of cracked black pepper.
8. Fold the foil around the fish tightly and place in preheated oven. Bake for about 20 minutes or until the fish is flaking when poked with s small knife.

✓ Chef's Tip 1: Serve with steamed baby potatoes.
✓ Chef's Tip 2: This recipe is GFCF.

Cabillaud Gratiné au Parmesan. *Cod au Gratin with Parmesan*

Marinated with lime, this moist fish is then covered with a thin layer of cream and Parmesan cheese before being baked for added flavor. This dish will give you a good serving of omega-3 fatty acids.

Servings: 4

Oven Temp: 350F

Cost per person: $4.38

- 4 cod fillets or 1 lb
- 1 tsp sea salt
- Freshly ground black pepper to taste
- 2 cloves garlic, minced
- 2 Tbsp fresh lime juice (2 limes)
- ½ Tbsp olive oil
- 4 oz (1/2 cup) half and half cream
- 2 Tbsp grated Parmesan cheese

PROCEDURE

1. Preheat your oven at 350F.
2. Place the fish fillets on a plate. Season them with salt, pepper, garlic and lime juice. Cover with plastic wrap and allow to rest for 15 minutes.
3. Coat an oven dish with olive oil. Arrange cod fillets in it. Pour cream over fish and sprinkle with grated Parmesan.
4. Brown at 350F for about 20 minutes. Serve immediately.

✓ Chef's Tip 1: Serve on brown rice and with a small side salad.
✓ Chef's Tip 2: For my GFCF friends, substitute the cream with coconut creamer and the cheese with soy cheese.

Cannellonis au Thon. *Cannelloni with Tuna*

This is a good winter recipe to prepare on the weekend. It is a little time consuming, but gives you wonderful results. It's a great dish for lunch leftovers.

Servings: 4

Prep Time: 90 min

Oven Temp: 350F

Cost per person: $4.42

INGREDIENTS

- 8 lasagna sheets
- 12 oz home-made tomato sauce (see Spring recipes)

Tuna stuffing:

- 2 small cans tuna in water, drained
- 4 oz (1/2 cup) green peas (frozen)
- 1 slice whole wheat bread, crumbles

Cheese sauce:

- 2 oz butter
- 2 oz flour
- 8 oz milk
- 2 oz grated Swiss cheese for the sauce
- Sea salt, pepper and nutmeg to taste
- 2 oz grated Swiss cheese as topping

PROCEDURE

1. Warm the homemade tomato sauce.
2. Prepare the stuffing: Drain tuna and mash with a fork. Mix in the peas, bread crumbs, salt, pepper and Italian herb mix. Fold this with one third (4 oz) of the tomato sauce. Adjust seasoning if needed.
3. Soften the lasagna sheets one by one in hot water. Lay on a towel. Stuff them with the tuna mixture and roll. Make sure the seal is on the bottom.
4. Oil an oven dish. Pour another third of the tomato sauce in it. Arrange the cannelloni on top of the sauce. Pour the remaining sauce over the stuffed lasagna.
5. Prepare the white cheese sauce: melt the butter in another pan, add flour, whisking well until the preparation turns golden. Remove from heat and whisk in the milk gradually to get a béchamel. Heat again and bring to a boil, stirring constantly until the sauce thickens. Add the grated cheese, nutmeg, salt and pepper.
6. To finish: Pour the cheese sauce over the tomato sauce. Sprinkle with remaining grated cheese and bake for 30 minutes at 350F or until the cheese is golden brown.

✓ Chef's GFCF Tip: Replace flour with cornstarch, milk with alternative milk and the cheese with soy cheese.

VIANDES - MEAT

Daube de Bœuf à la Provençale. *Provencal-style Beef Stew*

My mother-in-law, Helene, prepared this dish wonderfully. Unfortunately, she passed away before I could ask her for her secrets. I suspect it had a lot to do with the well-seasoned "daube" pot she used. After long research, this is the version I feel tastes the closest to her divine stew. This is a meal to share with friends around a lively table. It adds to the goodness of this dish.

Servings: 8

Prep Time: 40 min.

Cooking Time: 4-5 hours

Cost per person: $3.66

INGREDIENTS

- 2 pounds of beef stew meat: shank or chuck, cut into 3 ounce pieces (ask your friendly butcher)
- 2 Tbsp olive oil
- 2 medium onions, peeled and sliced thin
- 3 carrots, peeled and sliced thin
- 1 celery stalk, sliced thin
- 2 garlic cloves, peeled and sliced thin
- 2 parsley sprigs with their leaves
- 6 whole peppercorns, crushed coarsely
- 2 pinches of coarse sea salt

PROCEDURE

1. In a large enameled cast iron pot, toss the meat along with the vegetables, herbs, spices, salt and pepper; sprinkle with the olive oil and cover with the red wine. Stir together well. Cover and marinate at least 6 hours, or overnight at room temperature. Note: If you feel uncomfortable with leaving this marinade out overnight, refrigerate overnight, but the flavors will not develop the same way. If you are marinating during the day, stir every two hours.

2. The next day, take the meat out and put aside; strain the marinade, saving the vegetables and the liquid separately. Dry the pot to be reused right away.

3. In that same pot, melt the butter, and cook the cubed bacon and meat together for about 5 minutes; add the drained vegetables and cook for another 5 minutes; finally, cover with the marinade liquid. Bring to a gentle boil. If you own a heat disperser, place it on the flame and keep the heat to the level where the stew is barely simmering.

4. Cook covered for 4 to 5 hours until the

- 1 knife tip of ground nutmeg
- 4 juniper berries, crushed coarsely
- 1 fresh orange peel, cut in strips
- 2 whole cloves
- 2 fresh thyme sprigs
- 2 bay leaves
- 1 bottle of deep dark red wine with strong tannins

- 2 Tbsp butter
- 2 oz lean bacon in one thick slice, cut into dices

- 4 cups (8 oz) of large egg noodles, macaroni or bow tie pasta, or GF pasta cooked in a large pot of salted water.

meat is falling apart.

5. When the meat is ready, cook your noodles in a large pot of salted water for 12 minutes or al dente. Drain. Place the cooked pasta on the bottom of your serving dish, and cover with the stew. Serve pasta and meat separately and allow each guest to help themselves to their heart's content.

✓ Chef's Tip 1: One of the old folks' secrets when it comes to this stew is that you should top the stew pot with a large plate and fill it with a cup of red wine (or water). When the wine or water evaporates, add some more until the meat is cooked. What this does is to allow the steam from the stew to condense against the cool lid filled with liquid and fall back into the stew to develop a better flavor. As a matter of fact, if you visit the South of France, you can buy a "daube" earthenware pot with a special lid that allows you to add liquid on top.

✓ Chef's Tip 2: Some chefs believe that adding tomatoes or tomato paste to this "daube" makes it more special. As you already know, every chef will add his own twist to any recipe. I don't recall Helene using tomatoes in hers, but if it works for you, give it a try and let me know how it tastes.

✓ Chef's Tip 3: This recipe is GFCF if served with GF pasta.

Hachis Parmentier. *Shepherd's Pie*

No matter what the English translation may infer, a shepherd did not invent this dish. This gratin is named after the chemist Antoine Parmentier, who created it and had Louis XVI taste it. Parmentier was convinced that the potato (considered an exotic tuber) could effectively vanquish the famine raging through France at the time.

Servings: 8

Prep Time: 60 min

Oven Temp: 400F

Cost per person: $2.76

INGREDIENTS

Mashed potatoes:

- 1 lb potatoes – I like Yukon Gold
- Salted water to cook potatoes
- 4 oz (1/2 cup) milk
- 2 oz butter
- 1 pinch ground nutmeg
- Sea salt and pepper to taste

Meat:

- 1 Tbsp olive oil
- 12 oz ground beef
- 1 white onion, chopped
- 2 garlic cloves, minced
- 1 carrot, diced small
- 1 small tomato, diced

PROCEDURE

1. Start your mashed potatoes: Peel, wash and cut the potatoes into large cubes (note: I personally like my mashed potatoes with the skin on). Plunge them into boiling salted water. Cook 20-25 min or until tender. Drain.

2. Cook the meat: Meanwhile, heat the olive oil in a skillet. Add the onions and garlic with a pinch of salt. Sauté until wilted, about 5 minutes.

3. Add the meat, cubed carrots and tomatoes; salt and pepper to taste. Mix well and cook for 15 minutes over medium heat while stirring.

4. Preheat your oven at 400F. Butter a large glass baking dish.

5. Finish the mashed potatoes: While the potatoes are still hot, mash them with the milk and butter. Add a pinch of nutmeg. Adjust consistency as needed with more milk.

6. To finish: Place meat in the baking dish. Top with the mashed potatoes and grated Swiss cheese. Let it brown in the oven for 20 minutes; broil it if you need added color.

7. Sprinkle with chopped parsley. Serve very hot.

small
- Sea salt and pepper to taste

To finish:

- 2 oz grated Swiss cheese
- 5 sprigs parsley

✓ Chef's Tip 1: This recipe is larger than usual because it's hard to do just a small amount. It's perfect for lunch leftovers. If you have a meat grinder, this is also a great way to recycle leftover roast beef or pot roast.

✓ Chef's Tip 2: For my GFCF friends: Make the mashed potatoes with plain almond or soymilk. Replace the butter with olive oil and replace the grated cheese with your favorite CF cheese.

Le Presque Célèbre Chili Con Carne d'Alain. *Alain's Almost Famous Organic Chili Con Carne*

I know, I know! This does not sound French and it is not. But we have adopted this recipe, added a little twist here and there and made it our own pretty quickly. If you don't believe me check out how many Tex-Mex restaurants you will find in France during your next trip. Feel free to experiment a little with the spices and herbs. Make it your own.

Servings: 12 at 6 oz each

Prep Time: 30 min

Oven Temp: 400F

Cost per person: $1.28

INGREDIENTS

- 1 Tbsp olive oil
- ½ ea white onion, diced
- 2 garlic cloves, minced
- ½ green bell pepper, diced
- ½ red bell pepper, diced
- 1 lb grass fed ground beef
- 1 Tbsp chili powder of choice
- 1 Tbsp ground cumin
- 1 tsp sea salt
- ½ tsp cayenne pepper
- ½ tsp ground coriander
- ½ tsp dried oregano
- ½ tsp ground allspice
- ¼ tsp ground cloves

PROCEDURE

1. Diced and chop all your veggies. Toss together.
2. Prepare your herbs/spices mix.
3. Heat the olive oil and sauté the onions, garlic, and peppers until tender.
4. Add the ground beef, herbs/spices and continue to cook until the beef is done.
5. Add the beans and tomatoes; bring back to boil and simmer about 20 minutes to allow the flavors to blend. Cool a little and serve with brown rice ($0.20/serving) if you wish.

✓ Chef's Tip 1: This recipe will feed you for a couple of days. Add a side salad ($1.00) and a fruit ($0.75) and voila! A complete meal. Actually, if you can wait that long (I seriously doubt it), this chili will taste a lot better the next day. A good thing since you will take some of this with you at work, right?

✓ Chef's Tip 2: This recipe is GFCF.

- 3 cans (15 oz) red
  beans or pinto beans
- 1 can (15 oz) fire-
  roasted tomatoes

Côtelettes de Porc Sauce Framboises et Oignons Marinés. *Raspberry-Glazed Pork Chops with Pickled Onions*

I love these pork chops with their fruity sauce. The pickled onions and fresh raspberries add that special sweet and sour addition to please your palate. The thick flavorful sauce, rich pork chops and pickled onions all come together in an explosion of flavors and textures.

Servings: 4

Prep Time: 30 min

Cost per person: $3.85

IINGREDIENTS

Pickled onions:

- 1 small onion, thinly sliced
- ¼ cup raspberry or red-wine vinegar
- 2 Tbsp maple syrup or honey
- 1 tsp fresh thyme leaves, divided
- 1/8 tsp sea salt
- Black ground pepper to taste

Sauce:

- 1 pint fresh raspberries; save 8 nice one for decoration
- 1 small onion, thinly sliced
- ½ cup white wine or chicken broth

PROCEDURE

1. Whisk raspberry (or red-wine) vinegar, 2 tablespoons maple syrup, 1 teaspoon thyme, 1/8 teaspoon salt and pepper together in a medium bowl. Add the first sliced onion; toss to coat well. Cover and set aside to pickle.

2. About 15 minutes before you're ready to cook the pork chops, combine 1 1/2 cups raspberries, the remaining onion, wine or broth, maple syrup, balsamic vinegar, salt and pepper in a blender or food processor. Blend or process until pureed. Pour the sauce through a fine-mesh sieve or chinois into a small bowl; stir and press on the solids to extract all the sauce. Stir in the remaining 1 teaspoon thyme. Set aside.

3. Sprinkle both sides of the pork chops with sea salt and a generous grinding of pepper.

4. Place a large cast-iron or heavy-bottomed skillet over medium-high heat until hot; add oil and the pork chops and cook until browned, 2 to 3 minutes per side. Transfer the chops to a plate and keep warm.

5. Reduce heat to medium; add the raspberry sauce and boil, stirring constantly, until the sauce is reduced by

- 2 Tbsp maple syrup or honey
- 1 Tbsp balsamic vinegar
- ¼ tsp coarsely ground pepper
- 1 tsp fresh thyme leaves
- Sea salt and pepper to taste

Cook the meat:

- 1 Tbsp olive oil
- 4 bone-in, center-cut pork loin chops, ½ inch thick, about 4 ounces each

half, about 3 minutes.

6. Return the chops and any accumulated juices to the pan and cook on medium heat, turning the chops to coat with the sauce, until they register 145°F on an instant-read thermometer, 1 to 2 minutes.

7. Drain the pickled onions (discard the pickling mixture or save for another use). Gently toss with the remaining raspberries. Serve the chops with the pan sauce and top with the pickled onions and raspberries.

✓ <u>Chef's Tip 1</u>: These chops would be wonderful on top of pasta or mashed potatoes.

✓ <u>Chef's Tip 2</u>: This recipe is GFCF.

Roulés de Dinde à la Moutarde à l'Ancienne. *Old Fashioned Turkey Rolls with Mustard*

Nothing is as easy as this healthy recipe! Made from turkey cutlets, smoked turkey, cottage cheese and old-fashioned mustard. What could be better? Serve this with a nice salad and voila! A complete healthy meal.

Servings: 4

Prep Time: 30 min.

Cost per person: $1.51

INGREDIENTS

- 4 thin turkey cutlets (ask your friendly butcher)
- Sea salt and pepper to taste
- 2 slices of oven-roasted or smoked turkey breast
- 4 oz cottage cheese
- 4 tsp old-fashion mustard or Dijon
- 1 Tbsp coconut oil

PROCEDURE

1. Spread the turkey cutlets and flatten them as much as possible. Salt and pepper to taste. Cover them with the cottage cheese, then spread 1 teaspoon of mustard on each.

2. Cut each oven-roasted turkey breast slice in 2 and put a half on each cutlet. Roll and tie them with string or attach them with wooden toothpicks.

3. Heat coconut oil in a frying pan and brown the rolls on each side, then reduce heat, cover, and cook for another 15 minutes.

4. Remove the strings and slice into pieces to serve. If there is some sauce at the bottom of the pan, coat the slices with it.

✓ Chef's Tip 1: For my GFCF Friends, replace the cottage cheese with spreadable soy cheese.
✓ Chef's Tip 2: Serve with pasta tossed with a little butter and chopped parsley.

ACOMPAGNEMENTS - SIDE DISHES

Chou Rouge Braisé au Fromage de Chèvre. *Braised Purple Cabbage with Goat Cheese*

This is a warming dish favored during winter. Make sure there is enough cooking juice left to use as a sauce when eating with pasta or rice. The cheese will add protein and make this a complete meal.

Servings: 6

Prep Time: 15 min

Cooking Time: 2 hours

Oven Temp: 325F

Cost per person: $1.18

IINGREDIENTS

- 2 Tbsp olive oil
- 1 head red cabbage, shredded (~2 lbs)
- ½ cup balsamic vinegar
- ¼ cup water
- 2 Tbsp raw sugar
- Salt and pepper to taste
- ¼ cup goat cheese

PROCEDURE

1. Preheat your oven to 325F.
2. Heat a Dutch oven or a large pot to medium. Once it's warmed up a bit, add the oil and the cabbage. Stir well and sauté for 2 minutes to tenderize the cabbage.
3. Add the vinegar, water, sugar, salt and pepper and combine.
4. Cover and braise in the oven at 325 degrees for 2 hours. Stir every half hour or so. Keep an eye on the liquid level. Before the liquid completely evaporates, add a little extra water.
5. Remove from the oven. Serve while hot. Break off small chunks of goat cheese with your fingers and evenly dot the cabbage with it.

✓ Chef's Tip 1: This warming dish goes well on top of whole wheat or rice pasta or brown rice.

✓ Chef's Tip 2: for my GFCF friends, omit the cheese or replace with your favorite cheese substitute.

Crêpes aux Champignons et Epinards. *Mushroom and Spinach Crêpes*

This is one of my favorite crepe dishes. I serve to my friends every year for Mardi Gras. I hope you like it too!

Servings: about 10 crepes, or 5 servings

Prep Time: 45 min.

Oven Temp: Broil

Cost per person: $1.34

INGREDIENTS

- 1 cup whole milk, or plain almond or soy milk
- 2 eggs
- ½ tsp sea salt
- ¼ tsp ground black pepper
- 1 cup (4 oz) unbleached pastry flour, buckwheat or GF flour mix
- 2 oz butter, melted, or olive oil
- 8 oz mushrooms of your choice (Paris, Cremini, shiitake, or more exotic if you can afford it)
- 4 oz baby spinach
- 2 Tbsp butter or olive oil
- 1 tsp Herbes de Provence mix

PROCEDURE

1. In your food blender, weight/measure the milk, eggs, salt and pepper. Blend well. Add the flour and blend without lumps. At the end, add the melted butter or oil and blend until smooth.

2. Pour into ceramic or glass bowl. Cover and let rest for at least 30 minutes. Heat buttered or oiled frying pan at medium heat. Adjust crepe batter to right consistency with added filtered water. Pour 4 oz of batter (more or less according to your pan's size) and cook until the edges are turning light brown. Lift and flip with a metal spatula. Finish cooking. Reserve on a plate covered with a kitchen towel. When all are cooked, fold the towel over to keep the crepes warm and flexible.

3. Meanwhile, heat the butter (or oil) and sauté your mushrooms with salt, pepper and herbs. When they have rendered their juices, add the baby spinach and cook gently. Allow the juices to evaporate or this filling will be too runny for the crepes. Allow to cool a little.

4. Preheat your oven to broil.

5. Fill each crepe with the filling. Fold over and roll in a cannelloni shape. Place in a buttered or oiled baking dish.

6. Sprinkle with the cheese and place in the oven. Broil until the cheese melts. Serve

- ½ tsp sea salt
- ¼ tsp freshly ground pepper
- 2 oz grated Swiss or Parmesan cheese

hot.

✓ Chef's Tip 1: Unsweetened crepes can be filled many things: ham and cheese, eggs, asparagus, mushrooms, shrimp or any other filling of your choice. Fold over or roll. Sprinkle grated cheese on top and broil until cheese is melted.

✓ Chef's Tip 2: This dish can be made GFCF by using the alternate ingredients listed.

Curry de Lentilles Rouges a la Noix de Coco. *Red Lentil Coconut Curry*

I know this is not a classical French dish, but I warned you I would go exotic on you. Besides, French people are increasingly eating healthy dishes coming from all over the world. Filling, very tasty, and loaded with goodness.

Servings: 6

Prep Time: 1 hour

Cost per person: $1.15

IINGREDIENTS

- 1 tbsp olive oil
- ½ a large onion, chopped
- 2 garlic cloves
- 1 Tbsp ginger root, peeled and minced
- 2 tsp curry powder
- ½ tsp each: ground turmeric, ground cumin, pepper
- ¼ tsp each: cayenne pepper, ground cinnamon
- 2 bay leaves
- 1 14-oz can coconut milk
- 2 Tbsp GF soy sauce
- ½ cup tomato sauce
- 1 cup (6 oz) dried red lentils, rinsed
- 2.5 cups water
- 1/2 medium head cauliflower, cut into florets (1 lb)
- 1 medium sweet

PROCEDURE

1. In a large soup pot heat olive oil at medium heat; sauté onion until translucent, but not brown.
2. Peel and cube the sweet potato.
3. Add minced garlic, ginger and all the spices and reduce heat to medium-low. Cook for 3 minutes, stirring frequently. Do not let the spices burn.
4. Add coconut milk, soy sauce and tomato sauce and simmer on low heat for 20 minutes, stirring occasionally.
5. Meanwhile, cook the lentils in water for 15 minutes. Drain them and add to the soup.
6. Add the cauliflower and sweet potato. Add additional water to cover the veggies and cook until just tender, about 15 minutes.

✓ Chef's Tip: This is a complete meal and is GFCF.

potato (12 oz)
- 1/4 head cabbage,
  thinly sliced (1 lb)

Gratin Dauphinois. *Gratin Dauphinois*

This is one of those classic poor folks' dishes that has become famous the world over. As you can imagine, there are as many versions as there are cooks. Here's my version of this warming winter dish. By the way, don't worry too much about the amount of garlic. Its flavor will disappear during the cooking.

Servings: 6

Prep Time: 60 min.

Cost per person: $1.18

INGREDIENTS

- 2 lbs firm cooking potatoes like Yukon Gold, peeled and sliced thin
- 4 garlic cloves, chopped
- 1 garlic clove for rubbing dish
- 4 oz butter
- 8 oz whole milk, plain soy or almond milk
- 4 oz heavy cream
- ½ tsp ground nutmeg
- Sea salt and freshly ground pepper to taste
- 2 oz grated Swiss or Emmentaler cheese

PROCEDURE

1. Preheat your oven to 400F.
2. Rub an earthenware dish with the garlic love and butter it. Place a layer of sliced potatoes across the bottom of the dish (in a layer so). Sprinkle with salt and pepper, butter and chopped garlic.
3. Repeat the previous step (layer of potatoes, salt, pepper, butter, and garlic) as many times as necessary until you get to 3/4 of the dish's height.
4. Mix the milk with heavy cream. Add nutmeg, salt and pepper to taste. Pour the liquid in until it is visible through the potatoes. <u>Note</u>: you should see the milk but do not drown the potatoes. Top with the grated cheese.
5. Put in oven and bake for about 45 minutes. If the dish appears dry, add more of the milk mix. Bake until the cheese is gratiné and the potatoes are tender.

✓ <u>Chef's Tip 1</u>: Serve hot, with pork chops for example. This is a wonderful dish reheated for leftovers. Bon Appétit!
✓ <u>Chef's Tip 2</u>: This dish is GF. It can be made CF if you replace the milk/cream mix with soy creamer.

Purée de Patates Douces de Sante. *Healthy Mashed Sweet Potatoes*

This full flavored sweet potato dish is quick and easy to prepare, as well as being an interesting and healthy way to serve potatoes. You will find the flavors of the spice mixture along with the orange juice a wonderful complement to the potatoes.

Servings: 4

Prep Time: 20 min

Cost per person: $0.72

INGREDIENTS

- 2 medium sized (8 oz each) sweet potatoes or yams, scrubbed and sliced thin for quick cooking
- 2 oz vegetable broth
- 1 fresh orange, juiced
- 1 Tbsp olive oil
- ½ tsp Garam Masala or Curry spice mix
- Sea salt to taste
- White pepper to taste

PROCEDURE

1. Bring lightly salted water to a boil in a steamer with a tight fitting lid.
2. Scrub or peel your sweet potatoes; slice them and add them to the steamer basket. Cook them, covered, for about 10 minutes, or until tender.
3. When tender, mash with vegetable broth, orange juice, oil and spices. Adjust seasoning if needed.

✓ Chef's Tip 1: If you need to adjust the consistency, add a little more broth or oil. It will give it a richer taste.

✓ Chef's Tip 2: This recipe is GFCF.

DESSERTS et GATEAUX - DESSERTS and CAKES

Pommes au Four aux Amandes et au Miel. *Baked Apples with Almonds and Honey*

This simple recipe will perfume your whole home while you're preparing dinner. Just the smell will make everyone happy. If you feel creative, you can replace the almonds with other dried nuts or fruits. Serve warm with a scoop of vanilla ice cream or fruit sorbet.

Servings: 6

Prep Time: 45 min

Oven Temp: 400F

Cost per person: $1.54

INGREDIENTS

- 6 apples (3 red and 3 yellow)
- 4 Tbsp local honey
- One orange, juiced and zested
- 4 oz sliced or chopped blanched almonds
- 2 oz butter

PROCEDURE

1. Preheat your oven at 400F.
2. Wash and core your apples without peeling. Cut into slices about ½ an inch thick.
3. Place apple slices in layers in a baking dish, preferably earthenware.
4. In a bowl, mix the honey, orange zest, juice, and almonds.
5. Pour over apples. Sprinkle with butter pieces here and there.
6. Cover with aluminum foil and bake for about 30 minutes.
7. Remove the foil and cook for another 10 minutes or until the apples color.

✓ Chef's Tip 1: This desert is perfect by itself or serve with a scoop of vanilla ice cream.
✓ Chef's Tip 2: This dessert is GFCF.

Salade d'Oranges à la Cannelle. *Cinnamon Orange Salad*

Dessert is a stressful time for those watching their weight. No need to panic--Chef Braux to the rescue! With this fragrant orange salad, no more guilt trip!

Servings: 4

Prep Time: 20 min plus cooling time

Cost per person: $1.90

INGREDIENTS

- 4 large oranges
- 1 Tbsp dark rum
- 1 Tbsp orange flower water
- 2 Tbsp powdered or raw sugar
- ½ tsp ground cinnamon

PROCEDURE

1. Cut the rind off the oranges, trying to eliminate as much white part while leaving only the flesh.
2. Cut the oranges into slices between the section's skins over a ceramic bowl. Make sure to collect the juice drippings.
3. Add the remaining ingredients. Mix gently.
4. Cover with plastic wrap and allow to marinate for 1-2 hours in your refrigerator.

✓ Chef's Tip 1: If you feel decadent, serve over a scoop of vanilla ice cream or orange sorbet.
✓ Chef's Tip 2: for my GFCF friends, no changes. Serve over orange sorbet.

Truffes au Chocolat et à la Prune. *Dark Chocolate Prune Truffles*

Try this winning combination of chocolate and prunes! And think of all this good fiber coursing through your digestive system. It's also loaded with antioxidants. Who said chocolate can't be good for you?

Servings: 4 - 6

Prep and Cook Time: 15 minutes

Cost per person: $1.18

INGREDIENTS

- 8 oz pitted prunes
- 4 oz pitted dates
- 6 Tbsp almond butter
- 1 Tbsp maple syrup
- 4 Tbsp unsweetened cocoa
- 1 cup finely grated unsweetened coconut

PROCEDURE

1. Place the prunes and dates in a food processor. Pulse a few times to chop. Scrape the processor bowl.
2. Add the almond butter, maple syrup and cocoa powder and run until the mix is smooth and thick.
3. Roll the mixture into 24 one-inch balls and roll in coconut to coat. Refrigerate for at least 1/2 hour.

Compote de Rhubarbe et Pommes. *Rhubarb and Apple Compote*

This recipe reminds me of Mamie. She used to grow rhubarb in her garden and would trade for a few apples at the market. Although she never gave me her recipe (I don't think she had one), this is the closest I could come from my memories of this dessert.

Servings: 8

Prep Time: 50 min

Cost per person: $0.80

INGREDIENTS

- 1 lb rhubarb
- 1 lb apples of your choice: Granny Smith, McIntosh, Gala, Braeburn
- 8 oz raw or turbinado sugar
- 1 lemon zest
- 1 tbsp vanilla extract

PROCEDURE

6. Wash rhubarb, peel it and cut it into small even sections.
7. Peel, core and cube apples.
8. Put it in a saucepan with the sugar, zest and vanilla.
9. Cover and cook over medium heat for about 40-45 minutes while stirring once in a while until it turns into a sauce.
10. Allow to cool and enjoy.

✓ Chef's Tip 1: In France, we like this sauce this way but if you feel adventurous, add any combination of exotic spices: cinnamon, cardamom, ginger, allspices, etc.

✓ Chef's Tip 2: This sauce is wonderful by itself but you can serve it over vanilla ice cream. There will be plenty of leftovers for lunch. Enjoy!

✓ Chef's Tip 3: This dessert is GFCF.

Gâteau Exotique Aux Carottes. *Exotic Carrot Cake*

This is a cake I created for my GF customers at Peoples Pharmacy and they love it. I can barely keep up with demand. I hope you will enjoy it too!

Yield: One 9" double-layer cake

Oven Temp: 350F

Prep Time: 50 min

Icing Time: 20 min

Cooling Time: Overnight

Cost per person: $1.83

INGREDIENTS

- 1 lb 8 oz carrots, grated
- 6 oz walnuts pieces
- 4 oz coconut, shredded
- 4 oz dried currants
- 4 oz candied ginger, chopped
- 8 oz pastry flour or GF pastry flour
- 2 tsp baking powder
- 2 tsp baking soda
- 1 tsp cinnamon, ground
- 1tsp ginger, ground
- ½ tsp sea salt
- ½ tsp allspice, ground
- 8 oz whole eggs (4)
- 4 oz olive oil
- 6 oz turbinado sugar
- 4 oz apple sauce
- 2 tsp vanilla extract

Cream Cheese Icing for

PROCEDURE

1. Preheat your oven to 350F
2. Weigh carrots. Grate them in the food processor fitted with a medium grating plate.
3. Place mixing bowl on the scale. Add grated carrots, walnuts, coconut, currants and candied ginger. Mix together with the paddle attachment for a minute to blend well. Let sit to allow the moisture of the grated carrots to be absorbed by the dried fruits.
4. Meanwhile, prepare your pans. Take two 9" spring form pans. Spray them with olive oil spray. Cut two pieces of baking paper to fit the pans' bottoms. Place them carefully at the bottom of each pan. Spray the paper as well. Place the two pans on two separate baking sheets.
5. In a separate bowl, weigh all the dry ingredients and mix together with a hand whisk. Set aside.
6. Add the eggs, olive oil, sugar, applesauce and vanilla to the carrot mix. Blend well. Add the flour a little at a time and continue to blend until all the flour is absorbed.
7. Weigh out 2 lbs 2 oz of batter per pan. Bake at 350F for 15 minutes. Turn and switch cakes around to insure even baking. Bake another 15 minutes or until a small knife's blade comes out clean.
8. Refrigerate overnight or at least 2 hours before icing.
9. When ready to ice the cake, prepare the cream cheese icing: in the mixing bowl,

one cake

- 8 oz butter
- 8 oz powdered sugar
- 1 lb 8 oz cream cheese
- 2 tsp vanilla extract

Dairy-Free Cream Cheese icing for one cake

- 8 oz GF powdered sugar
- 8oz dairy-free soy margarine (non-hydrogenated)
- 24 oz (3-8 oz) dairy-free cream cheese, such as Tofutti
- 2 tsp vanilla extract

weigh the powdered sugar, then add the butter cut in small pieces. Using the paddle attachment, start mixing at slow speed. When butter and sugar are mixed together, switch to high speed and cream well. Add the room-temperature cream cheese a little at a time until all ingredients are well blended together. Mix in vanilla extract.

10. **Dairy-free icing.** Use the same procedure but let it "set" before you ice the cake.

11. Ice and decorate the cake your favorite way. This cake should serve at least 12 people with generous slices.

✓ Chef's Tip: This cake is GF when made with GF pastry flour. It can be made CF if using the dairy-free icing above.

ACKNOWLEDGMENTS

I created this book to answer the ever challenging question: "How can I eat on a budget?" I heard this from many of my own clients and hear it over and over again where I work at Peoples Pharmacy in Austin, Texas.

I created this book to answer these questions. I sincerely hope it will help you in developing a healthy diet for you and your family even if you have a restricted food budget.

In the endeavor, I was helped tremendously by a small group of enthusiastic friends and professional wanting me to spread the good news: yes, you can eat healthy on a budget. Not only that but it is possible to eat a healthy and gourmet diet – French or otherwise - with beautiful, fresh and flavorful food. In this culinary travel, I would like to thank the following people for their constant inspiration, professional and volunteer help.

My grand-mother **"Mamie"** for teaching me by example that healthy food should come from one's kitchen garden, freshly picked, prepared quickly and with love, but does not have to be complicated or expensive to taste wonderful.

My mother, **Bernadette Moulin-Braux,** who encouraged me to discover and apply my culinary and baking abilities. My mother-in-law, **Helene Jaboulay,** for opening my eyes to what Mediterranean cuisine is all about. She always amazed me with her ability to feed her family with simple but flavorful home-cooked "Cuisine du Midi".

Janet Zand for being my first supporter even before I started writing my first food word. She has been my model and inspiration all along. Thank you Janet for your kind support. You are my writing fairy God Mother.

My very creative team:

My caring, patient, talented and very patient editor, **Kathleen Thornberry** for her loving work on my "charabia" or Frenglish gibberish. When it comes to food and health, we are kindred spirits and this project would have been almost impossible without her astute suggestions and reinterpretation of my "Frenchisms" while preserving the spirit of my writing.

Nathan Stueve for designing a beautiful and practical web site and an original book cover.

My dear friend **Athena Danoy** for capturing that special spark in me in her portraits of me.

Beth McCall for being my tireless, enthusiastic and knowledgeable reviewers and for her watchful eye in proofing this "ouvrage."

The newest member of my creative team is **Laura Stevens**, a very talented and creative marketing lady that knows what it takes to promote a book on an Indie's budget. Their creative efforts supported my vision for this book. I literally could not have done without them.

<u>My esteemed predecessors and guiding mentors:</u>

Hippocrates 460-377 B.C., the father of us all in the "food as a healing medium" movement, who affirmed, "Let thy food be thy medicine and thy medicine be thy food".

And I cannot forget my daily inspiration for writing this book: **Jonny Bowden, Ph. D.** and **George Mateljan**. My Chef's hat off to both of you for proving that we can still hack it even if we're not in our 30's or 40's or even in our 50's.

To **Dr. Janet, Dr. Amy** and **Dr. Liz** for reading and approving my manuscript.

My boss, **Bill Swail** for allowing my books to be sold in his stores and for providing me the safety and security I needed during the writing of this book.

Tim and Barbara Cook for their spiritual guidance and encouragements.

Last but by no means least, my son **Gilles Braux** for inspiring me to be the best I can, just by being himself no matter what. I hope this and my other books will show him the way to healthy living.

And finally, my **Healthy Cuisine Friends** and **Healthy Cuisine Champions** that have been supporting me through my belief that fresh and good-tasting food is the source of good health. Thanks again for your continuing support over the past few years.

To the people that offered their own homemade and budget-conscious recipes, thank you all very much (in country and alphabetical order):

- ✓ **Georgette "Mamie" Moulin.** Laval, France.
- ✓ **Moulin-Braux,** my mom. Nice, France

- ✓ **Isabelle Braux,** my sister. Nice, France
- ✓ **Helene Jaboulay,** my mother in law. Nice, France
- ✓ **Amanda Love,** The Barefoot Cook. Austin, TX
- ✓ **Françoise Pointeau.** Austin, TX.
- ✓ **Jackie Powell.** Austin, TX
- ✓ **Lauri Raymond.** Austin, TX
- ✓ **Marie Reed,** especially for her contribution in the book as well. Austin, TX
- ✓ **Paula Tuttle** – Austin, TX

Thank you all from the bottom of my Healthy (I hope) French heart.

Love and Dark Chocolate,

Chef Alain Braux.

DO YOU WANT TO KNOW MORE ABOUT CHEF BRAUX?

If you are interested in:

➢ Consulting privately with me regarding your health issues
➢ Me creating a customized diet for your specific food allergies situation
➢ Finding out about my cooking and baking classes
➢ Me creating a cooking or baking classes for your Cooking School
➢ Asking me questions about this book
➢ Hiring me as a Health Food and Gluten-free consultant for your restaurant
➢ Interviewing me for a featured article
➢ Inviting me as a Health Speaker at your event
➢ Talking to me about any other health-related opportunities…

Feel free to check my constantly updated web site:
http//www.alainbraux.com

Contact me on my web site's Contact page or send an email to:
alainbraux@gmail.com

Thank you again for reading my book and "see" you soon in my next book.

Sincerely,

Chef Alain Braux

CEPC, CMB, B.S. in Holistic Nutrition, Macrobiotic Counselor.

CHEF ALAIN BRAUX'S BIO

Award-winning chef (two gold and three silver medals) and nutrition-therapist Alain Braux has worked in the food industry for more than 40 years. He is a **Certified Executive Pastry Chef** with the **American Culinary Federation** and a **Certified Master Baker** with the **Retail Bakers of America**. He earned a **Bachelor of Science** degree in **Holistic Nutrition** and is a macrobiotic counselor. Chef Braux currently lives in Austin, Texas, where he is the executive chef at **Peoples Pharmacy** and in private practice as a nutritherapist with **A Votre Santé**.

Chef Braux started his training in France at **Confiserie Patisserie Auer** in Nice, France. He then decided to improve his skills at some of the highest-rated hotels, restaurants and pastry shops of Europe. He refined his trade at **Grand Hotel du Cap d'Antibes** near Cannes, France; the **Moulin de Mougins** in Mougins, France; the famous **Lenotre** in Paris, France, and **Patisserie Wittamer** in Brussels, Belgium.

While in Paris, he was offered his first U.S. job at **Dumas Pastry Shop** in New York, NY. He then held the Executive Pastry Chef position in various companies such as **Délices la Cote Basque** in New York, NY; **Lenotre Paris Inc.** in Houston, TX; **The French Hearth Bakery and Café** in Sarasota, FL and **Texas French Bread** in Austin, TX.

In 1988 Chef Braux opened his own business, **Amandine French Bakery and Café** in Austin, TX. Amandine Bakery was written about in numerous publications including the **New York Times**, **Texas Monthly**, the **Austin American Statesman** and the **Austin Chronicle** and won a few "Best of Austin" awards over its 10 year lifetime. Please check Google to see copies of these articles.

After closing Amandine, Chef Braux found a new home at the **Barr Mansion** for his elegant cakes and fine pastries. Chef Braux then became the Pastry and Baking instructor for the **Culinary Academy of Austin**. Currently, Chef Braux is the Executive Chef and Nutrition Therapist at Peoples Pharmacy in Austin, Texas.

Chef Braux authored his first book called *How to Lower your Cholesterol with French Gourmet Food* in 2009. This book won the **Cookbook Award** at the **2010 Paris book Festival**, was one of the **Finalists** at the **2010 Indie Excellence Book Award** and earned an **Honorable Mention** at the **2010 New York Book Festival** and the **2010 San Francisco Book Festival**.

Chef Braux published his second book entitled *Living Gluten and Dairy-free with French Gourmet Food* in 2010. So far, this book has won the **Best Cookbook Award** at the **2011 Paris Book Festival**, was the **Winner** in the **Nutrition Category** at the **2011 Indie Excellence Book Award**, and an earned an **Honorable Mention** at the **2011 New York Book Festival**.

Chef Braux's third book, *Healthy French Cuisine for Less Than $10/Day* will be published in October 2011. Let's hope it will win a few awards of its own.

14378281R00157

Made in the USA
Charleston, SC
08 September 2012